D1357187

WITHDRAWN
KT 2316860 9

THE FEARLESS BENJAMIN LAY

ALSO BY MARCUS REDIKER

Outlaws of the Atlantic: Sailors, Pirates, and Motley Crews in the Age of Sail

The Amistad Rebellion: An Atlantic Odyssey of Slavery and Freedom

The Slave Ship: A Human History

Villains of All Nations: Atlantic Pirates in the Golden Age

The Many-Headed Hydra: Sailors, Slaves, Commoners, and the Hidden History of the Revolutionary Atlantic (with Peter Linebaugh)

Between the Devil and the Deep Blue Sea: Merchant Seamen, Pirates and the Anglo-American Maritime World, 1700–1750

THE FEARLESS BENJAMIN LAY

The Quaker Dwarf Who Became the First Revolutionary Abolitionist

MARCUS REDIKER

VERSO
London • New York

First published in the UK by Verso 2017

1 3 5 7 9 10 8 6 4 2

Verso
UK: 6 Meard Street, London W1F 0EG
US: 20 Jay Street, Suite 1010, Brooklyn, NY 11201
versobooks.com

Verso is the imprint of New Left Books

ISBN-13: 978-1-78663-471-9
ISBN-13: 978-1-78663-473-3 (UK EBK)

British Library Cataloguing in Publication Data
A catalogue record for this book is available from the British Library

Printed in the UK by CPI Mackays

To my children,

Eva, Ezekiel, and Greer,

with hope that you

and your generation

will take inspiration

from this life story

CONTENTS

INTRODUCTION

PROPHET AGAINST SLAVERY

ON SEPTEMBER 19, 1738, Benjamin Lay strode into a large gathering of Quakers in the Burlington, New Jersey, meetinghouse for the biggest event of the Philadelphia Yearly Meeting. Benjamin had journeyed almost thirty miles on foot, as was his way, arriving four days earlier and subsisting on "Acorns & peaches only." Presiding over the gathering were John Kinsey, clerk of the Philadelphia Yearly Meeting, and Israel Pemberton Sr., assistant clerk, leaders of the Society of Friends in the Philadelphia region and the Quaker-dominated legislature of Pennsylvania. Benjamin had a message for them and indeed for all of the assembled.[1]

Benjamin surveyed the room and took a conspicuous location. He wore a great coat, which hid a military uniform and a sword from his fellow Quakers, who, back in 1660, had embraced the "peace testimony," refusing all weapons and warfare. Beneath his coat Benjamin carried a hollowed-out book with a secret compartment, into which he had tucked a tied-off animal bladder filled with bright red pokeberry juice. Because Quakers had no formal minister nor church ceremony, people spoke as the spirit moved them. Benjamin, a man of spirit pure and unruly, waited his turn.

He finally rose to address this gathering of "weighty Quakers," many of whom owned African slaves. Quakers in Pennsylvania and New Jersey had grown rich on Atlantic commerce and many bought human property. To them Benjamin delivered a chilling prophecy. He announced in a booming voice that God Almighty respects all peoples equally, rich and poor, men and women, white people and black alike. He explained that slave keeping was the greatest sin in the world and asked, How can a people who profess the Golden Rule keep slaves? He then threw off his great coat, revealing the military garb, the blade, and the book to his astonished co-religionists. A collective murmur filled the hall. In a rising crescendo of emotion, the prophet thundered his judgment: "Thus shall God shed the blood of those persons who enslave their fellow creatures." He pulled out the sword, raised the book above his head, and plunged the sword through it. The people in the room gasped as the red liquid gushed down his arm; several women swooned at the sight. To the shock of all, he spattered "blood" on the heads and bodies of the slave keepers. Benjamin prophesied a dark, violent future: Quakers who failed to heed the prophet's call must expect physical, moral, and spiritual death.

The room exploded into chaos, but Benjamin stood quiet and still, "like a statue," remarked Kinsey. Several Quakers quickly surrounded the armed soldier of God, picked him up, and carried him from the building. Benjamin did not resist. But he had made his point. As long as Quakers owned slaves, there would be no "business as usual" if Benjamin could help it. His brothers and sisters had made peace with the devil, so he used his body to disrupt their hypocritical, pious routines.

This spectacular prophetic performance was one moment of guerrilla theater among many. Benjamin repeatedly dramatized what was wrong in both the Society of Friends and the world at large. For a quarter century he railed against slavery in one Quaker meeting after another, in and around Philadelphia, confronting slave owners and slave traders with a savage, most un-Quaker-like fury. Whenever he performed guerrilla theater, his fellow Quakers removed him by physical force as a "trouble-maker" or "disorderly person" as they had done in Burlington. He did not struggle against eviction, but back he came, again and again, undeterred, or rather more determined than ever. He began to stage his theater of apocalyptic outrage in public venues, including city streets and markets. He refused to be cowed by the rich and powerful as he freely spoke his mind. He practiced what the ancient Greeks called *parrhesia*—free, fearless speech, which required courage in the face of danger. He insisted on the utter depravity and sinfulness of "Man-stealers," who were, in his view, the literal spawn of Satan. He considered it his Godly duty to expose and drive them out.

His confrontational methods made people talk: about him, his ideas, the nature of Quakerism and Christianity, and, most of all, slavery. His first biographer, Benjamin Rush—physician, reformer, abolitionist, and signer of the Declaration of Independence—noted that "there was a time when the name of this celebrated Christian Philosopher . . . was familiar to every man, woman, and to nearly every child, in Pennsylvania." For or against, everyone told stories about Benjamin Lay.[2]

The zealot carried his activism into print, publishing in 1738 one of the world's first books to demand the abolition of slavery: *All Slave-Keepers That Keep the Innocent in Bondage, Apostates*. All enslaved people were innocent, Benjamin believed, so he called for all to be emancipated, immediately and unconditionally, with no compensation to slave owners. Slave keepers had transgressed the core beliefs of Quakerism in particular and Christianity in general: they should be cast out of the church. Benjamin wrote his book at a time when slavery seemed to many people around the world as natural and unchangeable as the sun, the moon, and the stars in the heavens. No one had ever taken such a militant, uncompromising, universal stand against slavery in print or in action. Benjamin demanded freedom *now*.

Perhaps because he had little education, Benjamin ignored the rules of convention in writing his book. It made for odd reading, then and since, but it is a veritable treasure trove for a historian: a mixture of autobiography; prophetic Biblical polemic against slavery; a commonplace book into which he dropped writings by others as well as his own thoughts on a variety of subjects; haunting, surreal descriptions of slavery in Barbados; an annotated bibliography of what he read; and a vivid, scathing account of his own struggles against slave owners within the Quaker community. It is a founding text of Atlantic antislavery.[3]

Benjamin knew that Kinsey, Pemberton, and the other members of the Quaker Board of Overseers—who vetted all publications—would never approve the book. Most of them owned slaves. So he went directly to his friend, the printer Benjamin Franklin, and asked him to publish it. When Franklin saw a confused jumble of pages in a box he expressed puzzlement about how to proceed. Lay answered, "Print any part thou pleaseth first"—assemble the materials in any order you like. As one exasperated reader later noted of the different parts of the book, "the head might serve for the tail, and the tail for the body, and the body for the head, either end for the middle, and the middle for either end; nay, if you could turn them inside out, like a glove, they would be no worse for the operation." (Lay was one of the world's first postmodernists.) Franklin agreed to publish the ringing rant against slavery, knowing full well that the wealthy Quakers assailed in it would howl in protest. He quietly left the printer's name off the title page.[4]

Part of Benjamin's guerrilla theater was his distinctive appearance. He was a dwarf or "little person," standing a little over four feet tall. He was also called a "hunchback," meaning that he suffered from over-curvature of the thoracic vertebrae, a medical condition called *kyphosis*. According to a fellow Quaker,

> His head was large in proportion to his body; the features of his face were remarkable, and boldly delineated, and his countenance was grave and benignant. He was hunch-backed, with a projecting chest, below which his body became much contracted. His legs were so slender, as to appear almost unequal to the purpose of supporting him, diminutive as his frame was, in comparison with the ordinary size of the human stature. A habit he had contracted, of standing in a twisted position, with one hand resting upon his left hip, added to the effect produced by a large white beard, that for many years had not been shaved, contributed to make his figure perfectly unique.[5]

Benjamin's wife, Sarah, was also a "little person," which caused the enslaved Africans of Barbados to remark in delighted wonder, "That little backarar [white] man go all over world see for [to look for] that backarar woman for himself." Yet Sarah was more than a help-meet; she was a principled abolitionist in her own right. Benjamin was by some definition "disabled," or handicapped, but I have found no evidence that he thought himself in any way diminished, nor that his body kept him from doing anything he wanted to do. He called himself "little Benjamin" but he also likened himself to "little David" who slew Goliath. He did not lack confidence in himself or his ideas.[6]

Benjamin Lay is little known among historians. He appears occasionally in histories of abolition, usually as a minor, colorful figure of suspect sanity. By the nineteenth century he was regarded as "diseased" in his intellect and later as "cracked in the head." To a large extent this image has persisted in modern histories. Indeed David Brion Davis, a leading historian of abolitionism, condescendingly called Benjamin a mentally deranged, obsessive "little hunchback." Benjamin gets better treatment by amateur Quaker historians, who include him in their pantheon of antislavery saints, and by the many excellent professional historians of Quakerism. He is almost totally unknown to the general public.[7]

Benjamin was better known among abolitionists than among their later historians. The French revolutionary Jacques Pierre Brissot de Warville gathered stories about him almost three decades after Benjamin's death, during a visit to the United States in 1788. Brissot wrote that Benjamin was "simple in his dress and animated in his speech; he was all on fire when he spoke on slavery." In this respect Benjamin anticipated by a century the abolitionist leader William Lloyd Garrison, who was also "all on fire" about human bondage. When Thomas Clarkson penned the history of the movement that abolished the slave trade in Britain, in 1808, a moment of triumph for that country, he credited Lay, who had "awakened the attention of many to the cause." Lay possessed "strong understanding and great integrity," but was "singular" and "eccentric." He had, in Clarkson's view, been "unhinged" by cruelties he observed in Barbados between 1718 and 1720. When Clarkson drew his famous graphic genealogy of the movement, a riverine map of abolition, he named a significant tributary "Benjamin Lay." On the other side of the Atlantic, in the 1830s and 1840s, more than seventy years after Lay's death, the American abolitionists Benjamin Lundy and Lydia Maria Child rediscovered him, republished his biography, reprinted an engraving of him, and renewed his memory within the movement.[8]

Benjamin is not the usual elite subject of biography. He came from a humble background and was poor most of his life, by occupation and by choice. He lived, he explained, by "the Labour of my Hands." He was also considered a philosopher in his own day, much like the ancient Greek Diogenes, the former slave known for speaking truth to power. (He refused Greek nationality and insisted that he was, rather, "a citizen of the world.") Benjamin lived a mobile, far-flung life, in England, Barbados, Pennsylvania, and on the high seas in-between, all of which shaped his cosmopolitan thinking. Unlike most poor people, he left an unmediated record of his ideas.[9]

We are unusually fortunate to have three distinct bodies of evidence with which to write Benjamin's intellectual history "from below." The first is his own book, *All Slave-Keepers . . . Apostates*, a rich and remarkable body of evidence by any measure. The second set of sources is Quaker records, generated in Colchester, London, Philadelphia, and Abington, the places where Benjamin lived and worshipped. In the aftermath of George Fox's reforms in the 1660s and 1670s, Quaker congregations became careful record keepers, partly in order to discipline recalcitrant spirits such as Benjamin. The third collection of records grew from Benjamin's guerrilla theater, which generated endless stories. Some of these were published in newspapers after Benjamin's death. In the early nineteenth century Benjamin's second biographer, Quaker philanthropist Roberts Vaux, interviewed elderly Quakers who knew Benjamin. Born in the early 1730s, they had encountered Benjamin as children, teenagers, and young adults. With this unusual combination of sources we can explore in detail the thoughts and actions of someone who, with clear and canny prescience, saw that slavery must be abolished.[10]

Benjamin's radicalism was a rope of five strands: he was a Quaker, philosopher, sailor, abolitionist, and commoner. As a free thinker he drew on a wide variety of books and intellectual traditions, combining them creatively to serve his own values and purposes. He was first and foremost an *antinomian* radical—someone who believed that salvation could be achieved by grace alone and that a direct connection to God placed the believer above man-made law. Taken from the Greek, meaning "against all authority," antinomianism emerged in the heat of revolution and civil war in England. As heresiographer Ephraim Pagitt wrote of religious radicals such as the Diggers, Levellers, and Seekers, in 1647, "The Antinomians are so called . . . because they would have the Law abolished." They offered a deep critique of power in all its forms in a "world turned upside down," as Christopher Hill called the revolutionary era. Against institutions, the state, and all "outward forms," conscience reigned supreme. Benjamin was, in short, a free spirit. Antinomianism was the foundation of his thought.[11]

Benjamin combined Quakerism with abolitionism and other radical ideas and practices that were uncommon for his time and rarely thought to be related: vegetarianism, animal rights, opposition to the death penalty, environmentalism, and the politics of consumption. He lived in a cave for the last third of his life, cultivated his own food, and made his own clothes. For Benjamin these beliefs and practices were all part of a consistent, integrated, ethical worldview—one that could save a planet desperately in need of salvation. He showed that multiple forms and traditions of radicalism could all be part of the same consciousness. He believed that abolition must inform a revolutionary revaluation of all life, premised on a rejection of the capitalist values of the marketplace. Benjamin Lay was, in several ways, a curiously modern man whose story has never been fully or properly told. He is a radical for our time.

In the aftermath of numerous successful abolition movements, now that almost everyone agrees that slavery was, and remains to this day, morally wrong, it is not easy to recover the profound hostility Benjamin encountered for espousing antislavery beliefs in the early eighteenth century. Benjamin himself noted how people flew into rages when they heard him speak against bondage. They ridiculed him; they heckled him; they laughed at him. Many dismissed him as mentally deficient and somehow deranged as he opposed the deep "common sense" of the era. The scorn was based in economic interest and racial prejudice but also in bias against him as a little person. Each reinforced the other in cruelty and rancor.

Efforts began after Benjamin's death to remember the enmity he suffered. A New Jersey abolitionist who wrote under the pen name "Armintor" noted in 1774 how few were the number of advocates who, early on, dared to speak out on behalf of Africans, "this poor oppressed part of creation." He singled out "the despised Benjamin Lay" as the "foremost" among them. Quaker Ann Emlen, wife of abolitionist Warner Mifflin, noted in 1785 that Benjamin's confrontational ways in meetings met strong resistance from Friends, even though he spoke "the truth" about slavery.[12]

Roberts Vaux made the hostile response to Benjamin a major theme of his biography, published in 1815. Indeed he wrote his memorial against the repression that had obscured and sullied the activist's memory. As a philanthropist and abolitionist himself, Vaux sought to set the record straight among his fellow Quakers and the public at large. He used strong words to describe precisely what Benjamin encountered as he witnessed against the beast of bondage: opposition, antipathy, prejudice, ridicule, hostility, intolerance, persecution, oppression, and violence. Vaux noted that Benjamin faced "vigorous opposition from every quarter" and found himself "an almost solitary combatant in a field where prejudice and avarice . . . had marshalled their combined forces against him." The response from his fellow

Quaker abolitionist and philanthropist Roberts Vaux was Lay's second biographer, publishing *The Memoirs of the Lives of Benjamin Lay and Ralph Sandiford, Two of the Earliest Public Advocates for the Emancipation of the Enslaved Africans* in 1815.

Quakers in particular was "so general and so intense," it was enough "to make a wise man mad." Benjamin was, in 1738, the last Quaker disowned for protests against slavery. It would take another twenty years for Quakers to agree even to the possibility of disowning a member for slave-trading and an additional eighteen years to begin to excommunicate slave owners. It was not easy to be so far ahead of one's time.[13]

Prejudice ballooned into repression. Fellow Quakers not only denounced Benjamin's book about slavery but also denied his right to speak on the subject in their gatherings. As John Kinsey made clear in 1737, the leaders of the Philadelphia Monthly Meeting objected to how Benjamin was "presumeing to preach" in "publick Meetings." Once known for their open-to-all "mechanick preaching," Friends now decided that they "could not approve of his Ministry." They simply could not bear to hear what he was saying.[14]

Campaigners against slavery who came before Benjamin could not always take the pressure. According to Quaker John Forman, Benjamin's fellow Essexman John Farmer made "a very powerful testimony against the oppression of the black people" in 1717–1718. After Farmer addressed a

Quaker congregation in Philadelphia, "a great man, who kept negroes . . . got up and desired Friends to look on that man as an open enemy to the country." Other Friends sided with the great man and together they forced Farmer to "make something like an acknowledgment" that he had been wrong. This event had a crippling effect: Farmer "sunk under it" and "declined in his gift" of ministry. He never returned to England. On his deathbed he declared himself "easy" about everything in his life except "flinching from his testimony at that time, and in that manner."[15]

Benjamin got greater pressure, over a longer period of time, and additional derision for being a little person, but he never sank, declined, flinched, or retreated. At the same time his determination and conviction made him an awkward and difficult person, to say the least. He was loving to his friends, but he could be a holy terror to those who did not agree with him. He was aggressive and disruptive. He was stubborn, never inclined to admit a mistake. His direct antinomian connection to God made him self-righteous and at times intolerant. The more resistance he encountered, or, as he understood it, the more God tested his faith, the more certain he was that he was right. He had reasons both sacred and self-serving for being the way he was. He was sure that these traits were essential to defeat the profound evil of slavery.

The ill will expressed toward Benjamin in Barbados and Pennsylvania came from both above and below—from political and religious leaders like Kinsey and from ordinary people, all of whom supported the institution of slavery in one way or another. To make this point, Vaux quoted Rome's great lyric poet, Horace, of whom Benjamin would certainly have approved, as he loved the writers of antiquity:

> *The just man who is resolute*
> *will not be turned from his purpose*
> *either by the rage of the crowd or*
> *by an imperious tyrant.*

It took fortitude and courage to face the kind of opposition that confronted Benjamin over the last forty years of his life. Fortunately for him, and for posterity, those virtues were never in short supply. He demonstrated the power of saying no to slavery. His life is a story of fearlessness in that cause.[16]

CHAPTER ONE

EARLY LIFE

THE FORMATIVE EARLY influences in Benjamin Lay's life were family, region, religion, and work. He was born in 1682 to people of modest but growing means in Essex, a part of England known in the seventeenth century for textile production, protest, and religious radicalism. He was a third-generation Quaker and eventually one more fervently dedicated to the faith than either his parents or grandparents. He studied the history of Quakerism and drew inspiration from its origins in the English Revolution. And he had a broad set of work experiences—rural and urban, regional and international—as a shepherd, glove maker, and sailor. How and where Benjamin made his living would shape his evolving view of the world.

COPFORD: COMMONER

Benjamin's family had lived in the small village of Copford, County Essex, about sixty miles northwest of London, for several generations. Copford was part of the manor of the Bishops of London during the tenth and eleventh centuries, under the rule of England's later Saxon kings. The bishops held the manor until 1559, when the new Protestant queen, Elizabeth I, dispossessed Copford's bishop, Edmund Bonner, for refusing to take an oath of allegiance. The lands of Copford were then offered for private purchase, but local commons remained. The village chapel was known for its twelfth-century Norman wall paintings and for a sheet of flayed human skin—probably that of a poacher—that hung on a door as a dreadful warning. Originally dedicated to St. Mary, the chapel would be renamed St. Michael and All Angels Church, based on the storied clash between good and evil in the Book of Revelation.[1]

Benjamin's grandparents, William and Prudence Lay, possessed modest property in Copford, as revealed by the hearth tax levied in Essex in 1670. "Willelmus Lay" owned a cottage with one fireplace: it was home to himself, his wife, and three children: son William (Benjamin's father), born 1654; daughter Susan, born 1659; and son John, born 1662. The village itself was small. Only twenty-two households had taxable hearths. One family, obviously the local gentry, had six; two had four; five had three; nine had two; and five, including the Lays, had one. An additional "nine poor persons" were omitted from the list, while another seventeen had exemptions, perhaps because they too were poor or were renters. Among the forty-eight households noted in the hearth tax record, the Lays were squarely in the middle, at the lowest end of the propertied. The village would consist of fifty to sixty households over the next century.[2]

William and Prudence were moved by the revolutionary ferment of the 1640s and 1650s, joining the Quakers sometime after 1655. A dozen years later William was still a dissenter: he was indicted at the Essex Quarterly Court for not attending Church of England services. In 1672 he was appointed by the Quaker Colchester Monthly Meeting (CMM) to look for a proper meeting place for the local congregation. This is the only reference to William or Prudence in early Quaker records, other than notations of the births of their children. They appear not to have been active in the CMM, perhaps because they, like other members of the congregation, lived "3 Miles & so to 5, 8 & 10 Miles Distance" from the meeting place.[3]

Benjamin's father—let us call him William II—was more active in the congregation, though not without controversy. He apparently married as a young man outside the Quaker faith, producing two sons, William III and John, neither of whom became Quakers, as far as can be told, and a daughter, Susanna, who did. In 1679, presumably after the death of his first wife, William II went before the CMM and "declared his intention of marriage wth Mary Dennis" (or Dennish) of Layer Breton, about five miles south of Copford. Even though Mary was apparently William's first cousin, no objections were raised, and the union was consummated. Years later, in 1687, the CMM asked whether "marrying one so near a kin" was appropriate and added that they were "unsatisfied whether they be married or not." At the very next meeting William presented a marriage certificate, but this caused more strife because the ceremony had been performed by an Anglican priest, which was unacceptable to the Quaker congregation. After a discussion of the case, the CMM scribe noted that William "declares that he is sorry" and accepted the "testimony of condemnation against himself & ye evil works." All seems to have been forgiven, for in 1712 William II and his friend Robert Tibbal "conveyed a piece of Land at Copford to the meeting for a [Quaker] burial ground." But even this act of generosity was tainted as something was wrong with the deed. The CMM concluded that "William Lay forsakes Truth, so a new deed is made mentioned in this book at ye Monthly Meeting."[4]

William's marriage to Mary Dennis apparently raised the family's fortunes dramatically. He had grown up in a small one-hearth home in Copford, but in 1684, a mere nine years after he turned twenty-one, he listed in his will three substantial properties he now owned, almost certainly through Mary. He willed to his son William III "free and copy hold Lands with a Barne thereon built standing lying and being in ffordham [Fordham] and Westbergholt [West Bergholt] called or known by the names of Bishopps and Moorcrofts." He willed to his other son, John, "all those ffree and copy hold houses and Lands whatsoever standing lying and being in Mount bures [Mount Bures] and Colne Wakes." To wife Mary he left "free hold Houses and Lands standing lying and being in Layer Bretton," with the provision that on her decease the property would go "to my youngest sonn Benjamin Lay," who was then two years old. William may have worried about Benjamin's longevity, perhaps because of his dwarfism, for he added, "If my said Sonn Benjamin shall dye before hee shall accomplish his full age of one and twenty years or day of majority," the "Houses and Lands" would go to his older sons. Meantime William III and John moved onto their properties and turned them to immediate advantage. When they wrote up their wills years later, in 1722 and 1735, respectively, they listed themselves as "yeomen"—commoners who possessed and cultivated their own free or copyhold land. The family was moving up in social rank.[5]

Benjamin was born April 26, 1682, in the small, dark, smoky cottage in Copford and named for his maternal grandfather, Benjamin Dennis. He was followed in the family by a sister, Mary, twenty months later. Despite the upward mobility of the half-brothers, education was not yet a significant family achievement. John could not sign his own will and Benjamin himself was afforded only limited schooling. He does not appear in the "Register of the Scholars Admitted to Colchester School" between 1637 and 1740. He may have received some informal schooling within the Quaker community, even though the first official Friends school was founded too late for him, in 1698. In any case, according to Roberts Vaux and the older Quakers he interviewed, Benjamin was given nothing "more than the rudiments of learning, as taught in the lower order of English schools." He would spend the rest of his life educating himself, becoming an autodidact known for wide reading in "theology, biography, poetry, and history."[6]

Benjamin's home region was dominated by the textile industry. In the late seventeenth century it was known for producing "bays and says," coarse cloths made of combed, not carded, wool, the precursors of the contemporary cloths, baize and serge. The know-how had been brought to Essex by Dutch refugees in the 1560s and 70s. A century later, after sheep herding and spinning had proliferated across the countryside, woolens were the region's most important export. Local chronicler Philip Morant wrote in 1768 that in Essex, "the poor are employed in spinning Wool, in most parts of the County." When Benjamin migrated to Philadelphia in 1732 he took with him the textile culture of his home region. Among items he listed for sale were "a parcel of Wool or Worsted Combs and Wool Cards." And Benjamin was himself a spinner, as visitors to his cave noted: skeins of yarn hung in wild profusion all about the interior. These he used to make his own clothes, suggesting a history of skill and familial involvement in textile production.[7]

Essex had a long tradition of popular protest that would be part of Benjamin's patrimony. Major disturbances rocked the region in 1549, the year of Kett's Rebellion against enclosure in Norfolk, and in 1566 conspiracy and resistance wracked the textile towns of northeast Essex. In 1642 thousands plundered the opulent estate of Sir John Lucas in the most dramatic attack on property committed during the English Revolution. Morant remembered the history more than a century later, remarking that the lower sort of the region were "always too much inclined to plunder." Popular protest in Essex was many-headed: commoners protested the enclosure of common lands, unfair elections, the allocation of grain, weavers' wages, and the authority of ministers and the church.[8]

Essex was relatedly a hotbed of religious radicalism, beginning in the early fifteenth century with the Lollards, whose heretical rejection of wealth would roil the region for more than a century. Inspired by the Oxford theologian John Wycliffe, who attacked the clergy and translated the Bible into the vernacular, Essexmen joined the Lollard Revolt of 1414; executions followed, creating many a martyr over the next century. By 1440 the heretics were refusing oaths and claiming that all property should be held in common. Later they kept their hats on during prayer, practiced fierce anticlericalism, and criticized the "covetousness" of the Church of England. According to Christopher Hill, the textile region around Colchester was "a breeding ground for Lollardy." The same was true for a new heretical movement, the Family of Love, or Familists, led by Henry Niclaes. Alongside the knowledge of bay- and say-making in the Dutch migrations of the late sixteenth century came radical religious ideas.[9]

Lollardy and Familism took root in the very region where the Lay family lived and where Quakerism would emerge in the middle of the seventeenth century. Indeed Copford's Robert Tibball, who was surely a descendent of the Essex Lollard leader John Tyball, was apparently a lifelong friend of Benjamin's father. William married Mary Dennis at Tibball's home in 1678, and the two men worked together, many years later, in 1712, to procure a Quaker burial ground for the CMM. As historian Adrian Davies has shown, religious radicalism had a long underground existence in Essex. The Lays were part of it.[10]

QUAKER

Quakerism emerged in the English Revolution within a motley crew of uppity commoners who used the quarrel between Cavalier (Royalist) and Roundhead (Parliamentarian) elites to propose their own solutions to the problems of the day. During the 1640s, as armies warred and censorship broke down, and during the interregnum of the 1650s, Protestant radicals such as Levellers, Seekers, Ranters, Diggers, and Quakers fought to deepen and radicalize the English Revolution, establish a godly republic, and advance the principles of democracy and equality. Many of these radicals were denounced as "antinomians"—people who believed that no one had the right or power to control the human conscience. Early Quakers epitomized the type. Benjamin never used the word—it was largely an epithet used by enemies—but he was deeply antinomian in every nuance. This was the wellspring of his radicalism and of the endless conflict and controversy that were his life.[11]

Led by the charismatic James Nayler of Yorkshire, a long-time soldier in the New Model Army, and George Fox, a shoemaker from Leicestershire known for his convulsive—quaking—manner of preaching, Quakers built a national movement in the 1650s. Nayler and Fox drew together men and women who had been Levellers, Seekers, Ranters, and Diggers to attack the Church of England: they shouted down ministers and refused to pay tithes. One Quaker recruit wrote, "I was struck with more terror before the preaching of James Naylor [*sic*] than I was before the Battle of Dunbar, when we had nothing else to expect but to fall a prey to the swords of our enemies." Another man screamed at Fox: "Don't pierce me so with thy eyes! Keep thy eyes off me!" Quakers believed that God was in each person in the form of a divine "inward light." Deeply anticlerical, they rejected ministerial mediation between God and the believer, reserving special wrath for "hireling ministers" who "preached their bellies." Quakers also insisted that wicked laws need not be obeyed. The early Quakers shared an affinity with the ultra-antinomian Ranters, who took their name from their rants against ungodly ministers and believed that to the pure of heart, all things were pure.[12]

Quakerism came to Benjamin's native Colchester in the militant spirit of eighteen-year-old itinerant James Parnell in 1655. Influenced by Familism, Parnell thought the time was right "to turn the world upside down; and this is the cause why the world rages." From Colchester jail he warned the wealthy to "weep and mourn" before the coming judgment: "the Lord is coming to burn you up as stubble before him." Another Quaker incarcerated in Colchester was Martha Simmonds, who disrupted church services and "was moved to walke in sackcloth barefoote with her hayre spread & ashes upon her head, in the toun in the frosty weather, to the astonishment of many." Parnell died in the jail in Colchester Castle in 1656 after a ten-month imprisonment and a ten-day fast; Simmonds went on to wilder antinomian controversy.[13]

Three principle characteristics of early Quakerism are crucial to understanding Benjamin's life and activism two generations later: public rants against established ministers, the refusal of "hat honor," and provocative street theater. Many Quakers, including Fox himself, routinely disrupted the services of the Church of England and other denominations. They would enter a Sunday service, sit in the congregation, wait for the minister to speak, then stand up and loudly denounce both speaker and sermon as unrighteous and unholy. Leo Damrosch has written that among the early

Quakers the denunciation of ministers was "understood to be a prophetic duty, and if it gave offense, so much the better." Best of all would be if serious persecution should follow, for this was a sure sign of God's favor. Quaker disruptions became so frequent, Oliver Cromwell issued a national proclamation in 1655 to prevent the heckling of ministers. Hundreds of Quakers were prosecuted and imprisoned for the practice, in Colchester and across England. Benjamin would continue the tradition of speaking truth to power, after which he was physically removed from many a meeting and even jailed on occasion.[14]

Quakers gave new meaning to an old form of protest in England when they refused to doff their hats in the presence of a so-called social superior. Such acts of deference were crucial to maintaining harmony in a class-riven society, so the Quaker refusal was considered not only a breach of social etiquette but an act of leveling equality. Radical Quakers took the practice further: John Perrot claimed that he received "an express commandment" directly from God that men should not take off their hats during prayer. After all, God was present in all believers—all were divine and equal—so what was the point? George Fox, who thought Perrot was "Nayler risen from the dead," was infuriated by this ultimate antinomian act, so he clamped down against the practice. But Perrot had preached in Colchester in 1657 and attracted numerous followers there, including members of the influential Furly family. The hat controversy would smolder on in the region and Benjamin would carry the practice into the eighteenth century.[15]

Early Quakers acted out high religious drama in public in order to shock people out of their sinful complacency. They conducted religious services anywhere and everywhere, in a private home, a barn, an open field, or in the streets, because they believed that a church was not a physical structure but rather any congregation of godly people. They frequently performed deliberately wild and eccentric acts such as "going naked for a sign" or burning a Bible in public to emphasize the primacy of the "inward light." One Quaker "came naked through [Westminster] hall, only very civilly tied about the privities to avoid scandal, and with a chafing-dish of fire and brimstone upon his head did pass through the Hall, crying, 'Repent! Repent!'" Women often played leading roles in these apocalyptic dramas.[16]

The most famous piece of Quaker guerrilla theater featured James Nayler, who, surrounded by Martha Simmonds and other Quaker women singing hosannas and laying flowers in his path, reenacted Christ's entry into

This hostile image of the early radical Quakers, depicted "going naked for a sign," emphasized their antinomian disdain for law. They were "above ordinances."

Jerusalem by riding into Bristol on a donkey in October 1656. Nayler was at the time the leading writer and theologian among Quakers, a coleader with Fox of a rapidly growing, already national, deeply subversive movement. When questioned by Bristol magistrates, Simmonds gave an antinomian explanation of her actions: she acted "in obedience to the power on high." Parliament seized the moment to try to break Nayler and the Quaker insurgency. After a debate lasting twelve sessions—about whether to execute him or torture him nearly to death—MPs condemned Nayler to three floggings, a bored tongue, a branding of the letter *B* (blasphemer) on his forehead, and incarceration, a savage set of punishments from which he never recovered. After the flogging it was said that Nayler had no skin left between his hips and his shoulders. He left prison a broken man in 1659 and died a year later.[17]

George Fox thought Nayler's extravagant actions had harmed the Quaker movement and took action. Against the antinomian ways of Nayler, Simmonds, Perrot, and many others, he led something of an internal counterrevolution in the 1660s and 1670s, instituting a series of reforms that would discipline or drive out the free spirits in his midst. His efforts to tame the radical Quakers occurred in the larger context of the restoration of

King Charles II and a reign of terror against those who had made the English Revolution, including and perhaps especially the Quakers, who were the most successful and longest-lasting of the radical religious groups that sprung up in the 1640s and 1650s. Fox declared the "peace testimony"—a vow of pacifism, an enduring and defining feature of Quakerism—in 1660, partly in reaction against the carnage of war and partly in a shrewd preemptive bid to lessen the violence he knew would be enacted against his own people. In the 1660s, furious at Perrot and his ilk, he implemented a new hierarchical meeting system that imposed self-censorship and collective discipline on the radical wing of the faith. He implemented a certificate system that required all Quakers to get approval from their local meeting before launching an itinerant ministry or changing congregations. He created separate meetings for women, who could be quite unruly. The original spontaneous, democratic style of Quakers was slowly but surely replaced by "a more rigid, authoritarian, catechetical technique" to preserve order. Quaker elders and leaders were *not* to be opposed. Not surprisingly, the reforms met opposition: in the 1670s the Story-Wilkinson group objected to subordination of the inward light to a new national hierarchy. But Fox carried on, waging and winning a twenty-year struggle against his own antinomian wing, creating in the end what Barry Reay has called a "Quaker ruling class." Fox won the battle with Nayler decisively, and Quakerism was profoundly changed between 1660 and 1700. Fox and his fellow rulers had effectively transformed a boisterous part of a revolutionary movement into a disciplined sect. Benjamin spent much of his life battling the mechanisms that Fox put in place to discipline free spirits such as himself.[18]

Benjamin, born two generations later, was in many ways a throwback to Nayler, Simmonds, Perrot, and other early radical Quakers. As we shall see, he followed their lead by visiting houses of worship to rant against the ungodliness of minister and congregation, all in a fierce effort to level church hierarchy and restore the proper egalitarian order of things. He observed leveling principles by keeping his hat upon his head during sermons and prayers. He engaged in street theater to shock people into a renewed sense of proper, ethical behavior. He shared with the early Quakers a love of the apocalyptic Book of Revelation, which became a cornerstone of his political theory. Many of the behaviors his contemporaries regarded as "mad" about Benjamin were actually antinomian survivals from the early history of Quakerism.

Radical Quakerism was the foundation of Benjamin's worldview. He self-consciously stood within a tradition of Protestant radicalism and indeed he constructed his own genealogy of it in *All Slave-Keepers . . . Apostates.* It began with Jesus, the apostles, and the "primitive Christians," who held "all things in common," according to the book of Acts (4:32). It continued through the heretical Waldensians, who arose in twelfth-century France, and carried on through the Reformation, to the Lollards, the Family of Love, and the antinomians of the English Revolution. To Benjamin, the glorious historical arc of Protestant radicalism reached its apotheosis with the "primitive," antinomian Quakers of the 1650s. These brothers and sisters lit the path to glory.[19]

FORDHAM: SHEPHERD

During the late 1690s, a teenage Benjamin left his parents' cottage in Copford and traveled about fifty miles northwest to work on the farm of his half-brother William in Fordham, a prosperous village located in eastern Cambridgeshire. Benjamin's work during this time was the care of sheep, whose wool drove the regional economy. He also formed a lifelong attachment to William's family, wife Sarah and their six children, none of whom, it appears, were Quakers. Benjamin seems to have had a special relationship with one of the younger sons, Philip, whom he would remember fondly in his will of 1731.[20]

Benjamin loved the work of the shepherd, as he recalled in *All Slave-Keepers . . . Apostates*: "I remember about 40 years ago I kept my elder Brother's Sheep, and the pretty Lambs and their Dams would be quietly sweetly and prettily feeding together, a very beautiful and comely Sight to see." All was not idyllic, however: at times, Benjamin, like many shepherds, got "a little careless and sleepy," whereupon his brother's sheep "would go wandring about over Hedge and Ditch, and get into my Neighbour's Corn, and do Mischief." It was no easy matter to recover them all: "Sometimes it would cost me many Tears before I could get them in to order again." Even more worrisome was the trouble caused by roving dogs, which would scatter the sheep and occasionally kill them. This would be a "Grief" to his brother and a "Reproach" to himself. Yet all things considered, Benjamin loved tending the "pretty pretty dear Lambs."[21]

Lambs and sheep would come to play an important part in Benjamin's thinking about the world. He used the gentle creatures as metaphors throughout his writing. As a seeker of the true church he saw all genuinely Godly people as "dear lambs." He regarded Jesus as the most dutiful shepherd, "who laid down his Life for his Sheep and Lambs." He considered slave-owning ministers to be wolves in "Sheeps Cloathing." Benjamin's ideal for a Quaker meeting was one in which the assembled were "as silent as a Flock of Sheep and Lambs in a Field, sweetly feeding, without Noise of Words." He was of course drawing on Biblical verse and a major theme in Christian theology, even if he rarely kept silent himself.[22]

Yet the lamb also had a more specific—and militant—meaning for Benjamin and indeed for many Quakers, who since the 1650s had seen themselves as engaged in the "The Lamb's War"—the desperate fight against satanic forces as they sought to build the "New Jerusalem" on earth. *The Lamb's War* was the title of an influential pamphlet written by James Nayler, originally printed in London in 1657 and republished in 1716. Nayler and George Fox, like Benjamin, drew on the apocalyptic Book of Revelation in explaining the war of good against evil, the archangel Michael against the Great Red Dragon, who, once defeated, was exiled to earth and brought Satan's dominion with him. This parable, in which the lamb was a central actor, would guide Benjamin in his view of Christianity, divinity, Quakerism, and in the end slavery. The roots of this life-forming interpretation lay in an early experience of work.[23]

COLCHESTER: GLOVER

When the time came for Benjamin to leave his half-brother's household and begin life on his own, his father apprenticed him to a master glover in Colchester. Glove making was a low and unpleasant craft, one of the "stinking trades"—the glover worked primarily with the skins of dead animals. Families of modest means often bound their children to glovers, tailors, or shoemakers as these crafts required only a modest payment to the master to train the child. Because glove making took "neither much Strength nor Ingenuity," it was rapidly proletarianized in the eighteenth century, including ever-larger numbers of women. The tedious work was also known as "a sedentary Stooping Business."[24]

According to an eighteenth-century survey of the crafts in London, the glover worked primarily with the skins of sheep, goats, and deer, dressed with allum and salt. The glover cut the leather into different sizes and shapes, then stitched them together, sometimes lining them with rabbit fur. Better-off glovers (unlike Benjamin) might put the cut leather pieces out to seamstresses for stitching, while those who had wealthier patrons might also make muffs and tippets, sometimes with ermine. Like the tailor, the glover depended on shears and needles, his main tools. Indeed, the inventory of Benjamin's material possessions taken at his death in 1759 included "a pair of Glovers Shairs," gloves of various kinds, and twelve thousand pins!

Benjamin loved being a shepherd, but he did not like being a glover, which is probably the main reason he ran away to London to become a sailor when he reached the age of twenty-one in 1703. Even though he returned to the craft of glove making after he left the sea, practicing it for a number of years in London and Colchester, he would eventually escape it. During the 1730s, not long after he moved to Philadelphia, Benjamin decisively rejected a line of work that depended on violence against animals. Like Thomas Tryon, who made beaver hats and would later, as a writer and a founding father of vegetarianism, have a great influence on Benjamin's view of the world, the experience of life and work in a "stinking trade" would contribute to a radical rethinking of the relationship between human beings and the rest of the animal world.

LONDON: SAILOR

A young and independent Benjamin took off for London, the swarming metropolis of six hundred thousand souls who stood at the center of England's global empire. He was happy to escape his work as a glover, but he also had positive reasons for moving to the London waterfront. According to Roberts Vaux, Quakers who had heard Benjamin's stories of his life at sea said that he sought "to gratify *the leading inclination of his mind*, which withdrew him from the interesting and innocent employments of agriculture, to encounter the hardships and perils of the life of a sailor." Benjamin was curious and he was brave; he wanted to see the world more than he feared the dangers of life at sea. This is especially significant given his father's promise that on the death of Benjamin's mother, Mary, he would inherit a family farm in Layer Breton. Benjamin could have bided his time and eventually become a settled, propertied yeoman like his half-brothers. But he looked to the horizon and wanted to see what lay beyond it. He was nothing if not headstrong about anything he decided to do.[25]

Benjamin picked an extraordinary year, 1703, to head toward the docks along the River Thames. On November 26 a cyclone tore through southern England: eighty-mile-per-hour winds toppled hundreds of windmills and chimneys. Wreckage was extreme in Essex and in London, where dozens of sloops, schooners, brigs, snows, and ships were either sunk or pitched together in a confused tangle of splintered masts and torn rigging. As many as ten thousand seafaring lives were lost during "the great storm." This was perhaps the greatest catastrophe ever visited upon the Thames waterfront.[26]

Edward Barlow, who had been sailing the high seas on English ships for almost half a century, offered a class-conscious interpretation of the origins and meaning of the storm: it was a "warning of God's anger . . . for no man values his word or promise, or matters what he doth or saith, so that he can but gain and defraud his neighbour. All commanders and masters of ships are grown up with pride and oppression and tyranny." "I want words," he concluded in frustration, "to lay out the business and unworthy dealings of many men I have met with, not acting like Christians." If Benjamin was already in the city, he escaped the wrath of nature unharmed. If not, he later entered a city in great need of maritime labor. He had chosen a line of work menaced by both natural and man-made dangers.[27]

For the next dozen years Benjamin would live alternately in London and, for months at a time, in a new social world all its own—the deep-sea sailing ship, the most advanced and consequential machine of its day. This engine of wood, canvas, and hemp, and the men who sailed it, had made possible the vast blue-water empires of Portugal, Spain, the Netherlands, France, and England. Benjamin lived in cramped quarters with multiethnic fellow workers, cooperating within a strict hierarchy beneath a captain with extreme powers of discipline, to move ships and their cargoes around the world. Gangs of sailors messed together, spun yarns, set sails, and maintained the ship. Their lives were profoundly collective.

Benjamin climbed aloft to work the sails, remembering at all times the saying, "one hand for the ship, one for yourself." He heard the captain bawl his commands against the wind as it whistled through the rigging. In stormy seas the timbers groaned as the vessel rocked and rolled; sailors defied the elements with their curses. In better weather Benjamin felt the sun and spray in his face as the ship clipped along with a brisk wind in its sails. He watched majestic sunrises and sunsets. He scanned the horizon and surveyed the ever-changing seas, always looking for clues about what omnipotent nature might do next to a lonely, brittle ship. He would test his physical strength and mental resolve to the limit, risking his life in a dangerous calling. This was the price of seeing the world and learning the ways of its peoples. His inquiring mind had taken him to sea: he filled it with the cosmopolitan knowledge that only a well-traveled sailor could acquire.[28]

Benjamin's years at sea created a lifelong identity. In *All Slave-Keepers . . . Apostates*, published in 1738, Lay called himself a "common sailor," even though he had not worked at sea for almost a quarter century. He was a "plain dealer"—he spoke simply, directly, and without deference, as seamen were known to do. He ate from a simple wooden bowl and slept in a hammock, sailor-style. And at the end of his life he made a request that shocked his friends and acquaintances: he asked a man to "burn his body, and throw the ashes into the sea." Benjamin repeatedly used his seafaring experience to explain who he was. He had imbibed the traditions of seafaring during a formative phase of life.[29]

Several people who knew Benjamin recalled one of his stories about "ocean wandering." On a Mediterranean voyage he visited Samaria in the southern part of the Ottoman Empire, in search of a place important to Biblical history. He probably jumped ship in a Turkish port, got aboard a small craft, sailed south to the port of Haifa, then hiked inland, over mountainous terrain, to visit the spot where Jesus met with the "woman of Samaria." When he arrived Benjamin did what Jesus had done after a long journey: he "refreshed himself by a draft of water from *Jacob's Well*." What he later found significant about both the Biblical story and its setting was that it was a woman who carried the divine word about the messiah to the Samaritans. As Benjamin explained in *All Slave-Keepers . . . Apostates*, "Male and Female are all one in Christ the Truth." He used his seafaring travels to explore the history of Christianity and later to make a statement about gender equality.[30]

Sailing around the world gave Benjamin a hard-earned, hard-edged cosmopolitanism. He appealed to his proletarian experience as the basis of his authority in writing his book against slavery: "I know what I write by large experience, for many Years, in several Nations, where my lot hath been cast." Like many sailors, Lay saw his "lot" as having been "cast" rather than "chosen." Such was the case for most picaresque proletarians. Still, he had traveled the globe and could claim to know "Mankind, in all Nations, Colours, and Countries in the World." He spoke proudly of his cosmopolitan experience, and indeed he announced it on the very cover page of his book. The author, he declared, "truly and sincerely desires the present and eternal Welfare and Happiness of all Mankind, all the World over, of all Colours, and Nations, as his own Soul." This was enlightenment from below.[31]

Like other sailors, Lay adapted strategies of resistance to a reality of incessant movement. The seafaring sage "Barnaby Slush" (pen name) noted that early-eighteenth-century sailors responded to the excesses of authority with "an unchangeable Resolution of deserting at the first opportunity." Lay used this approach in late 1717. He faced a dilemma when he decided to ask Sarah Smith to marry him. He needed a certificate from his own Devonshire House Monthly Meeting in London affirming that he was clear of debt and marital obligations; no problem there. But he was in trouble with local "weighty Quakers" for having opposed ministers in public meetings. Benjamin therefore decided to sail from London to Salem, Massachusetts, and to request a marriage certificate from the local Quaker meeting *over there*. He likely worked the voyage over, stayed a couple of months, made the request, ranted against the pompous Puritan prelate Cotton Mather, and sailed back home. The stratagem eventually worked: Benjamin and Sarah married July 10, 1718.[32]

Benjamin used the same strategy of mobility repeatedly in subsequent years as he fought one Quaker meeting after another about issues of hierarchy and power, whether in London, Colchester, or Philadelphia. Almost every move Benjamin made after he retired from the sea was an escape from a system of religious authority designed to control radicals like himself. He remained, throughout his life, always restlessly in motion, traveling widely and visiting, for example, Quaker meetings in Pennsylvania, New Jersey, New York, and New England, many miles at a time. He always traveled on foot as he opposed the exploitation of horses.[33]

Benjamin's knowledge of slavery began at sea, with a sailor's yarn. He sailed to the Mediterranean: "I was near 18 Months, on board a large Vessel of 400 Tons in a Voyage to *Scanderoon* [Iskenderun] in *Turkey*." This was a big ship on a long voyage with a crew as large as fifty men—quite a concentration of worldly experience and knowledge. Benjamin met "four Men that had been 17 Years Slaves in *Turky*." He carefully took in their yarns, then later compared what he learned to the stories he heard from other sailors who had worked in the African slave trade. Benjamin heard accounts of rape in the infamous Middle Passage—that "the Captain [kept] 6 or 10 of 'em in the Cabbin, and the Sailors as many as they pleased," all to satisfy "their lusts." He identified not with the crew but their female victims. He also understood that in Africa the trade tended to the "Destruction and the Ruin of the whole Country." He concluded that the four men enslaved in Turkey were not as "badly used" by Muslims "as the poor Negroes are by some called Christians."[34]

Benjamin's cosmopolitan experience as a sailor resonated with a Biblical passage (Acts 17:26) that would eventually become a centerpiece of the abolitionist movement: God "hath made of one Blood all Nations of Men for to dwell on all the Face of the Earth." Benjamin took to heart this assertion of the spiritual equality of all humankind, saying confidently to his fellow Quakers that God "did not make others to be Slaves to us." His Quaker belief and maritime experience sailing the "Face of the Earth" joined to produce a radical assertion of unity at a time when race and slavery were rapidly dividing up global humanity. Benjamin never once used the word "race" in *All Slave-Keepers . . . Apostates*, preferring always the more neutral, more objective, less divisive "color." His insistence that people were "of one blood" deracialized and denationalized his arguments against slavery.[35]

Benjamin demonstrated his commitment to equality in the very language he used to describe people of African descent. He said not a word about any of them being "savage," "barbaric," "inferior," or "uncivilized," the standard racist tropes of his day. He reserved the word "barbarity" strictly for the European mistreatment of Africans. He evinced no condescension, no paternalism. He wrote that if the hundreds of thousands in slavery were given "the same Education, Learning, Conversation, Books, [and] sweet Communion in our Religious Assemblies," they would "exceed many of their Tyrant Masters in Piety, Virtue and Godliness." This he knew because he had talked with a great many Africans; he knew firsthand what he called "their bright Genius." Enslaved people deserved liberty, which is "life" itself.[36]

Because of their collective labor in a dangerous environment sailors were known for their solidarity, to one another and to other workers. Their cry "one and all" was heard in mutinies, strikes, and waterfront riots around the Atlantic. Lay's class experience created in him a lifelong sensitivity to issues of labor and an empathy for those who worked under difficult, sometimes deadly conditions. Dependency on the money wage and the reality of being bilked by captains taught him and other sailors something about the labor theory of value. Benjamin recognized that slave owners, including Quakers, paid no regard, as Edward Barlow noted, to "Equity or Right, not heeding whether they give them [the enslaved] any thing near so much as their Labour deserveth." He linked seafaring and slavery back to the Bible, to Jeremiah 22:15: "Wo unto him that buildeth his House by Iniquity, and useth his Neighbour's Service without Wages, and giveth him not for his Work."[37]

Benjamin used his seafaring knowledge to indict slave traders as a class of murderers. He was perhaps the first ever to do so. Here he anticipated an argument made a century later by Friedrich Engels, who claimed, in *The Condition of the Working Class in England* (1845), that factory owners in England who caused workers to live in deadly conditions were in fact guilty of "social murder." Benjamin saw that the operation of the slave trade routinely and systematically produced death, and he held the organizers of that trade personally responsible. In *All Slave-Keepers . . . Apostates* he noted that slavers were so puffed up with pride that they thought themselves beyond the Bible, beyond law, beyond "*Abraham*, Prophets, [and] Patriarchs." They were beyond all moral sense. They had come to "*Cain* the Murtherer," and Benjamin insisted they were beyond him too, for Cain had "Murthered but one." He said to the traders directly, you, *you*, have killed "many Thousands, or caused 'em to be so."[38]

Conscious of the long, lethal history of the slave trade, Benjamin went further in his indictment: "for ought I know," slavers may have murdered "many Hundreds of Thousands." At the very moment he wrote these words, two and a half million Africans had already been transported through a nightmarish Middle Passage to the plantations of the Americas. His estimate was right: "Hundreds of Thousands" had already been murdered. The actual number was almost half a million—lifeless bodies thrown over the rail of ships to the sharks that followed the slavers across the Atlantic. Benjamin not only denounced the murderers of enslaved Africans; he also glimpsed the magnitude of their crime. The sailor-turned-abolitionist was also one of the first to condemn the maritime holocaust perpetrated by Atlantic slave traders.[39]

. . .

By the time Benjamin reached his early thirties he was a working man of the world: he had known pastoral labor, sheep herding; he had experienced the urban crafts as a glover; and he had survived rigorous proletarian work at sea as a "common sailor." He had lived in a small village, a manufacturing town, an imperial metropolis, and on big ships, on the oceans and in port cities around the world. All of these experiences shaped his consciousness, expanding a core of radical Quaker concerns, values, and practices. As a throwback to the "primitive Quakers" and the English Revolution, Benjamin would challenge his fellow Quakers in London and Colchester on a wide variety of issues.

CHAPTER TWO

"A MAN OF STRIFE & CONTENTION"

DURING THE EIGHTEEN years after Benjamin retired from the sea, his main preoccupations—the dangers of false ministers and the evils of slavery—took shape amid intense engagements with the Quaker communities of London, Bridgetown, Barbados, and Colchester. Benjamin's "zeal" became more pronounced and more public as he repeatedly conflicted with his fellow Quakers over matters he considered intolerable but they did not. Behind both themes was his worry that "covetousness" was destroying Quakerism. What slowly developed into a struggle for the soul of the faith became in the end something much bigger: a campaign to save the world from itself. Between 1714 and 1732 Benjamin walked a treacherous path toward prophecy.

LONDON, 1714–1718

The earliest record of Benjamin's active participation in organized Quakerism originated in America. Even though he was based in London at the time, he had sailed to Boston to request a certificate of approval from local Quakers to marry Sarah Smith of Deptford, England. The Quaker meeting (actually located in Salem) in turn sent a letter to Benjamin's home congregation, the Devonshire House Monthly Meeting (DHMM) in London, asking if he was a Friend in good standing and therefore eligible for marriage within the faith. Three London Quakers were appointed to look into "his Conversation & Clearness in Relation to marriage."[1]

The committee gathered information and noted that Benjamin had joined the congregation about three years earlier, in 1714, and that "he is clear from Debts and from women in relation to marriage." But the report added that Benjamin "hath given dissatisfaction to divers Freinds in severall Meetings" and suggested that this concern be expressed in the certificate as a warning to Quakers in Massachusetts. In an official document of June 1717 twenty-six signatories of the DHMM said of Benjamin:

> We believe he is Convinced of the Truth but for want of keeping low and humble in his mind, hath by an Indiscreet Zeal been too forward to appear in our publick Meetings to the Uneasiness of ffriends, we therefore in Good Will Exhort him to Lowliness of mind, that he may know how to behave himself peaceably in the Church among you and Else where to ffriends Satisfaction and leave it to friends to act towards him in Charity, according to their freedom, and as he may deserve.

So convinced of the truth as to be arrogant, zealous, belligerent, and aggressive, the "Quaker comet," as Benjamin was later called, made his first appearance in the skies of historical documentation. A lifelong pattern of troublemaking would follow.[2]

The woman Benjamin sought to marry, Sarah Smith, was born in Rochester, County Kent, near the Medway River, in 1677. Like Benjamin, she was a dwarf and a hunchback. Her deceased father, John Smith, had been a plaisterer, a middling artisan who specialized in plastering and whitewashing walls and ceilings. At some point the family moved to Deptford, located on the southern bank of the Thames River across from the Isle of Dogs and home of the first shipyard of England's Royal Navy. Sarah converted to Quakerism "in her young years" and soon demonstrated a gift for preaching. By 1712 she had earned so much respect from the Quaker community of Deptford as to be designated an "approved minister." She traveled widely and represented the local congregation. Around that time, one of the many sailors who passed through Deptford may have been Benjamin Lay. The two probably met at the Deptford Quaker Monthly Meeting.[3]

Benjamin and Sarah would settle down in a part of London called St. Ethelburga, located in the ward of Bishopsgate in northeast London. Benjamin left the sea and resumed his trade as a glover. Around this time he commenced what would be a lifelong practice: in "divers Places of this City and suburbs" he visited a variety of churches and even several different Quaker meetings to learn about their preachers, their ideas, and their congregations. He was a "Seeker" of the pure church. He was a member of the DHMM in Bishopsgate, but he also attended the Wheeler Street (Spitalfields), Gracechurch Street, Peel, Bullhill, and Bull and Mouth Quaker meetings. Through these meetings he cut a path of turmoil that would lead to his first disownment.[4]

Six months after Benjamin was exhorted to "Lowliness of mind," he got into more serious trouble when he confronted two "Publick Friends" (approved ministers), William Selkald and Richard Price, during worship services at the Devonshire House and Wheeler Street Meetings. He did not like their preaching. The holy spirit, he was sure, was not in them. They were "preaching their own words," not God's truth, so Benjamin bid them "to be Silent, and sit down," adding for good measure that Price was a hypocrite. Benjamin later described the kind of preaching he objected to: many, he wrote, "are grown restless and uneasy in sitting in silence." Those who had "a strong Opinion of their own Performances, and a rich Conceit of the great good they do," started speaking, "hammering and tampering." They went to work "with Noise of Words, and oftentimes no Sense." Conceit was vanity, and silence, so crucial to Quaker worship, was being disrespected, so Benjamin took it upon himself to enforce an old tradition. The leaders of Devonshire House disapproved. They appointed three Friends to speak with Benjamin, "tenderly," about his outburst and to encourage him "to come to a sense of his offence." The meeting officially condemned his acts and required that he affirm the condemnation in order to be reinstated.[5]

When questioned by the deputed Friends, Benjamin was ornery. He refused to provide direct answers and would not admit guilt. Rather, he "justifyed the Practice." When he showed up a month later at a worship service, he was given a copy of the article drawn up against him. He replied that he hoped he would not grieve his friends any more by his actions. Two weeks later, when he reappeared, the article was read aloud in what amounted to a ritual of public shaming. He replied that he "would not joyn with the Meeting" in condemning what he had done. Urged again to admit his "Disorderly Practice," Benjamin stated that he had nothing more to say. He was sure he was right and would not admit wrongdoing.[6]

A month later Benjamin submitted to the DHMM what was essentially the same apology in writing: "It appearing that freinds have been greived on my account, which I am sory for. And hope my conduct for the future will be such as to give no occasion to freinds." It only "appeared" that Friends were "greived" and Benjamin merely "hoped" that he would do better in the future. Not surprisingly the DHMM did not accept the grudging apology. Moreover, until Benjamin demonstrated "sincerity and unity of Spirrit with us," they decided to withhold the final, official copy of the marriage certificate he needed to marry Sarah. Their resolve had been stiffened by another recent event: Benjamin had gotten so angry at another "Publick Friend" that he shook a cane in his face after a meeting.[7]

Whatever their complaints about him, Benjamin insisted, they had no right to withhold his marriage certificate. He went over their heads with an appeal directly to the London Quarterly Meeting, which appointed ten Friends from all over the city to look into the matter. They conducted interviews with all parties and issued a report, saying that "wee absolutely disapprove of Benj Lays behaviour in his open opposition to some Publicke friends," but the LQM added that the DHMM ought to give Benjamin the marriage certificate, which in fact they did. Benjamin had won the battle, and he and Sarah were married July 10, 1718. But tensions within the local meeting lingered as Benjamin never gave satisfaction for his disruptive behavior. Two months later Benjamin and Sarah set sail for Barbados to begin a new chapter of life.[8]

BARBADOS, 1718–1720

The Lays arrived in Barbados in fall 1718, putting Benjamin's ruckus with his fellow Quakers in London behind them, at least for a time. Perhaps they chose the island destination because Benjamin had sailed there during his time at sea. Undoubtedly they wanted to live in a place that had a Quaker community, which Barbados, the first cradle of Quakerism in the Americas, did, although it was now small and declining. Once disembarked in the leading port of Bridgetown, the former sailor followed the path of many seafarers who aged out of a body-breaking occupation:

he set up a small shop to serve those who worked on the bustling docks—from merchants and artisans to sailors, indentured servants, and those who slaved on the waterfront and sold their own produce there on "market day." There is no evidence to suggest that Benjamin caused controversy or courted disownment among the Quakers of Barbados, but he certainly did create discord—of a bigger, more explosive kind—during his eighteen months on the island.[9]

Benjamin and Sarah had landed in the world's leading slave society, the crown jewel of the British imperial tiara. Only a few years before they arrived, Thomas Walduck, a military man who had spent fourteen years in the West Indies, had drawn a rich portrait of their new island home. Walduck was no abolitionist but he nonetheless gave a vivid, critical, now humorous, now acid account of both the origins and material reality of Barbados slave society. He wrote that the first settlers "were a Babel of all Nations and Conditions of men, English, Welch, Scotch, Irish, Dutch, Deans [Danes], and French." Each group made a singular contribution: "The English brought with them drunkenness and swearing, the Scotch Impudence & Falshood, The Welch covetousness & Revenge, the Irish Cruelty & perjury, the Dutch and Deans Craft & Rusticity and the French Dissimulation & Infidelity." He added to the motley crew a significant Jewish population and many thousands of enslaved Africans from "the Guiney Angola and Weda [Ouidah] Coast." The combination of nine thousand people of European descent and more than seventy thousand Africans added up to "the worst scene of all quarrells and contentious pride and poverty drunkenness and debauchery."[10]

Slavery defined the island for all peoples who lived there: a master class ruled and terrorized an army of African slaves. The planters, observed Walduck, are "unmercifully cruel to their poor slaves by whome they get their living without a wet finger." They forced bondsmen and women to work eighteen hours a day without rest. The sugar they produced brought huge profits: "It is a common saying amgt the planters that if they give 30 [pounds] for a Negro and he lives one year he payes for himself." The planters, according to Walduck, were, as a class, "Unjust in their words & Dealings one to the Other," as well as, "Horrible profane and rude in their Discourse and Conversation." They possessed no moral code and no proper religion. They thought of God only in their "Curses & Blasphemies." They took better care of their horses than the workers on whom they depended.

Walduck concluded one of his letters with "An Acrostick upon ye Island of Barbadoes & ye Inhabitants thereof":

> ***B**arbadoes Isle inhabited by slaves*
> ***A**nd for one honest man ten thousand knaves*
> ***R**eligion to thee's a Romantick Storey*
> ***B**arbarity and ill gott wealth thy glory*
> ***A**ll Sodom's Sins are Centred in thy heart*
> ***D**eath is thy look and Death in every part*
> ***O**h Glorious isle in Vilany Excell*
> ***S**in to the height thy fate is Hell.*

Benjamin and Sarah saw right away that in this land of "Barbarity and ill gott wealth" the struggle against slavery began with sheer existence. They witnessed enslaved people so weak they fainted and collapsed in the street. Some were "ready to perish with Hunger and Sickness." Exhausted, emaciated workers staggered into their waterfront shop, buying, begging, and sometimes stealing small items and food. Early on, Benjamin responded to the theft in anger, lashing a few of the culprits, but he soon understood that this monstrous slave society called Barbados had been built by bigger thieves, who sought not subsistence but riches. Wracked with guilt for having behaved like a slave master, Benjamin decided to educate himself by talking with the enslaved and learning about their lives. He heard stories of violent mistreatment: "One Says, *My Master very bad Man; another, My Mistress very bad Woman.*"[11]

Benjamin saw with close intimacy the bloody dialectic of torture and resistance that would haunt him for the rest of his life. He got to know an enslaved man, "a lusty Fellow, a Cooper," who made his master, Richard Parrot, "7 s. 6 d. a day." The man was highly skilled and extremely valuable, but Parrot was a cruel master who "used to whip his Negroes on Second-day [Monday] Mornings very severely, to keep them in awe." The unnamed man complained to the sympathetic Benjamin: "*My Master* Parrot *very bad man indeed, whippe, whippe poor Negro evee Munne Morning for notin tall! me no bear no longer.*" The cooper kept his dreadful word: on a Sunday night he took his own life because, as Benjamin explained, "he would not be *whippe Munne Morning.*"[12]

On another occasion Sarah visited "a plain coat," a fellow Quaker and a slave owner, in Speightstown, a dozen miles up the coast from Bridgetown. Outside the Friend's house she was startled to encounter "a Negro stark naked" suspended in the air, probably by chains. Below his "trembling and shivering" body lay a "Flood of Blood." Tender-hearted Sarah froze in speechless horror. But "at last a little recovering," she went indoors and begged the Quaker to explain. Not only did he show no remorse over the cruel treatment; he railed against the man, who had dared to run away for "a day or two." The Quaker justified the torture Sarah saw outside his door.[13]

This was no uncommon event in Barbados. By "conversing, trading, and living daily" with the enslaved, Benjamin and Sarah witnessed, up close, a gruesome array of tortures: many people, Benjamin lamented, "are Murthered by Working hard, and Starving, Whipping, Racking, Hanging, Burning, Scalding, Roasting, and other Hellish Torments," routine practices that were "very sorrowful to consider." He witnessed public events staged to create terror and ensure planter control of their workers. He saw fatal accidents in the industrialized production of sugar. Slaves were mangled, sheared-off body parts fell into boiling sugar vats, and sugar itself ended up containing "Limbs, Bowels, and excrements." Long before anyone campaigned against the extreme violence of plantation production, Benjamin knew that "sugar was made with blood." He asked ruefully, "O when will there be an end of these things?"[14]

The Lays began to hold meetings and serve meals at their home, which drew ever larger crowds of enslaved people, many in defiance of their masters. Eventually "many hundreds" turned up, creating a public spectacle and fierce disapproval from the white population, who began to "clamour" against the Lays. At these gatherings the host and hostess denounced slavery, drawing the attention and, finally, the wrath of the island's ruling class, which sought to banish them for their subversive fraternization with slaves and their growing opposition to slavery. In truth Benjamin and Sarah themselves had already decided to leave. Shocked by the crimson cruelties of daily life, they feared their hearts would harden and they would be "leavened too much into the Nature of the People there." Would they come to resemble these "Masters and Mistresses of Slaves"? Would they take on their "Pride and Oppression" and compromise their own souls? They had already seen this happen to fellow Quakers.[15]

After eighteen months the Lays returned to London, but the look of death in Barbados had transformed them. Benjamin would remain haunted—one might say tormented—for the rest of his life by his encounter with slavery. He later wrote of the trauma he suffered in Barbados, noting that his "afflicted mind" had been "tossed as with a Tempest at times, above 17 Years, on this sad Account [of] Slave-Keeping." He remembered that time as a turning point, when he converted to abolitionist principles. He would never forget the desperate hunger of the enslaved nor the vicious violence of the masters. Amid the gilded depravity of Barbados, Benjamin found a new Babylon. He would make it his life's purpose to tear it down.[16]

LONDON, 1720–1722

Benjamin and Sarah sailed back to London in the fall of 1720, deeply shaken by their experience in Barbados. They returned to worship at the Devonshire House Monthly Meeting (DHMM), no doubt hoping to put past troubles behind them and to make yet another fresh start. But less than a month after their return, Benjamin was once again challenging Quaker ministers in public. His fellow Quakers in London already knew his disputatious ways—he had, after all, never atoned for his previous transgressions. Their patience soon wore out.

The trigger was an encounter in late October 1720 with a minister named Zachary Routh at the Quaker meeting on Wheeler Street. Benjamin and Routh apparently had some history. Benjamin spoke out against him as he preached, then insisted to several Quakers after the meeting that Routh was "a Drunkard and a Swine." When asked to justify the charges Benjamin added that the man was "Drunk with wind": he preached "in his own spirit and not from the Spirit of Truth." Those who heard the charge were scandalized and reported Benjamin's "vile accusations" to the DHMM, whose leaders once again investigated and asked Benjamin to retract his comments and repent, all for the sake of "the Peace of our Meeting." Quaker Joseph North delivered the article to Benjamin, who was not willing to comply.[17]

When Benjamin appeared a month later at a worship meeting, the article about his disturbance at Wheeler Street was read aloud before the full congregation, again in order to shame him. Would he, in public, admit wrongdoing and renounce his attack on Brother Routh? He would not.

He would not be shamed. Once again Benjamin refused the advice and discipline of the meeting and justified his criticism. After further deliberation the exasperated leaders of the DHMM turned to their most potent sanction: "the Meeting Doth Intirely Disown—and Him also—untill he repent and Acknowledge his Offence." Three months after his return from Barbados, the man to whom Quakerism meant so much was now no longer a member of the community.[18]

Yet the DHMM did not give up on Benjamin. Two months later, in early March 1721, Joseph North once again tried to deliver to Benjamin the article that had been drawn up against him and to ask him to give satisfaction. North found Benjamin in his glover's workshop in St. Ethelburga. Benjamin was not in a mood to receive the complaint. When North handed the paper to him, he looked at it, then "slighted it and threw it out of his shop window." North dutifully retrieved the document, returned to the shop, and placed it on Benjamin's counter, where he conducted business. But the glove maker ignored both the message and the messenger. Meantime, Benjamin continued to attend Quaker worship meetings and continued "to oppose Publicke ffriends in their Testimony." The man was self-righteous—and stubborn. Three months after the London Quarterly Meeting received official news of his disownment, Benjamin decided to do what he had always done when confronted with deep and abiding conflict: he took to his feet and moved, this time back to his native Colchester.[19]

COLCHESTER, 1722–1726

When Benjamin moved to Colchester in 1722 he returned to a historic city in whose shadow he had grown up, four miles away in Copford. Over the centuries Colchester had suffered Roman, Saxon, Danish, and Norman conquerors. Philip Morant, chronicler of the city's history and "antiquities" in the eighteenth century, added English revolutionaries to the list when he described the siege of the city by Sir Thomas Fairfax and the New Model Army in 1648: "This poor and unhappy Town," he wrote, was "brought under the tyranny of an Army, the most undesirable of Masters, and what is worse, an Army of Enthusiasts." (William Dell and John Saltmarsh, whose ideas Benjamin would embrace, were two of the invading army's leading enthusiasts.) When Benjamin arrived, the city still bore the marks of the siege in Colchester Castle's "batter'd walls" and breached turrets. He and

Sarah took up residence inside the walls in the oldest part of the city, near St. Peter's, the medieval church noted in *The Domesday Book* of 1086. He opened a glover's shop, but, ever the rebel, he did not register with the city as a "freeman," for which he was soon indicted "for keeping open Shop being a foreigner." He lived not far from "Red-Row" on High Street, later called "The Exchange," where rich merchants gathered to organize the textile trade. A couple of blocks to the northwest, in "Quaker Alley," stood the "Great Meeting House," built in 1663 and consisting of three large rooms and a gallery, where Benjamin and Sarah worshipped. This was the home of the Colchester Two Weeks Meeting (CTWM). A slowly declining community of five hundred Quakers lived in the city and the surrounding region.[20]

By August 1722 Benjamin was renewing the history of "enthusiasm" as he attacked one local minister after another. He had "in a disorderly manner undertaken to charge some Public Friends with preaching their own words, and going beyond the leads of the Spirit of God." His reputation for such behavior had preceded him. Knowing that Benjamin had been disowned in London and that he "threaten[ed] yet further the disturbance of Friends Meetings in this Town," the leaders of the CTWM wrote the London Committee of Sufferings and the DHMM to ask what to do about this man they considered to be in a "Dark disordered Condition." Benjamin had apparently inquired about membership, so he would be reminded that he had to make amends with the DHMM before the request could be considered.[21]

Seven elders of the CTWM summoned Benjamin to attend a meeting to discuss his "disorderly and irregular practices." He refused. The CTWM then took decisive action, as announced in an official minute:

> We therefore in concurrence with our Friends of Devonshire House Monthly Meeting do signify our great dislike to and dissatisfaction wth his irregular disorderly & evil practices tending to Confusions as well as at London as amongst us wherefore we can have no Unity with him until he has given ye Friends of ye Monthly Meeting of Devonshire House Satisfaction for his Offense during the time of his Residence in London and Afterwards gives this meeting satisfaction also.

The declaration of "no unity" was essentially a second disownment, although technically it would not count as such because Benjamin would have had to be reinstated at Devonshire House before he could be officially disowned again in Colchester. Once again he took less than three months to mire himself in deep conflict with his own congregation.[22]

Benjamin and Sarah looked for a more congenial meeting and found it in the Colchester Monthly Meeting (CMM), where Quakers gathered from villages outside Colchester proper: Copford (Benjamin's place of birth), Bentley, Birch, Boxted, Harwich, Horkesley, Manningtree, Oakley, Osyth, and Thorpe. This was the meeting to which Benjamin's parents and grandparents had belonged. Many Quakers from these scattered villages lived far from their monthly meeting place, so business meetings were usually small—and often dominated by women. An important part of the history of the CMM was its decision in 1692 to reject a national trend among Quakers toward separate meetings for men and women and to unite the two into a single deliberative body. It was collectively decided that the two would "meet together & not apart upon ye monthly meeting daies . . . to manage ye affairs of business except upon some peculiar occasions yt may happen."[23]

As conflicts about Benjamin raged in the CTWM during the years 1723–1724, Sarah quietly shifted her allegiance and membership. She presented her certificate from Deptford, where she had lived before she married Benjamin, to the CMM, whose members readily accepted it. Among the women who welcomed her were Elizabeth Kendall, with whom she engaged in a traveling ministry, and Mary Bundock and Elizabeth Dennis, who were members of Benjamin's extended family. At this very moment relations between the CTWM and the CMM turned hostile, and it seems that the Lays were at the center of the dispute. According to local Quaker historian Stanley Fitch, the two meetings ceased to cooperate, tensions lasting until 1759, the year of Benjamin's death.[24]

Meantime, Benjamin continued to attend the meetings of CTWM at least some of the time, probably because his glover's shop was only a few blocks away. He also continued to cause trouble, opposing those he considered to be false ministers and keeping his hat resolutely on his head when they prayed. (Quakers barred disowned members from business meetings, where group decisions were taken, but not from worship meetings, which were always open to all.) By May 1723 the meeting had formed a new committee to draw up fresh charges against Benjamin. The plan was to read them aloud the next time he attended a meeting.[25]

Benjamin somehow found out about the list of charges and requested a copy of it. The antinomian who considered himself above the law suddenly got legalistic: he challenged messenger Richard Freshfield, a representative of the meeting, asking "whether Friends ought not to have proved what they charged him with before they ordered ye Paper to be read against him." Freshfield stated that he would convey the message to the meeting, to which Benjamin replied angrily, "he had no Message to send to ye Meeting." He added that "in a proper time" he would insist on Friends proving the charges against him. He would then "dispute those Charges." He was in no hurry.[26]

The CTWM wanted an immediate showdown, not least because they had learned of the move by Benjamin and Sarah toward the CMM, whose members they warned against the disowned Friend. Meantime, Benjamin asked that he be allowed to meet with a committee from the CTWM at a time when Sarah could attend, for "She hath laid some Blame on Friends as if they had dealt too hardly by her Husband." In response Freshfield told Benjamin that they should meet at "ye Mens Gallery at ye Great Meeting House." Sarah could be present and so should some "indifferent [i.e., impartial] persons . . . to judge whether ye Matters Charged were proved." Benjamin rejected the proposal, saying that "neither he nor his Wife should meet Friends on that Accot." Benjamin apparently thought the meeting was rigged against him. Emotions ran high and reverberated back to London. In October 1723 the Yearly Meeting sent an epistle to all localities "against any Disorder of keeping on ye Hat in time of Prayer or other appearance of Disunion." Benjamin's protests were becoming a national issue.[27]

The leadership of the CTWM could not figure out what to do about this impossible man in their midst: "he still continues to come to our Meetings, and gives us frequent disturbances." In an act of desperation they resolved to go to the local Justice of the Peace, an office long involved in the harassment and repression of Quakers, in Colchester and around the country. Two weeks later they quietly abandoned the idea as too extreme. They decided instead to draw up a new indictment against Benjamin—adding "gross & abominable Practices"—and to read it aloud whenever he disrupted a future meeting. This would shame him and simultaneously make it clear to all that he was not a member of their community.[28]

On May 13, 1724, Benjamin dramatically escalated the conflict. He went to the women's section of the Great Meeting House during worship services "& appeared in a very Rude & Audacious manner to ye great Disturbance of many friends in ye Meeting." What he said and did was not recorded, but the symbolism of speaking from the women's quarter was unmistakably subversive. Benjamin believed that male and female were "all one in Christ," so he apparently did not accept the artificial division of meeting space by gender. Outraged, the leadership took another unprecedented step: they appointed three men, including Cyrus Scott, the grave digger in the Quaker burial ground, as an internal police force, "to keep him out of ye Gallery for ye future." The pacifists would now use physical force to prevent Benjamin's protests.[29]

To break the impasse, Benjamin decided to appeal his case to the Essex Quarterly Meeting (EQM). On June 8, 1724, he charged the CTWM "with doing him injustice & desired that he might have Liberty to appeal to ye sd Quarterly Meeting to hear the Matter between ye Meeting and him." The Quakers at the EQM did not want to get involved and "signified that they had nothing to do with it." They referred the matter back to the CTWM, who constituted yet another committee to chart a way forward. When two members visited Benjamin, he told them that "he refused to come to a hearing, and said he did not think the Meeting to be proper to judge concerning him, he signifying that several members of the Meeting are prejudiced against him." The statement was probably true. By now Benjamin had many enemies, some of them quite determined to drive him out. The leaders of the CTWM in turn felt that they had been falsely and unfairly impugned before the EQM, which polarized the situation further.[30]

A few months later, Benjamin was ready to talk. In a letter to the CTWM dated December 7, 1724, he declared his readiness to have his case "decided by ffriends," as long as they were "indifferent," by which he meant impartial about him and the issues. He went on to explain who such "indifferent men" had to be: "Men fearing God, full of the Holy Ghost, far from, or hating Covetousness." This phrase illuminates Benjamin's understanding of the struggle. In his mind, the Quaker community in Colchester was being undermined by wealth and its profanation of values as it moved from its plebeian origins to a more prosperous, bourgeois social composition. To Benjamin and perhaps others like him, the covetous did not fear God and did not embody the Holy Ghost, the antinomian beat in the heart of radical Quakerism. Benjamin had surely attacked "the covetous" in meetings, and he knew that they would now sit in judgment in the CTWM.

Benjamin wanted fair and virtuous judges, not those who were, in his eyes, destroying the faith.[31]

The showdown finally took place in late February 1725. Benjamin faced several accusers and a committee of eight men who would prepare a final report on the meeting. The details of the discussion are unknown, but Benjamin was in some measure contrite. He wanted to be readmitted. A postscript to the report said, "The above Committee do further report that Benjn Lay acknowledg'd to them that he has known sorrow for his unwarrantable Actions, wch gives this Meeting hopes, that his future conversation may be such, as may shew forth Sincere Repentance." Despite the apology, the committee ruled against Benjamin: his "Corrupt" practices and principles were plainly proven "by Divers Witnesses." But his penance had limits: as he left the meeting he insisted that "he was misunderstood."[32]

Benjamin soon gave up on the CTWM and focused on making peace with the DHMM, the original source of his disownment. He began a letter of March 1725 in a warm and conciliatory tone, addressing himself to his "Dear & Loving Friends." But he immediately laid bare the antinomian spirit that had led him into open opposition in the first place: "while I lived in ye Compass of your Quarter, it appeared to me in ye Light of ye Lord & in ye openings of his Pure truth in my Soul yt there was many appearances yt was not right in your Meetings." God had directly revealed to him the shortcomings of the meeting and he considered it his duty to point them out. This was not the stuff of apology.[33]

Benjamin then switched suddenly from self-certainty to self-doubt and blame: he admitted that a "forward Zeal" had crept into his soul and "drew me forth to make opposition." He saw the agency of the devil in his actions: he had fallen victim to "many cunning Snares & Subtill Stratagems strong Temptations and sore Buffetings of ye Enemy of our Souls." He affirmed that the meeting was right to admonish him and added, "I did repent." He concluded in regret: "I remain dear Friends your sincere true & Loving although Exercised & at times Sorrowful & much afflicted Brother." He was in turmoil, but his message was clear: if God had forgiven him, how could the Friends at Devonshire House do otherwise? Trusting, perhaps desperately, that the DHMM would show mercy, Benjamin petitioned for reinstatement.[34]

Devonshire House received the letter but was not convinced: "Our meeting not being fully satisfied wth his first Letter did therefore postpone writing till he renewed his Solicitation." They would keep him in limbo for a while to see if his sorrow, affliction, and repentance grew. Several months later, in November 1725, Benjamin wrote a follow-up letter:

> Dear Friends, whereas I left a Paper with you near a Year ago, I think; Desire you will be pleased to let me hear once from you; for you may well think (if you can believe I have any sincerity) that it is no small Exercise to me to be separated from my Brethren whom I dearly love. I am your true & loving friend & Brother.

Benjamin wrote again in April 1726, reiterating his apology. At this point the Devonshire House Meeting softened, perhaps because they had not seen Benjamin's antics firsthand for more than three years. They wrote to the CTWM saying that they could forgive Benjamin—if the Colchester Meeting could too.[35]

The Colchester Friends could not and would not do it. They wrote a long response to Devonshire House, explaining that Benjamin's behavior had not improved, even since he wrote the letter of apology: he had continued to oppose ministers in public and he "kept on his hatt in time of Prayer," contrary to the directive of the London Yearly Meeting. He was, in short, "ye same Restless Uneasy & troublesome Spirit" as ever. To make matters worse, he was disturbing churches all over town—Anglicans, Presbyterians, Independents, Baptists, and Quakers. It was true, Benjamin had apologized for his "unwarrantable Actions," but locally, in conversation, he minimized them as "Slight folleys," then he denied making a confession at all and even ridiculed the charges by the CTWM against him, calling them a "Bull," a formal proclamation by the Pope detested by Protestants such as Quakers. He also attacked in meetings the Quakers "who were concern'd in ye Convicting him." Personal animus and revenge were now intertwined parts of the struggle.[36]

On at least one occasion Benjamin's practice of visiting local churches and ranting against ungodly ministers and their practices caused an uproar that landed him in the Essex Court of Quarter Sessions. In August 1723 a group of Essex gentlemen, including Mayor Robert Price and five justices of the peace, swore a grand jury to hear charges against him: "Benjamin Lay . . . stood Indicted for depraving the Sacrament of the Lords Supper." It is not clear exactly what he did to provoke these charges as no details about his action were recorded. But it seems that he not only ranted but took some physical action to disrupt Anglican Communion. The use of the verb "to deprave" suggests that he engaged in an antiritualistic act of desecration, as indeed had been common practice among the "primitive Quakers" of the 1650s. In any case, Benjamin faced the gentlemen and jury defiantly and pleaded not guilty. When asked if he could provide surety that he would appear at the next Quarter Session for trial, he could not. When offered release on his own recognizance, he refused. He was determined to go to jail. The court scribe wrote that "he was ordered to be committed and he was committed accordingly."[37]

In May 1726 Benjamin decided to try again with the CTWM, to whom he wrote a long letter of apology. He explained that he had "for several days been under very close Exercises of mind concerning War." He sat in the "Coolness & Still" of his workshop and asked the Lord for direction. He mused on "outward War" in which "many were kill'd & Wounded" and, with characteristic honesty, on the inward, or spiritual, war that was raging among him and his "Brethren & of ye same Pretious Faith." He was moved by God to seek forgiveness "for ye many offences I have given you by disturbing of your Meeting in making Publick Opposition & by over Shooting myself in a forward Zeal in disturbing other Assemblys." He added that he had been "too familiar wth several women here in Colchester near 4 years Agoe & yt wch aggravated ye Cause." He admitted that he was wrong in refusing to attend disciplinary meetings and that he did not submit with "Meekness & Quietness of mind as I ought to have done." He had continued to speak taunting words and now regretted them. Yet Jesus, he knew, would forgive: he said "unto his followers yn & so now if you are Reviled[,] Revile not." Benjamin wrote that he had already confessed all these things to God with "Strong Cries & many tears." God had now showed mercy and forgiven him; of this he was certain. He concluded, I "humbly Intreat you will be pleas'd to Accept of this for your Satisfaction Doe Remain in true Simplicity & Godly Sincerity your truly Penitent & Christian Brother."[38]

Benjamin added as a postscript the authority for the letter and requested, "Dear friends be pleas'd to read these Scriptures": Galatians 6:1 (restore the wayward with meekness); II Corinthians 2:4–13 (about his "affliction and anguish of heart"); Colossians 3:13–14 (about forgiveness); Matthew 5:43–44 ("Love your enemies, bless them that curse you"). A second postscript added a personal touch, "I think I may say as one said Woe is me." His mother "hast born me a Man of Strife & Contention"—these had been lifelong traits. But now, confessed Benjamin, "I am very weary of ym & never Intend to be found in such Practices or Contentions any more." Thus ended the most searching and self-critical apology Benjamin ever wrote about his turbulent behavior.[39]

The CTWM received the letter and wrote back in clear, cold fashion, spelling out their conditions for acceptance. The meeting

> desires that for time to come, Benj Lay may bring forth Fruits agreeable to the acknowledgments he has made in ye Paper he sent to this Meeting yt thereby he may manifest ye Sincerity of his Repentance of ye evil Practices yt he has therein acknowledged & Condemned & yt thereby he may be capable of giving Satisfaction to Devonshire House Monthly Meeting until wch we cannot receive his Paper as Satisfaction by Reason they were first offended and the Letter he has sent them being Invalid, Inasmuch as he has been in the like Practice since the Delivery thereof.

When a messenger delivered the document to Benjamin, he "expressed a great dislike thereto." He told the bearer of the message that he intended to complain to the LYM. Benjamin had spoken from the heart, saying many things that were not easy for him to say, and in his view the CTWM had not responded in kind. Benjamin and Sarah both disappeared from all Quaker records for almost three and a half years. Their whereabouts during this time are unknown.[40]

COLCHESTER, 1729–1732

Perhaps the Lays had been peaceably attending the more sympathetic CMM all along, and this is the reason for the uncharacteristic silence about Benjamin in Quaker meeting records from 1726 to 1729. But it seems more likely that the Lays, or at least Benjamin, had withdrawn from meetings for a while. Sarah hinted at this in the first documentary reference to the Lays after the hiatus, in a letter she wrote to the DHMM in November 1729. She expressed her concern about Benjamin having "stood at a distance" from Friends and worried further about what might become of him when she made a long trip as a traveling minister. Her own standing among

Quakers had apparently not been affected by Benjamin's turbulent history. She humbly requested that "this meeting would consider their Cases and give them a recommendation to Friends of Colchester." She made a personal plea for help, not least, it seems, because the Lays had decided during Benjamin's period of withdrawal that they wanted to migrate to Philadelphia and would need reinstatement to secure a certificate to join a Quaker community there.[41]

The Devonshire House Meeting took the request seriously and considered it, writing to the CTWM for an update on Benjamin's recent behavior, hinting that they might be willing to forgive and reinstate him. The CTWM responded curtly: Benjamin "continues in a spirit of opposition & disorder." But they added a more important observation: he was never "a Member of their Meeting." He was disowned for what he had done in London, and what to do about that was entirely up to the good people of Devonshire House.[42]

A few months later the CMM weighed in on the controversy, writing Devonshire House with what may have seemed astonishing news: Benjamin had recently "behaved himself orderly as becometh the Truth." They added that Benjamin had also made clear "his Intention of going beyond the Seas." He needed a certificate of good standing to be able to join a Quaker community in Pennsylvania, but such could not be issued as long as his disownment stood. The CMM thus discreetly requested, said the Devonshire House scribe, "our advice & judgement therein." Everyone knew this was a delicate matter.[43]

When the CTWM heard that Benjamin and Sarah were trying to get around them by joining CMM, they were furious. In March 1730 it was noted in their minutes that "Benj Lay & his Wife desires to be Joyn'd to ye [Colchester] Monthly Meeting." This was objectionable because he lived "within [the] Compass of this Two Weeks Meeting." It was, after all, *their* meetings Benjamin had attended and frequently disrupted. The CTWM therefore sent a committee of three to explain this to the CMM, "but could get no Satisfactory answer." They wanted to emphasize that Benjamin "stands disown'd" by the DHMM and that it would be improper to let him join any meeting at all, which of course the CMM already knew. The simple truth was, the people of the CMM did not care what the CTWM thought.[44]

Meantime, in an extraordinary turn of events, Devonshire House discussed Sarah's plea and declared their sympathy for it. They were probably moved by fond memories of her as a member of their community between 1718 and 1720 and between 1720 and 1722. In any case, John Baker and Philip Gwillim, who had been appointed to look into the matter, wrote the CMM

> to signifie that if [Benjamin's] Conduct and Behaviour have been agreeable to ffrds in your Part since he made us that Acknowledgement and ffriends are willing to receive him as a member our Meeting will be Contented with what he formerly offered for Satisfaction.

The phrase "in your Part" was ambiguous. If it meant the members of the CMM, Benjamin's behavior was "agreeable." But if it meant the whole Colchester region, including the CTWM, that was a different matter altogether. The latter meeting responded to the DHMM reiterating that Benjamin had not changed his ways, but decided to "Leave it to your Prudence to do as you shall think proper concerning him." With the DHMM now satisfied and the CMM willing to grant membership, Benjamin and Sarah must have been overjoyed.[45]

Benjamin seized the moment to show largesse and good will to the people of the CMM and the broader region. In March 1731 he made out a will, leaving a considerable sum of money—£218 6s., approximately $50,000 in 2016 dollars—to family members, working-class friends, and the poor, many of them widows, who lived between London and Colchester, and in many of the small villages there around. It is impossible to know how many of these people were actually members of the CMM, for whom the bequest might have seemed a kind of bribery. Benjamin also left money to a few members of the CTWM. A big part of the bequest illuminated Benjamin's state of mind at the moment: he reserved almost half of the bequest, £100, for individual Quakers (£5 each), who, like himself, wished to immigrate to America. At this time Benjamin also made himself useful to the CMM in other ways—for example, bringing writings "Relating to metten [meeting] houses and bearing [burying] grounds." These documents may have come from efforts his father had made years earlier to secure buildings and lands for worship and burial in and around Copford, which was "within the compass" of the CMM.[46]

A couple of months later, an old struggle burst back into the open. Richard Price, one of the "Publick Friends" Benjamin had attacked fourteen years earlier, resurfaced and tried to prevent the CMM from granting him membership and a travel certificate. Price submitted an unsolicited letter about Benjamin to the CMM, but the members of the meeting immediately understood it as an act of revenge and rejected it decisively. It was unanimously agreed that Price's letter "was Contrary to the Order used among ffriends & the bringing the sd Letter being an Irregular proceeding is ordered to be taken off the ffile & no farther notice taken of same." The meeting rebuffed Price but he was undeterred. He wrote to the CTWM, fanning their flames of anger. The CTWM, still stung by Benjamin's criticisms to the EQM, mobilized rapidly to prevent the award of the certificate, even though they had encouraged the DHMM to handle the matter of Benjamin's disownment as they saw fit.[47]

It was too late. Devonshire House had sent a letter dated November 3, 1731, to the CMM "which clears Benj Lay from all offences committed against the same." That letter was acknowledged and "put upon the file." It was official. The CMM then moved quickly, unanimously making Benjamin a member of the meeting and voting to award a certificate to Benjamin and Sarah to permit them to move to Pennsylvania and join a Quaker congregation there. Most of the group who took these actions in the CMM were women—friends of Sarah, relatives of Benjamin, or both. As the outraged CTWM dispatched its representatives far and wide, to the CMM and the EQM, to carry on the now-desperate rearguard battle against the irrepressible antinomian rebel who had tormented them with debate and disruption for much of the past ten years, Benjamin and Sarah seized the moment. They took off for London, and in mid-March 1732 they boarded the *Elizabeth and Dorothy*, bound for Philadelphia.[48]

CHAPTER THREE

PHILADELPHIA'S "MEN OF RENOWN"

BENJAMIN PROBABLY HAD not been to sea for a decade or more when he and Sarah set sail for the City of Brotherly Love. They had booked passage on a large three-masted vessel with Captain John Reeves, a fellow Quaker, for a voyage that would take them first to Bermuda, then to their new home. They brimmed with joy and hope. After a dozen long, painful, strife-filled years in London and Colchester, they were finally in good standing among their beloved fellow Quakers and, with certificate in hand, they eagerly looked forward to joining William Penn's "Holy Experiment." Like the many thousands of others who had sailed to "this good land," as Benjamin called Pennsylvania, they anticipated a future of "great Liberty."[1]

Benjamin knew his way around a ship and therefore used the voyage to do precisely what he had done earlier in life: he educated himself. For eleven weeks the old salt talked with the captain and crew, swapping yarns over meals or when the ship clipped along under a full press of sail and the hands had little to do. The seamen of the *Elizabeth and Dorothy* had tales to tell, some adventurous, some gruesome. A few had been captured by pirates. Others—of greater interest to Benjamin—had sailed in the African slave trade: here was a special opportunity for learning. Under Benjamin's questioning some of these tars told "what cursed Work their former Captain and Sailors made with the poor Negroes in their Passage." They described sexual abuse, most of it, Benjamin later wrote, "too foul for me to mention, or for chaste Ears to hear." When Benjamin stepped ashore in Philadelphia, his luminous hope of a new beginning had been darkened by violent memories of the Middle Passage.[2]

Benjamin the mariner would have closely observed the Philadelphia waterfront: the wide Delaware River made for easy maneuvering and the deep-water wharves for close, effortless docking. Twenty-five vessels entered and cleared the port the week Benjamin and Sarah arrived, and dozens of other vessels of all sizes lay at anchor, disgorging and refilling with cargo through the back-breaking efforts of motley workers—English, Scottish, Irish, German, and African—under the watchful eyes of merchants and ship owners. They loaded hogsheads and casks of pork, beef, lamb, fowl, flour, and bread onto vessels bound for the slave plantations of the Caribbean; they lowered into the holds wheat, iron, timber, flax, and hemp for European ports. They brought ashore manufactured goods—especially textiles and metal wares—and sometimes labor: enslaved Africans and, more commonly, European indentured servants. The week of arrival a master offered for sale "a very likely Servant Maid" who had four and half years left on her indenture, while another advertised a "young Negro Man," "country-born" and who therefore "speaks the language." The waterfront buzzed with the story of a sailor who had just fallen from the round-top of his ship into the Delaware and drowned. The docks were a place of wealth, power, misery, danger, and death.[3]

Beyond the waterfront lay the rest of the new and dynamic city of twelve thousand people, who lived in a well-ordered grid of streets, amid dynamic marketplaces, in two thousand houses, many of them handsomely made of brick and three stories high. In the biggest mansions lived the merchants who ruled the city. During his "Gentleman's Progress" through the city in 1739, Dr. Alexander Hamilton had Quaker merchants in mind when he explained "the science of chicane": they "will tell a lye with a sanctified, solemn face." Sailors concentrated in poor neighborhoods north of Market Street. Benjamin would maintain his ties to the waterfront, developing friendships with Captain Reeves and a man named Samuel Harford, a "ship-keeper" and likely a worn-out sailor, who kept eyes on docked vessels.[4]

The prosperity of Philadelphia reflected the productive hinterlands around it. The Quaker colony was founded in 1682 as a "peaceable kingdom," a place without war, based in principle on fair treatment for all peoples and religions, including the indigenous Lenni Lenape Indians. Penn's treaty with the Lenni Lenape at Shackamaxon a year later opened vast tracts of high-quality land to European settlement and agriculture and reputedly made Pennsylvania the world's "best poor [white] man's country," although indentured servitude and poverty were common experiences for workers of European descent in Pennsylvania. Benjamin and Sarah would slowly settle into North America's largest city, which contained the world's second-largest Quaker community. They would meet Friends, attend worship services, and build a new life.[5]

Having left the sea years earlier, Benjamin now left the trade of glover, which he had never liked. He resumed his Barbados practice as a petty merchant, based on one of the deepest loves of his life: books. He would be a bookseller. To get started he brought "a large parcel of valuable Books" with him across the Atlantic. In October 1732, a few months after he arrived in Philadelphia, he announced in the *American Weekly Mercury* that he would offer them for sale. He featured the works of the "Ancient Friends," the founding generation of Quakers such as George Fox, Edward Burrough, Francis Howgill, and George Whitehead. He added works by the second generation: William Penn and Robert Barclay. He brought histories—William Sewel's history of Quakerism, as well as unspecified histories of England and the world—and he brought "large and small Bibles, Testaments, Psalters, Primmers, Hornbooks." Mindful of children and their education, his large parcel included "school books," works on "Aritmatick, Mathamaticks, Astronomy, Trogonomytry," even William Whiston's famous *The Elements of Euclid* (sixth edition, 1728). Classical authors such as Eusebius, Seneca, and Expectatus were on offer. All would be found at the shop of printer Andrew Bradford, at "the sign of the Bible" on Second Street, near the Delaware River. Benjamin meant the books to be "useful" to the new Quaker colony.[6]

COMMUNITY

The center of the Philadelphia Quaker community in 1732 was the "Great Meeting House," built in 1696 on the southwest corner of Market and Second Streets, to replace the decaying Bank Meeting House. Here was the home of the thriving Philadelphia Monthly Meeting (PMM). Among its leaders were Anthony Morris Jr., Robert Jordan Jr., Israel Pemberton Sr., and John Kinsey Jr., all of whom would play major roles in the drama surrounding Benjamin and his abolitionist agitation in coming years.

These "weighty Quakers" led both the religious and political life of the city and colony.[7]

Anthony Morris Jr. was born in London in 1682, the same year as Benjamin's birth sixty miles away in Copford. Morris Sr. moved the family to Philadelphia in 1686 and twenty years later gave his young son a large brewery on King Street, along the Delaware River. Morris Jr. linked his brewery to taverns he acquired, including the Crooked Billet and the Boatswain and Call, which catered to waterfront workers, as well as the Pewter Platter House, whose name suggested a more refined clientele. He also amassed real estate in Philadelphia and thousands of acres of land in Whitemarsh and Whitpain Townships, north of the city, and in Chester County to the west. Owner of a broad integrated complex of farms, granaries, mills, mines, urban businesses, wharves, and taverns, he lived in a mansion on Philadelphia's Front Street. His economic potency was complemented by political and religious power. He was a leader in the Pennsylvania Assembly during his five terms in the 1720s, and he served as a member of the Philadelphia City Council from 1715 until his death in 1763. He also participated in the Philadelphia Monthly, Quarterly, and Yearly Meetings, wherein he was known for a "deeply felt religious devotion."[8]

Robert Jordan Jr. was a leading Quaker minister in the PMM during the 1730s. His grandfather, Thomas Jordan, was the founding patriarch of a small Quaker community in Nansemond County, Virginia. In 1664, the elder Jordan hosted the antinomian John Perrot, who preached against "outward forms," creating division and confusion in the congregation and no doubt many a family story. Robert, born in 1693, became a traveling minister in 1718. He was three times imprisoned in Virginia in the 1720s for refusing to pay tithes to support the salaries of Anglican priests. As an "approved minister," Jordan traveled widely to meet with Quaker communities, from Virginia and Maryland to New England, the Caribbean, and Great Britain. After moving to Philadelphia and joining the Monthly Meeting in 1731, he took up residence in a seven-room house on Strawberry Alley, off Market and Chestnut, between Second and Third Streets, where he worked as a merchant, specializing in international fabrics. Jordan played a central role in the Philadelphia Yearly Meeting, the longest and strongest arm of Quakerism in the New World. He was known among his fellow Quakers for his "energetic and powerful ministry" and for zealous opposition to the "obstinate & perverse in principle or practice." Those latter words probably referred to Benjamin Lay.[9]

Israel Pemberton Sr. was the son of Phineas and Phoebe Pemberton, members of the founding generation of Pennsylvania Quakers. Born in Bucks County in 1685, Pemberton was apprenticed by his father to a wealthy slave-owning and slave-trading Quaker merchant, Samuel Carpenter, in whose footsteps the boy rapidly followed as he learned the arts of "merchandizing." Known by his fellow merchants to be "honest & extreamly diligt, Carefull & in a very good way," he amassed a fortune through West Indian commerce and diversified his economic assets to include multiple houses, stores, warehouses, and wharves. He acquired more than six thousand acres of land in eastern Pennsylvania and western New Jersey, creating one of the region's greatest fortunes. Pemberton sat at the apex of power as clerk of the PMM from 1727 until his death in 1754. He became the head overseer of the Philadelphia Quaker press in 1722, deciding what would and would not be published. He represented the PMM at the Philadelphia Quarterly Meeting and served as assistant clerk to John Kinsey in the Philadelphia Yearly Meeting. He also worked with Kinsey as a leader of the Pennsylvania Assembly from 1731 to 1749 and likewise served as a city councilman in Philadelphia from 1718 to 1752. Pemberton lived in a nine-room mansion on the corner of Second and Chestnut Streets.[10]

John Kinsey was the single most powerful Quaker in the Americas during the late 1730s and 1740s. Born in 1693 in Philadelphia to parents who soon moved the family to Woodbridge, New Jersey, the junior Kinsey was apprenticed to a wood joiner in New York City. According to a later acquaintance, Kinsey had "a Genius for something above his then employ" and turned to the study of law and a career in politics. In 1727, he was elected to the New Jersey Assembly and three years later made Speaker. Ambitious by nature and eager for a bigger stage, Kinsey moved back to Philadelphia in 1730 and ran successfully for election to the Pennsylvania Assembly. At the same time his star rose within the Society of Friends, first in Shrewsbury, New Jersey, then in Philadelphia. He became clerk of the Philadelphia Yearly Meeting in 1729 and worked with Israel Pemberton Sr. on the Board of Overseers, screening all publications. By 1738 Kinsey had become the leader of the Quaker oligarchy in the Pennsylvania House. In his "beautiful estate," called "Plantation House," on the eastern bank of the

Schuylkill River, Kinsey sat at the very pinnacle of the Quaker ruling class, within both religious and political institutions.[11]

As members of a coherent, highly organized ruling group, the connections among the "men of renown" were dense and strong. Kinsey and Pemberton together handled all the correspondence between the Philadelphia Monthly, Quarterly, and Yearly Meetings and the highest Quaker authority in the world, the London Yearly Meeting. Pemberton and Morris organized trading voyages and sold imported goods together. When Jordan died, John Kinsey took care of his estate, as well he should: he had allocated money to Jordan from the General Loan Office to buy a home. Israel Pemberton Jr. married Jordan's widow, Mary Stanbury Jordan. Kinsey in turn was related to the Pemberton family by marriage: Charles Pemberton was his cousin. When Kinsey died suddenly in 1750, Pemberton Jr. was not only a pallbearer at his funeral but also took charge of Kinsey's estate and business affairs. Afterward Pemberton succeeded Kinsey as clerk of the PYM. His brother James Pemberton acquired Kinsey's "Plantation House."[12]

Morris, Jordan, Pemberton, and Kinsey epitomized one side of the early history of Quakerism, in which Friends came to Pennsylvania to "do good" and in turn "did well"—very well indeed to judge by the wealth and power they amassed. We have no evidence of Benjamin's first impressions when he met these men, or other Philadelphia Quakers for that matter, but it is safe to assume that he would not have liked their materialistic pursuit of "worldly things" nor the vanity and pride reflected therein. He would have seen their wealth as a sign of "covetousness," which in his view destroyed both virtue and community. Most worrisome of all, three and probably all four of these leaders of the PMM owned slaves.[13]

SLAVERY REVISITED

Having lived the previous ten years in Colchester, England, where the sights of slavery were few, Benjamin experienced shock when he arrived in Philadelphia. To be sure, bondage in his new home was fundamentally different from what he had witnessed in Barbados more than a decade earlier: only one in ten persons was enslaved in his new city, compared to almost nine in ten on the island. The levels of violence and repression were also significantly lower in his new home. But make no mistake, bondage, violence, and repression were all present in the City of Brotherly Love. Benjamin was furious. The trauma he suffered in Barbados was deeply and disturbingly reactivated. His abolitionist principles were reengaged and reenergized, not least because he had such high hopes for his new godly community of Friends. In Philadelphia, Benjamin would have to defend Quakerism against itself.

Another difference between Barbados in 1718 and Philadelphia in the 1730s was the larger context of slave resistance: Benjamin had sailed into an explosive Atlantic cycle of rebellion that spanned the 1730s and affected British, French, Spanish, Dutch, and Danish colonies in the Caribbean and throughout the Americas, from Bermuda to New Orleans and from Guyana to New York. Between 1730 and 1742 unfree workers organized more than eighty conspiracies, insurrections, and mass runaways—six or seven times as many as in the dozen years before or after. On Danish St. John's, African rebels captured and held the island's main armory and fortress, Fort Christiansvaern, for seven months in 1733. In Savannah, Georgia, in 1736 Irish indentured servants plotted the "Red String Conspiracy" to burn the town and escape to Indian country. Rebels from Congo and Angola fought their way from Charleston, South Carolina, toward Spanish Florida in the Stono Rebellion in 1739. Throughout the 1730s, maroon wars in Jamaica and Suriname inflamed the colonial landscape and gave hope to rebels everywhere.[14]

Some of these events had common participants, for as Benjamin knew, slave owners sold rebellious slaves to unsuspecting buyers in places such as Philadelphia and New York. This is how Will, a veteran of the St. John's rising, came to play a leading role in the conspiracy of Antigua in 1735–1736 and again in the New York Afro-Irish conspiracy of 1741. He was "very expert at plots," said a judge in New York, "for this was the third time he had engaged in them." Governor William Mathew of the Leeward Islands described the unity of these events through the idiom of disease in 1737: rulers were plagued by a "contagion of rebellion." Governor Edward Trelawny of Jamaica expressed the issue more straightforwardly: he thought the rebellious decade was animated by a "Dangerous Spirit of Liberty."

The causes of this cycle of rebellion are not entirely clear, but two developments stand out. First, the 1730s witnessed an overproduction crisis in the sugar industry, causing prices to plummet and conditions on plantations throughout the Americas to deteriorate. Second, the "Coromantee Wars," as historian Vincent Brown has called them, led to the enslavement of many thousands of trained warriors on the Gold Coast of Africa and their shipment to the Americas, where they would play leading roles in the conspiracies and insurrections of the 1730s, especially, for example, in St. John's and Antigua, where a grand conspiracy—well reported in Philadelphia's *American Weekly Mercury*—was unfolding as Benjamin reengaged with slavery. Closer to home, enslaved Africans in Somerset, New Jersey, conspired in 1734 to kill their masters, torch their houses and barns, saddle their horses, and fly "towards the Indians in the French Interest." This cycle of rebellion stood behind Benjamin's bloody message of 1738 as recalled by an eyewitness in Burlington: "the sword would be sheathed in the bowels of the nation, if they did not leave off oppressing the negroes." He did not have to say to slave owners that God might not be the only one wielding the blade of vengeance.[15]

Benjamin closely observed the workings of slavery in and around Philadelphia, paying special attention to enslaved Africans and their Quaker masters on farms and in urban households and workshops. There was much to see as more than half the members of the Philadelphia Monthly Meeting owned slaves. Bondsmen, he noted, would "Plow, sow, thresh, winnow, split Rails, cut Wood, clear Land, make Ditches and Fences, fodder Cattle, run and fetch up the Horses." Benjamin met slave artisans, men like his friend in Barbados who committed suicide rather than suffer weekly floggings from his owner. He saw enslaved women busy with "Washing, cleaning, scouring, cooking very nicely fine and curious, sewing, knitting, darning, almost ever at hand and Command; and in other Places milking, churning, Cheese-making, and all the Drudgery in Dairy and Kitchen, within doors and without." These grinding labors he contrasted with the despicable idleness of the slave owners. He put the growling, empty bellies of the enslaved alongside the "lazy Ungodly bellies" of their masters. He found it "intolerable" that some of these slave keepers had come to America as "vile servants," experienced the hard life of indentured servitude, gained their freedom and acquired wealth, and now mistreated their own bond slaves. Worse, slave keepers, he explained with rising anger, would perpetuate this inequality by leaving the enslaved as property to "proud, Dainty, Lazy, Scornful, Tyrannical and often beggarly Children for them to Domineer and Tyrannize over." What Lay had learned of solidarity as a sailor laid a foundation of sympathy for the plight of the enslaved.[16]

SEEKING SANDIFORD

Benjamin's long-standing opposition to slavery—he began to oppose the "Hellish Practice" in 1718—coupled with the rising tensions surrounding slavery, caused him to seek out people who shared his concerns soon after he arrived in Philadelphia. The most important and notorious of these was Ralph Sandiford, a merchant who wrote a fierce indictment of slavery, *A Brief Examination of the Practice of the Times*, and submitted it to the Quaker Board of Overseers for approval in 1729. Kinsey, Pemberton, and the rest of the mostly slave-owning members of the board refused to publish it. Kinsey in particular "threatened him with severe penalties, if he permitted it to be circulated." Sandiford in turn refused to be silenced. He published the short book at his own expense, distributed it *gratis*, then brought out a new, expanded edition of the book the following year, entitled *The Mystery of Iniquity; in a Brief Examination of the Practice of the Times, by the foregoing and the present Dispensation*. Controversy still swirled around the author and the book when Benjamin arrived in June 1732.[17]

The two abolitionists had much in common. Like Benjamin, Sandiford was an antinomian radical who combined Quakerism, experience at sea, and close personal exposure to the violence of slavery. Born in Liverpool, Sandiford sailed to the West Indies where he was captured by pirates and shipwrecked. Both men praised the primitive Christian church, when all members of the faith were "of one Heart and Mind, who had all in Common." Both foresaw a coming apocalypse, a "Day of Wrath" against slave owners. Sandiford had lived for years on Philadelphia's Market Street, where soul drivers sold human "cargo" just outside his window. He identified with the enslaved as indicated on the title page of his book: "Remember them that are in bonds, as bound with them; and them that suffer adversity, as being yourselves also in the body" (Hebrews 13:3). Sandiford was, like Benjamin, a pantheist: he expressed love, tenderness, and "a general Compassion to all Creatures." His consciousness of labor guided his critique of slavery, which he considered to be "a living Death." It was wrong in his view "to live on another's Labour by Force and Oppression." He expressed a deep anticlericalism as he wrote against the "ruling part" of the

Quaker community, many of whom owned slaves. Both men also rejected the ameliorative approaches to slavery taken by seventeenth-century writers such George Fox; they demanded instead immediate abolition. Sandiford concluded, "The holding of negroes in slavery is inconsistent with the rights of man, and contrary to the precepts of the Author of Christianity." Benjamin agreed from the bottom of his soul.[18]

When Benjamin met Sandiford in 1732, he found a man in poor health, suffering "many Bodily Infirmities" and, more disturbingly, "sore Affliction of mind," caused by persecution from Quaker leaders over the issue of slavery. Sandiford had recently moved from Philadelphia to a log cabin about nine miles northeast toward Bustleton, partly to escape the hostility of his enemies. Benjamin carried on "intimate Conversation" with Sandiford and soon befriended this "very tender hearted Man." Benjamin visited him regularly over the course of almost a year, the final time as Sandiford lay on his deathbed in "a sort of Delirium." He died "in great Perplexity of mind" in May 1733, at forty years of age. Lay explained that "oppression . . . makes a wise man Mad."[19]

Benjamin appreciated Sandiford as one of "Many worthy Men" who had "borne Testimony against this soul Sin, Slave-keeping, by Word and Writing," and indeed thought him one of the bravest to do so. Benjamin also relayed what Sandiford's detractors had said about the author and his book: they claimed that he wrote "in a Spirit of Bitterness" and that "he did not end his Life well," which was thought to reflect badly on both his character and his cause. Benjamin answered that he had "read his Book carefully, with Attention; and I do not remember a Word in it contrary to Truth." Quakers were supposed to embody the truth and Sandiford did so. Benjamin also used the Biblical parable of Judah's true prophet (Sandiford), who struggled against a false, "old lying Prophet" (Kinsey?). The latter, like contemporary Quakers ministers, carried people into "the Hellish Darkness or Smoak, of the Bottomless Pit."[20]

Benjamin mockingly assumed the voice of his friend's critics and wrote that his book "tells Tales to the World, sets forth to the World's People, what a Parcel of Hypocrites, and Deceivers we [Quakers] are, under the greatest appearance and Pretentions to Religion and Sanctity that ever was in the World." Sandiford made Quakers look bad, but according to Benjamin they deserved it. Yes indeed, he continued, "we'll censure him, and his Book too, into the Bottomless Pit, if we can, tho' we can't disprove a Word in it, for its undeniable Truth, and so unanswerable." We are, after all, "Men of renown . . . let who will or dare say nay."[21]

Benjamin was especially angry that the "weighty Quakers" continued to torment poor Sandiford after his death:

> we'll condemn *R.* in his Grave, and his Book and all that favour it, or promote its being spread abroad, or being read, that exposes us, and we'll expose that or especially him that writ it, by Calumnies and Slanders, and Surmises, and by insinuating all that ever we can hear or think of against him.

Now that he is "in his Grave," went their thinking, he "can't contradict or oppose us." But his friend Benjamin could. He would say nay again and again to the "men of renown," those who, in Benjamin's allusion to the Book of Genesis, had grown wicked and evil, grieved the Lord who had created them, and suffered destruction by flood. Benjamin would continue Sandiford's struggle against them.[22]

"CAPITAL SIN"

Benjamin arrived in Pennsylvania after a protracted, bruising struggle with those he identified as "the covetous" in Colchester, at a time when Quaker society was changing, in ways he did not like. The same process was going on in and around Philadelphia, where Quaker involvement in commerce and land speculation was rapidly producing wealthy "men of renown." Benjamin experienced these changes as a challenge to himself and to the faith. He fixed his gaze on rich slave-owning Quaker ministers as symbols of a trend that was, at its root, satanic. They were destroying his cherished religion.[23]

Covetousness, according to Benjamin, was the "worst Idol that ever the Devil set up in the World." He used the term interchangeably with greed and avarice, though much more frequently (twenty-seven times in *All Slave-Keepers . . . Apostates*). Benjamin followed the Apostle Paul—who himself had followed the ancient Greek Cynic philosophers—in explaining that covetousness, or love of money, "is the root of all Evil." He asked of his fellow Quakers "can there be a worse Devil, or more unclean Spirit or Root from which all Evil grows, or a worse Fountain than that from which all our Misery flows?" The impulse to material acquisition, which Benjamin emphatically rejected in his own austere way of life, was a "mighty, mighty, almost Almighty Monster, the chiefest of the Seven Devils and Supream Ruler, Head and Governor in Hell, *Babylon* and Bottomless Pit." He was convinced that "all Covetous Men are Beasts, Blasphemers, Lyers, Thieves and Murtherers as well as Idolaters" and that they damaged not only Quakerism but society as a whole: ministers and congregants, church and state. The wealthy were the "masters of misrule" in both politics and religion. And if they were bad in Colchester, they were worse in Pennsylvania: "I do believe here is in this Land of *America*, as selfish, sordid, greedy, Covetous, Earthly minded People of almost all Names, as any in the World." The covetous were predatory, like "Kites amongst Chickens, and Wolves with Lambs." All come "to devour," he announced; "it is their Nature."[24]

There was only one answer: war. Benjamin asked God for the "Strength and Courage to make War with, and engage against so Capital an Enemy that is so dishonorable to God, and all true Religion, destructive to Government and Mankind in general." He wanted God to "raise up" some "Couragious Valiant little *Davids*," furnish them with slings and "Smooth Stones taken out of the Brook of the Lord, the River of Life, that runs through or in the *Paradise* of God," and send them forth against Goliath. The soldiers of God would then "bring him down, cut off his Head, and give his Carcass, with all the uncircumcised Armies, in all Nations and Countries, to the Beasts of the Field." Benjamin went to war against "so Capital an Enemy."[25]

On one occasion Benjamin went so far in his critique of wealth as to suggest that slavery and violence were central to private property. In September 1736 he penned one of his most searing indictments. He wrote about Luke 11:21 and gave the passage his own distinctive, radical twist. He asked, "When the strong Man armed keeps the House, his Goods are in Peace: Is not this the Devil?" He continued, "Is not all his Goods Sin? Is not Slave-Keeping and Trading the greatest Sin in the World?" He then asked, when "this Capital Sin" appears "in the Heart, . . . does not the whole Creation, in the poor condemned or damned Creature groan, to be delivered?" Benjamin had worked as a craftsman, owning his tools and operating his own workshop in London and Colchester, and he had been a petty merchant, selling dry goods on the waterfront of Bridgetown and books in Philadelphia, but his thought evolved over time. His writing took a turn toward Hieronymus Bosch: "Then Hell-Torments, the Smoak and Darkness, of the Bottomless Pit arises and appears in the Soul; the Creature by some Glimmering of the Light sees itself in Darkness, feels itself in Hell tormented." It is high time, Benjamin concluded, "to bind the strong Man armed, the Devil and cast him out and spoil his Goods." The apocalypse was eminent: "here comes to be War in Heaven, *Michael* and his Angels fight, and the Devil or Dragon, which is one, and his Angels fight; for the Devil, Dragon, makes War with the Saints." The deliverance of Quakerism, and indeed the whole creation, required rescue from slavery, from "capital sin." Like a true prophet, Benjamin declared his mastery of the subject: "I know what I write, blessed be the Light, the Way, and the Truth." Jumping ahead two verses in the book of Luke (11:23), he quoted Jesus: "He that is not with me is against me."[26]

GUERRILLA THEATER

Benjamin began to stage public protests against the "men of renown" to shock the Friends of Philadelphia into awareness of their own moral failings about slavery. Conscious of the hard, exploited labor that went into making seemingly benign commodities such as tobacco and sugar, Benjamin showed up at a Quaker yearly meeting with "three large tobacco pipes stuck in his bosom." He sat between the galleries of men and women elders and ministers. As the meeting ended, he rose in indignant silence and "dashed one pipe among the men ministers, one among the women ministers, and the third among the congregation assembled." With each smashing blow Benjamin protested slave labor, luxury, and the poor health caused by smoking the stinking sotweed. He sought to awaken his brothers and sisters to the politics of the smallest, seemingly most insignificant choices.[27]

When winter rolled in, Benjamin used a deep recent snowfall to make a point to Quaker slave owners. He stood on a Sunday morning at a gateway to the Quaker meetinghouse, knowing all Friends would pass his way. He left "his right leg and foot entirely uncovered" and placed them in the snow. Like the ancient philosopher Diogenes, who also walked barefoot in snow, he again sought to shock his contemporaries into awareness. One Quaker after another took notice and expressed concern, urging Benjamin not to expose himself to the freezing cold. He would surely get sick. Benjamin listened carefully to their words, then replied, "Ah, you pretend compassion for me but you do not feel for the poor slaves in your fields, who go all winter half clad." He made two points: First, anyone without proper clothing in cold weather deserved compassion. Second, Quakers were not practicing a maxim central to their faith, drawn from Matthew 7:12, "Therefore all things whatsoever ye would that men should do to you, do ye even so to them: for this is the law and the prophets." So saith Benjamin the prophet.[28]

On another occasion, Benjamin called one morning on an unnamed gentleman "of considerable note," who politely invited him to sit down to breakfast with him and his family. As Benjamin began to take his place at the table he saw a man of African descent appear at the door of the dining room to serve the meal. Benjamin turned somberly to his acquaintance and asked, "Dost thou keep any Negro slaves in thy family?" When the gentleman answered yes, he did indeed keep slaves, Benjamin pushed back and stood up from the table. He announced, "Then I will not partake with thee, of the fruits of thy unrighteousness." Benjamin would have no intercourse with those who owned slaves. He walked out.[29]

Benjamin also began to disrupt Quaker meetings in and around Philadelphia. The nineteenth-century radical Quaker Isaac Hopper relayed the following story, which he had apparently heard as a child, to fellow abolitionist Lydia Maria Child:

> At the Monthly meeting of Friends [Benjamin] was a diligent attendant. At that time, many members of the society were slaveholders. Benjamin gave no peace to anyone of that description. As sure as any character attempted to speak to the business of the meeting, he would start to his feet and cry out, "There's another negro-master!"

Never afraid to point the finger of shame, Benjamin insisted that slave holding and Quakerism were utterly incompatible. "No justice, no peace" was his message.[30]

Benjamin carried his theater across the city, visiting a variety of churches and ranting at ministers he disliked, just as he had done in London and Colchester. According to Roberts Vaux, he "attended all places of public worship, without regard to the religious professions of their congregations," sometimes in sackcloth to emphasize his humility before God. He listened to the sermons and judged them, usually harshly. His responses "were sometimes so long and vehement as to require his removal from the house; an act to which he always submitted without opposition." When an ungodly minister owned slaves, as was not uncommon in Philadelphia, Benjamin doubled his wrath.[31]

These rants sometimes went awry. Ministers did not as a rule welcome a stranger's harangue, least of all in the presence of their congregation. When a Philadelphia preacher announced during a sermon that he heard "a voice from Heaven," Benjamin blurted out that "from thy life, and preaching, I question whether thou ever heardst a voice from heaven in thy life, and if thou didst, I am sure thou hast not obeyed it." Outraged, the clergyman seized a bullwhip and chased his critic from the church. Yet, not all congregants took Benjamin's interventions so seriously. On another occasion, Benjamin went to (Anglican) Christ Church in Philadelphia to hear the Reverend Robert Jenney preach about Judgment Day. As the congregation filed out of the church Benjamin stood at the door and asked person after person, "How can you, by such preaching as you have been hearing, distinguish the sheep from the goats?" A gentleman grabbed Benjamin's bushy beard, gave it a hard tug, and said merrily, "By their beards, Benjamin, by their beards."[32]

CONTROVERSY OF MEMBERSHIP

As Benjamin and Sarah got to know new people and surroundings, and as Benjamin agitated on the issue of slavery, the tumult left behind in Colchester rumbled onward in their absence. In March 1732 the Colchester Two Weeks Meeting (CTWM) made an official complaint to the Essex Quarterly Meeting (EQM) about the granting of membership and the certificate to Benjamin by the Colchester Monthly Meeting: the CMM, they claimed, had no right to admit Benjamin and give him clearance. The CMM responded to the power play by stalling for time. They eventually had to answer the charges, and when they did, in June 1732, the EQM meeting ruled against them. Benjamin "was not a proper Member of the Meeting," said the "weighty Quakers" of the EQM, and the CMM should not have given a joint certificate to Benjamin and Sarah. But the resistance of the CMM was not over: even after the ruling of the EQM, they sent a copy of the joint certificate to the Philadelphia Women's Meeting, which had requested it. Nor was the vengeance of the CTWM at an end. The long-churning conflicts in Colchester would soon follow the Lays across the Atlantic to Philadelphia.[33]

Even though the leaders of the CTWM had stated repeatedly that Benjamin was never a member of their meeting and that it was entirely up to the Devonshire House Monthly Meeting (DHMM), which had originally disowned him, to reinstate him, they now pursued the migrant Quaker with savage determination. They wrote a letter "to ffriends in Philadelphia or elsewhere, in America, Concerning the Irregular Certificate Benja Lay had from Colchester Monthly Meeting, with the Quarterly Meeting Minute concerning the same, and also an Accot of his behaviour &c among us." Knowing Benjamin's penchant for resistance by flight, and eager to bar him from any and all Quaker congregations, they sent a second letter to Philadelphia Friends two months later and urged them "to send it to any other part of America where Benjn Lay may settle." It was Benjamin's bad luck that letters from enemies in Colchester found their way into the hands of a new enemy in Philadelphia, Robert Jordan Jr., who had already become an object of public criticism by the boisterous, opinionated newcomer.[34]

Jordan may have been "covetous" like the people Lay attacked in the CTWM, but he was different from them in at least one respect: he was a slave owner. Indeed Jordan was descended from a long line of Quaker masters in the tobacco lands of Southside Virginia. Jordan and Lay became adversaries, partly because Jordan opposed Lay's membership in the Philadelphia Meeting but also because Jordan committed the worst sin in the world, as Benjamin revealed in *All Slave-Keepers . . . Apostates*. He listed the initials of several diabolical Philadelphia Quaker "Slave-Keepers," who had tormented him during his time in Pennsylvania; one of these was "R— J— n."[35]

Perhaps because of rising conflict with Jordan and other "men of renown," Benjamin and Sarah left Philadelphia by the end of March 1734, moving eight miles north to Abington. They likely chose their new home because Sarah was a dear friend of the charismatic Susanna Morris, an Abington woman who miraculously combined a traveling ministry with the mothering of thirteen children. She and Sarah had traveled together for months at a time in the 1720s to preach to Quaker congregations across England and Wales, often the "poorest sort" of God's people. On a voyage to Amsterdam they held each other in a tender, all-night embrace as their ship slammed repeatedly against a sandbar near Enkhuizen. They prepared for death. The ship was wrecked, "utterly lost," but Susanna and Sarah survived, learning, as Susanna later explained, to trust God for "help through all hardships."[36]

Once reunited, the Lay and Morris families would remain connected for many years, even after Susanna and her husband moved to Richland, Pennsylvania, in 1741. Benjamin became especially close to one of their sons, Joshua Morris, a landowner and sawmill operator who, under Benjamin's influence, became a convinced abolitionist. Having now moved to Abington, Benjamin and Sarah would require of the PMM a certificate stating that they were members in good standing to present to the local Quaker meeting in their new home.[37]

THE DEATH OF SARAH

Tragedy struck in late 1735 when Benjamin's beloved Sarah died, swiftly and unexpectedly it seems, for reasons unknown. Benjamin himself had been in poor health for a few years (he made out his will in 1731), but Sarah seems to have been vigorous and healthy, or so her extensive record of travel as an itinerant minister would suggest. From her time in Colchester through her years in Philadelphia and Abington, she served with other women such as Susanna Morris and Elizabeth Kendall, visiting and counseling the Quaker faithful far and wide, throughout England, Ireland, Scotland, Wales, the Netherlands, and North America.[38]

Upon her death, the Abington Monthly Meeting (AMM) issued the following memorial:

> About the latter end of the year 1735, died Sarah Lay late wife of Benjamin Lay of Abington. She was born in Rochester in the county of Kent in Old England, about the year 1677, and was convinced of the principles of Truth in her young years. She had a gift in the ministry bestowed on her in which she was serviceable & traveled in that service, with the concurrence of her friends in her native land and in Scotland & Ireland, as also to some adjacent parts on this continent. Her service therein being acceptable, aged about 58 years, a minister, about 23. She was buried at Abington.

The elderly Quakers interviewed in the early nineteenth century by Roberts Vaux remembered Sarah as "an intelligent and pious woman" who was "cordially united with her husband, in his disapprobation of slavery . . . [and] in his exertions to promote a change in the public sentiment, respecting the inhumanity and injustice of the custom." They added that she was a comfort to Benjamin as he underwent his own "trials" of mind.[39]

Sarah's death had a profound impact on Benjamin. He remembered her in *All Slave-Keepers . . . Apostates* as a "tender-hearted woman" who sympathized strongly with the enslaved. He recalled her acts of kindness and her horror over the grisly punishments of slave society. He fondly remembered the mirth and joy with which the enslaved Africans of Barbados reflected on the unlikely coupling of a "little backarar man" and a "little backarar woman." Benjamin wrote of Sarah often and lovingly in *All Slave-Keepers . . . Apostates*. Indeed it may have been her death that prompted him to write the book, which he began about six months later. By all available evidence, the couple who married late (Benjamin was thirty-six; Sarah, forty-one) had a devout, devoted, and happy life of seventeen years together.[40]

STRIFE RESUMES

The PMM appointed two Friends, John Bringhurst and Anthony Morris Jr., to look into granting a certificate for Benjamin, which required inspection of the previous one brought from England. Bringhurst and Morris would hardly have been neutral about Benjamin and his membership as both were slave owners. Indeed Morris may have had a greater commitment to the institution of slavery than perhaps any other living Quaker: he was the leading architect of Pennsylvania's slave code, "An Act for the Better Regulating of Negroes in this Province," passed in 1726. Morris and his legislative colleagues followed the examples of Barbados and Virginia, protecting property in slaves by reimbursing masters from state funds the value of rebellious bondsmen or women who were executed. The bill also sought to limit and control the free black community, stating that "free negroes are an idle, slothful people" who "afford ill examples to other negroes." The law made manumission more difficult and interracial marriages illegal. It also limited the autonomous mobility of free black workers, promising fines, whippings, and even re-enslavement for various transgressions of class and racial codes. (The law apparently did not help Morris a few years later when his slave, "a Mulatto boy, named Michael," ran away from him.) The Quaker pacifist Morris had no qualms about using state violence against enslaved and free people of color. Anyone who knew Morris would have known how he felt about Benjamin, who was already, in 1734, the colony's leading critic of slavery.[41]

Yet in truth it would not have required much prejudice against Benjamin for Bringhurst and Morris to recommend against his membership. The CTWM had written that the certificate provided by the CMM "was Irregularly obtained, it not being from the Meeting to which [Benjamin] properly belonged"—even though the CTWM had stated repeatedly that Benjamin had never been a member of their meeting and that his membership elsewhere was not their concern. The EQM nevertheless agreed with the complaint, declaring that the CMM should not have issued the certificate. The Philadelphia committee considered these negative comments an "Obstruction," and the meeting as a whole now revoked Benjamin's membership.[42]

Benjamin characteristically fought back. In both Philadelphia and Abington, he continued to attend meetings and to speak his mind about the denial of his membership and about the corruption of Quakerism by false ministers and slave keepers. Benjamin later described a confrontation at Robert Jordan's Philadelphia home, in which he began to "reason" with the "eminent Preacher" about the great Goliath, "Negroe or Slave-Keeping, which hath defied the little Army of the living God so many Years, and still continues so to do." Jordan, whose "Negro boy" may have been present as Benjamin spoke, replied in anger, saying, Benjamin later recalled, "that I loved the Negroes better than I did my Friends." Benjamin did not indicate his response to Jordan's challenge, but he likely held forth on the Quaker commitment to "the universal Love of God to all People, of all colours and Countries, without respect of persons." This confrontation, and probably others like it, disturbed Jordan, who, in a letter to Quaker elder Thomas Story in June 1736, worried about conflicts within the PMM, no doubt referring to the upheaval surrounding Benjamin's membership and antislavery ideas. This problem, in Jordan's view, was the "prevalence of Personal and Party Considerations." The former probably referred to Benjamin's fierce personality, the latter to his effect in dividing the congregation.[43]

The PMM reported, in June 1737, that Benjamin's preaching had been "very troublesome." Horrified that so many Quaker ministers and elders in Philadelphia owned slaves, Benjamin raised the stakes of the struggle, claiming in meeting after meeting that such people were apostates to the faith and should not be allowed to preach, or even to speak. Then he went further, arguing that none of them deserved to be Quakers at all and should be disowned. He denounced such Quaker ministers directly, personally, and vividly:

> For Friends, all you that are Ministers of Anti-Christ, whether in Pulpits or Galleries, you that are of the Royal Off-spring, of the King of the Locusts, and are creeping out of the Bottomless Pit a little, to see what Mischief you can do to Mankind, & Service for your King *Lucifer*, who was (and is now to you) as the Son of the Morning, and to see what good you can get for your God, your Bellies.

These covetous ministers were often, like Robert Jordan, full of "smooth Words," but be not deceived, was Benjamin's message to the congregation: such people were the devil's most effective instruments of evil. They scurried out of the depths of hell to serve the devil and damage the true church.[44]

It came as no surprise, to Benjamin or anyone else, that when he spoke such words in meetings the ministers and elders flew into rages and had him removed from one gathering after another. Indeed they appointed a "constabulary" to keep him out of meetings all around the Philadelphia area. When the PMM made its final move against Lay, they selected their two most powerful members "to draw up a testimony against him to be brought to the next Meeting." The first was Israel Pemberton Sr., who as clerk of the PMM essentially selected himself for the role. He chose as his partner none other than John Kinsey, clerk of the PYM. The choice of Pemberton and Kinsey—arguably the two most powerful Quakers in all of Pennsylvania—to draw up the report was, in a twisted way, a compliment to Benjamin and an acknowledgment of the power of his cause. It was simultaneously a sign of how determined the PMM was to crush the loud, fearless challenger.[45]

The statement, presented and affirmed by the PMM on August 26, 1737, claimed that Benjamin had not made satisfaction for his "Disorderly Conduct" and previous disownment in England, and that his certificate from the CMM was therefore invalid. This was patently false. The meeting then advised Lay to seek the reconciliation that would validate his certificate, but of course he refused, knowing that Devonshire House had already forgiven him and lifted the disownment, and that the CMM had properly admitted him. The PMM concluded:

> We have therefore thought fit to give publick Notice, that we do not esteem the said Benjamen Lay to be a Member of our religious Community but a disorderly & obstinate Person, one who slights the Advice of Friends, Imposes on them on his preaching & that he disregards the Peace of the Church.

With the help of the PMM, the CTWM had won the battle with Benjamin after all, at least in the short run. They pursued him, and they got him, even though they knew that his disownment had been lifted and he was a legitimate member of the CMM. At the same time the PMM went out of its way to indicate that Sarah Lay was a member in good standing—"she appearing to be of a good Conversation during her residence here"—but that Benjamin was not, effectively dividing the couple in their relationship to the Quaker meetings of America. This separation would be a source of lifelong bitterness for Benjamin, especially after he lost Sarah in 1735. He would not fail to let Jordan know how he felt, later accusing him of having been an instrument in "the Death of my Dear Wife."[46]

John Kinsey drew up the PMM ruling against Benjamin, and Israel Pemberton Sr. personally delivered it to the AMM, where Benjamin worshipped and where he had strong allies in the locally eminent Morris and Phipps families. But Benjamin had also made enemies in the congregation, one of whom was Nicholas Austin, an "approved minister" who had been born in New England in 1695. Active in the PQM and the PYM, Austin was a person of authority. Benjamin, however, did not approve of Austin's ministry. In response Austin angrily accused Benjamin of "setting up some ministers, and pulling down others." Benjamin replied that he would never pull down a true minister, nor would he ever approve of a false one, letting Austin know exactly where he stood. When told he was too judgmental, Benjamin answered, "Why, truly, I may say if we have no judgment in our goings and doings, we are in a very poor dark condition." Without "judgment," in Benjamin's view, false ministers such as Nicholas Austin and other "men of renown" will win the day.[47]

Eventually Austin and his allies prevailed, and Benjamin was disavowed once again. The scribe of the AMM noted: "It is ordered that Benjamin

Lay, be kept out of our Meetings for Business, he being no member but is a frequent Disturber thereof." This was effectively his fourth disownment: London, Colchester, Philadelphia, and now Abington. Probably no eighteenth-century Quaker was disowned more than Benjamin. The "Man of Strife & Contention" could never find a community that was simultaneously pure enough to suit him and tolerant enough to include him. But he was not yet done with false ministers and slave-owning Quakers. The biggest confrontation was yet to come.[48]

CHAPTER FOUR

HOW SLAVE KEEPERS BECAME APOSTATES

BEGINNING SIX MONTHS after the death of Sarah, and for the following two years, Benjamin spent much of his time writing *All Slave-Keepers That Keep the Innocent in Bondage, Apostates*, published by Benjamin Franklin in August 1738. The book represented an important advance in abolitionist thought. In a time when slavery seemed a normal, indeed unchangeable foundation of society in many parts of the world, Benjamin broke through the oppressive status quo and demanded an immediate, unconditional abolition of bondage. He wrote scathingly of wealthy slave owners, with whom there must be no compromise. He was the voice of a small but growing antislavery movement within Quaker meetings and in society at large. In calling for an end to human bondage he acted self-consciously as a prophet, drawing from the Biblical books of Isaiah, Jeremiah, and Ezekiel.[1]

Even though Benjamin was one of the very first to call for the abolition of slavery, his book has received remarkably little attention from scholars. Indeed, most have never heard of it, and, as Brycchan Carey has pointed out, even specialists have rarely read it. Not that *All Slave-Keepers . . . Apostates* is easy reading: on the contrary, it is a strange, unconventional, difficult book, but at the same time, a deeply revealing one. It shows how Benjamin arrived at an uncompromising position on the issue of slavery—one that would see him through ridicule, resistance, and repression. It shows how he reasoned, how he advanced the antislavery cause, how he found the courage

ALL
SLAVE-KEEPERS
That keep the Innocent in Bondage,
APOSTATES
Pretending to lay Claim to the Pure & Holy ChriſtianReligion ; of whatCongregation ſo ever ; but eſpecially in theirMiniſters,by whoſe example the filthy Leproſy and Apoſtacy is ſpread far and near ; it is a notorious Sin, which many of the true Friends of Chriſt, and his pure Truth, called *Quakers*, has been for many Years, and ſtill are concern'd to write and bear Teſtimony againſt ; as a Practice ſo groſs & hurtful to Religion, and deſtructive to Government, beyond what Words can ſet forth, or can be declared of by Men or Angels, and yet lived in by Miniſters and Magiſtrates in *America*.

The Leaders of the People cauſe them to Err.

Written for a General Service, by him that truly and ſincerely deſires the preſent and eternal Welfare and Happineſs of all Mankind, all the World over, of all Colours, and Nations, as his own Soul;
BENJAMIN LAY.

PHILADELPHIA:
Printed for the AUTHOR. 1737.

With the help of printer Benjamin Franklin, Lay published his furiously radical tract against slavery in 1738: *All Slave-Keepers That Keep the Innocent in Bondage, Apostates.*

to persevere in the face of overwhelming power arrayed against him. *All Slave-Keepers . . . Apostates* shows clearly why Benjamin was willing, long before most anyone else, to devote his life to the cause of antislavery.[2]

ORIGINS

By the time Benjamin published his book he had already become a controversial figure. He had performed guerrilla theater and been thrown out of many a Quaker meeting, as he himself noted, "in Philadelphia, Burlington and Concord, &c." The "&c." meant other places too numerous to be counted. He became so notorious, his reputation often preceded him, as when he attended a Quaker gathering in Horsham, Pennsylvania, on April 10, 1737. His appearance at the meeting caused "a great Bustle." Even though he was "sitting quietly," not "speaking a Word," he was seized and carried roughly out of the meeting. On another occasion, after he was tossed into the street on a rainy day, Benjamin returned to the main door of the meetinghouse, lay down in the mud, and required every person leaving the meeting to step over his supine body. Friends knew that if Benjamin walked through the meetinghouse door and encountered slave holders, combustion would follow. Gary B. Nash aptly called Benjamin a "living stick of dynamite."[3]

Knowing that the "men of renown" who threw him out of meetings would oppose his book, Benjamin began with a preemptive declaration of love for his fellow Quakers and an appeal to the "Impartial Reader." He stated on the title page that he intended the work for a "General Service," but he knew that most of his readers would be Quakers, and indeed they were his primary intended audience. He claimed, perhaps disingenuously, that his book would not offend or grieve his "very dear true and tender Friends"; on the contrary, "it is by their request and desire" that his thoughts were published at all. Yet he did understand that the book would cause turmoil, and that this might hurt the cause of antislavery, which gave him "some fear and trembling." He knew some would be sympathetic to his message and that others, already sworn enemies, would be adamantly opposed. He expected vicious, unremitting attacks.[4]

As a first-time author Benjamin knew that his book had shortcomings, especially in its organization and presentation. This is why he told printer Benjamin Franklin "to print any part thou pleaseth first." Given to a stream-of-consciousness flow of words and ideas, based on what Quakers called "openings" of the spirit, he apologized in the book for digressions in the narrative and added a postscript that some passages "are not so well placed as could have been wished." This was an understatement. He asked the "Courteous and Friendly Reader" to please bear in mind that the book was written by a "poor common Sailor." It appears that Franklin took the request for help to heart and did edit the book, for the dated sections do not appear in the chronological order in which they were written.[5]

Benjamin fretted about his own worthiness to write the book: "I being and seeing myself so very unfit almost every way," a man "of so very mean a capacity, and little Learning." Part of this feeling of inadequacy was humility before God as he faced a great and urgent task, but another part was his humble background. His parents had afforded him little schooling. Most of his learning was self-acquired, much of it likely at sea, where literate sailors often taught their less educated shipmates to read during slack times aboard ship. Benjamin came to love books and over time became well and broadly read, but he was always conscious of his class background and lack of education. Indeed he called himself in *All Slave-Keepers . . . Apostates* "an illiterate man"—after having written a book full of annotations about his extensive reading! His self-doubt also reflected the discrimination and condescension he experienced as a little person: "I know my self to be so very mean and contemptible in the sight of Men, almost in every respect."[6]

For these reasons Benjamin hoped God would "raise up and concern some worthy Friend or other, of more repute and Esteem amongst Men" to write the book condemning the greatest sin in the world. He prayed earnestly over the request "many Days and Nights, with great concern of mind," but God did not answer. Benjamin finally decided it was his duty—to God, his fellow Quakers, even to Christianity—to write the book, just as it had been his duty to speak out in meetings. Like all other Quakers, he conceived of the faith as God's Truth; they were commanded to tell it, unflinchingly, to all peoples. Benjamin took it as his task to "fix the Judgment of Truth" upon slavery. "Let us be faithful . . . let us be faithful . . . let us be faithful," he wrote. Yet even as he abased himself before God and man, he nonetheless saw his own role in the moral drama of slavery in grand terms. He would, like "little David," slay the Goliath of human bondage. He would, like Moses or Gideon, save the chosen people of Israel, his very own Quakers. He would "deliver his People from Captivity."[7]

Benjamin dated many of the entries in the book, the earliest of which was May 3, 1736. Why would he have begun the book at that moment? He had been in Pennsylvania almost four years, during which time his witness of bondage had rekindled the revulsion he felt toward slavery in Barbados between 1718 and 1720. He wrote, with obvious pain, about the enslaved, "Oh! my Soul mourns in contemplating their miserable, forlorn, wretched State and Condition that mine Eyes beheld them in then [in Barbados], and it is the same now." Trauma returned, with redoubled force. Moreover, his beloved Sarah had died six months earlier. The loss of her intimate companionship, coupled with his subsequent disownment by the

Philadelphia and Abington Monthly Meetings, may have moved him to seek conversation with a broader group of people through the written word. Even though he continued to attend worship meetings, he probably felt a growing sense of isolation, which was largely the result of his own polarizing ideas and tactics. His antislavery ministry was creating ever sharper tensions among Quaker communities as he completed the manuscript in July 1738. Six weeks later Franklin published the book, and less than a month after that Benjamin hoisted the "bladder of blood" above his head and ran his sword through it in Burlington, New Jersey. *All Slave-Keepers . . . Apostates* was thus part of a climax of confrontation with Quaker leaders over the issue of slavery.[8]

Benjamin wrote the bulk of the book in his cave in Abington, amid his library of two hundred volumes. He wrote about thoughts that came to his mind while he was working in the garden just outside the stone-lined entrance to the grotto. He wrote a couple of entries in Philadelphia. In good Quaker fashion he wrote when the spirit moved him, at all hours of the day and night: late morning, early evening, "between 3 and 4 this Morning," or "this Morning before day Light." He referred to the many books and pamphlets he had at hand. His writing was an outgrowth of his reading and his serious study of theology, history, and, especially, philosophy. Benjamin was an autodidact and an intellectual. He guarded against "pride," as any Quaker would, but there can be no doubt he took great satisfaction in his own hard-won ideas.[9]

Benjamin paid small attention to genre in writing the book. The only form he seems to have had in mind was the tried and true early modern commonplace book, a personal, popular, usually unpublished kind of writing distinct from a journal or diary. A commonplace book was essentially a multipurpose scrapbook, into which all kinds of facts, sayings, observations, and ideas might be inscribed and preserved, according to the interests of the compiler. People of all walks of life kept commonplace books, from poor women who preserved recipes, to poets and philosophers such as John Milton and John Locke, who recorded thoughts for future publications. The commonplace book suited Benjamin as a democratic form of expression.[10]

Benjamin's many entries over the 277 pages of his book were highly eclectic: he included Biblical passages, pieces of autobiography, personal reflections, letters he wrote to friends, notes on history, summaries of and observations on books he read, and, most importantly, arguments against false ministers and slavery, especially as those two themes reflected his own struggles within the Quaker community. Benjamin's sources for these items were as wide-ranging as the entries themselves. They drew on experience, conversations with people of all kinds, sea yarns, dozens of books (especially the Bible), oral histories, and popular memory.

All Slave-Keepers . . . Apostates is multi-vocal in the extreme, presenting the voice not only of the author but also of God, angels, devils, dozens of authors, fellow Quakers, and enslaved Africans who combine in a raucous cacophony of drama and protest. Even as Benjamin openly professed his limitations as a writer, he demonstrated rhetorical skill as he made his arguments. He wrote the book as he spoke—from the heart, in an intimate voice, directly to close acquaintances and fellow Quakers. The book is therefore conversational: it reads like spoken speech written down. This trait was not uncommon in the writings of autodidacts who grew up in oral cultures, as did Benjamin in rural Essex. His pages appeal to the ear as much as to the eye. One can almost hear the man speak from the page. Throughout he converses earnestly and urgently—and not without anger.

Benjamin often addresses his readers directly, introducing a remark with a highly personal invitation: "My dear Friends, I beg, I would intreat, in all Humility, with all earnestness of mind, on the bended Knees of my Body and Soul" that you consider this point or that. He also spoke directly to his opponents, using a technique of sharp personal interrogation. After discussing the thousands of deaths caused by the slave trade, he asked, "What do you think of these Things, you brave Gospel Ministers?" He knew they would be among his readers and that their silence was the sheerest hypocrisy.[11]

The intimacy of the book included prayer and rapture. Lay appealed directly to "O Lord God Almighty" to end slavery: "I trust, dearest One, thou wilt be pleased to stop and end this Practice, that is more like Hell than heaven, to be sure." Occasionally Benjamin ascends to exaltation: "Praises, Praises be given to his pure Name, for his holy glorious and pure presence in his holy Temple!" He assumes a more formal style when he conducts a question-and-answer session with himself, about, for example, the persecution of Quakers in England and New England, the implication being that Quakers were now doing the same thing to him and his "oppressed Friends" who had dared to speak out against slavery.[12]

It may come as a surprise that such a gravely earnest man sometimes used humor and sarcasm to make his points. He noted that the "Men of renown in the Congregation," the "chief Rulers in the House of the Lord," those who have "been so long in Power and Repute," most emphatically do not like to be contradicted. When someone dared to challenge them, he or she may "expect to be put in the Stocks . . . with little *Benjamin* their Brother"—who was already, always there, in perpetual trouble, and ready to receive them in solidarity. The elites might, on the other hand, find themselves "in the high Court of *Benjamin*," as they were surely doing as they read the pages of *All Slave-Keepers . . . Apostates*, for they were now being judged untrue to the faith! "Little Benjamin" ruled from on high. He had ample Biblical authority for this clever reversal: "And whosoever shall exalt himself shall be abased; and he that shall humble himself shall be exalted" (Matthew 23:12). Even his humor was subversive.[13]

On several occasions Benjamin resorts to a kind of ventriloquism, recording, for instance, the voices of enslaved Africans in the pidgin language of Barbados: "*My Master* Parrot *very bad man indeed, whippe, whippe poor Negro evee Munne Morning for notin tall! me no bear no longer.*" This kind of writing became quite common in the late-eighteenth and nineteenth centuries, both in racist and antiracist writings, but very few writers had listened closely enough to transcribe the sounds of African diasporan speech by 1738. Lay also put words in the mouth of a hypocritical Quaker slave owner: "Negro, fetch my best Gelding quickly, for me to ride to Meeting, to preach the Gospel of glad Tydings to all men, and Liberty to the Captives, and opening the Prison-Doors to them that are bound; but I'll keep thee in Bondage nevertheless, help thy self if thee can." Benjamin referred here to the Biblical Jubilee, the famous passage from the books of Leviticus (25:8–55) and Isaiah (61:1–11), promising "liberty throughout all the land." The pompous, hypocritical Quaker master preaches liberty and practices slavery.[14]

All Slave-Keepers . . . Apostates teems with metaphors, which Benjamin drew from a combination of Biblical reading and his own personal experience. True religion is often symbolized by "the Lamb," as Jesus was known, especially to the early Quakers, and of course the word had a special meaning to Benjamin, who fondly recalled his work as a shepherd. ("The Lamb" also had a specific theological significance as we shall see below.) Benjamin employed another farm animal to make a point about the preaching of false prophets: "in Truth it is hardly fit for Swine, nay, I think I may venture to say, the very Swine do not like it, it is so bad." When Lay criticized the poor preaching of ungodly ministers he described their cultivating the field of spirit "with the Ox and the Ass joined together; poor plowing with Beasts so ill matched, so unequal in their Nature and Stature, one drawing one way, and another way; and then the Field is sown with two Sorts of Seed, may-be a little good and a great deal of bad." The choice of words and concepts in many ways mirrored Benjamin's rural background and no doubt appealed to readers with an agrarian past. Benjamin the commoner instinctively reached for metaphors from the world of nature.[15]

MOVEMENT

One of the many roles Benjamin played in his book was that of chronicler—of an incipient antislavery movement. He included documents and commentary, folklore, Biblical exegesis, and anecdotes from personal experience, all in an effort to educate his readers, many of whom he regarded as ignorant of both fundamental facts and divine teachings on the subject. Benjamin was especially concerned that the ancient institution of slavery had been allowed to survive into "enlightened" times:

> It is true some may say, Christ in his great Love, hath forgiven Sins, committed in time of great Darkness and Ignorance; but if we should commit the grossest of evils now, in the clear light of this Gospel Day, continue in them, and plead for it too, . . . our Damnation would be just.

He therefore laid out a series of arguments against the world's greatest sin. Henceforth no one could claim that he or she did not know, least of all Quakers who always aspired to live in the light, within and without.[16]

Benjamin had two contradictory modes for writing about slavery. When he recounted the local history of opposition to slavery among Quakers, and even to some extent among non-Quakers, he wrote as if he were part of a small but growing movement to abolish the evil institution. But when he addressed the origins and morality of slavery, he tended to speak as a prophet—someone who battled massive forces of evil as a solitary, courageous individual speaking truth to power.

All Slave-Keepers . . . Apostates begins with a document written by William Burling, a Long Island Quaker Benjamin probably met during his travels. This is the most likely explanation of how Benjamin came to possess the document, which apparently was never otherwise published. It is not hard to see why Benjamin wanted to include it. It was dated 1718—a significant year, wrote Benjamin, because "I was convinced of the same Hellish Practice, I then living in *Barbadoes*." Burling was critical of the "elder brethren" among the Quakers—they were the "Transgressors in this Thing"—not only because they owned slaves but because they suppressed moral debate about the subject. Quoting his favorite prophet, Isaiah, Benjamin had written on the cover page of his book, "The Leaders of the People cause them to Err" and saw Burling as an ally in this view. Burling likewise saw the debate on slavery and Quakerism in stark terms: "the case admits of no medium." Benjamin could not have agreed more wholeheartedly.[17]

Benjamin used a change of fonts to enter into discussion with Burling, who was not merely an authority to cite but someone to argue with. When Burling made too mild a criticism of Quaker ministers, Lay interpolated into the text that ministers were the faithful's "worst Enemies in this case." Suddenly conscious of how radical his condemnation of ministers sounded, Benjamin then inserted a brief, humorous conversation with himself: "This is very pinching, B. L., canst thou prove thy Allegations? if not, what will become of thee?" He consoled himself by adding, "Never fear, Friend; Fear surprises, thou knows who; but the Truth is stronger than all the Powers of Hell." As long as he told the truth, all would be well.[18]

Benjamin traveled widely among Quaker meetings, across Pennsylvania, New Jersey, New York, and New England, and he talked to a lot of people like Burling. Based on these conversations, Benjamin broke Quakers into four basic groups on the issue of slavery: a small but growing number who were strongly and outspokenly opposed to slave keeping; a larger group who opposed the practice but remained silent; a third group who countenanced or actively supported slavery for a variety of reasons; and, finally, the wealthy merchants, artisans, and farmers who owned slaves and by word and example perpetuated the practice. His strategy, in the book and in direct action, was to unify the first group, get the second group to speak out, convert the third group, and either win over or drive out the final group. Success would simultaneously abolish slavery and revitalize Quakerism on holy principles.[19]

Benjamin's book also provides insight into the generational struggle going on among Quakers over slave keeping during the 1730s, supporting the views of historians Jean Soderlund and Brycchan Carey, who have emphasized that this period marked a turning point in Quaker attitudes toward the peculiar institution. Benjamin said repeatedly that his most determined enemies were "elders," which suggested both their age and influence within the meeting. Many of the elders were wealthy, like Anthony Morris, Israel Pemberton, and John Kinsey; others were ministers, like Robert Jordan. At one point the exasperated Benjamin stated that it was "Time for such old rusty Candlesticks to be moved out of their Places"! Benjamin was as old or older than all of these men, but he had the youth and power of a new idea. After he published his book in 1738, he made it a point to distribute it among the younger generation of activists, who would be led by Anthony Benezet and John Woolman.[20]

Benjamin was convinced that the "ancient worthy Friends," the founding generation of George Fox, James Nayler, Edward Burrough, and others, opposed slavery. They had criticized slavery before it was racialized, speaking against impressment, servitude, imprisonment, and the brutal poverty and sometimes wage labor that followed the loss of the commons. Even when members of the faith more recently, in places like Barbados and Pennsylvania, had joined with slave traders, "Men-Killers and Stealers for Gain," a small but "faithful Remnant" remained "zealous against this and all other Iniquity, to whom my Soul is nearly united in Spirit, blessed be the Lord my God, for so great a favour for evermore." These were his brothers and sisters in a righteous cause.[21]

Benjamin knew that many Quakers opposed slavery but did not speak out for fear of antagonizing their brethren, undermining consensus, and creating turmoil, all anathema to Quaker ideals of peace and harmony. He wrote: "I know and believe there is many Friends, that dare not touch with it, for any Profit whatsoever." By this he meant that many Quakers who would have benefited materially by owning and employing slaves nonetheless refused to buy them, just as Benjamin himself had refused to do in Barbados, despite the encouragement of many Quakers there. He added his hope that "there is some Thousands [who] will not bow the Knee to this *Baal* [a pagan god], nor kiss his Lips for an Ease or Gain." Here was Benjamin at his most optimistic: he thought a substantial minority of the approximately twenty-five thousand Quakers who lived in North America opposed slavery on principle.[22]

A larger, although diminishing number of Quakers, however, tacitly supported slavery for a variety of reasons. Some hoped to buy slaves themselves one day. Others sought to make marriage alliances with wealthy slave-owning Quaker families. Even those who harbored no such ambitions benefitted from the largesse of slave-owning Friends. Benjamin mockingly repeated excuses he had no doubt heard in various meetings: "we must not be too censorious, for we are often at their Houses, and Eat and Drink bravely, and have their negroes to wait on us, our Horses, Wives and Children." Benjamin saw that Quakers who owned no slaves but supported those who did were foundational to the system.[23]

Benjamin's comments make it possible to reconstruct part of the debate on the subject at a time when very little of the dispute was written down or published. Historian Rosemary Moore offers a global truth about Quakerism: after 1660 its oral culture was always more radical than its print culture, because elders, on the watch for antinomian radicalism and other deviations from Foxian orthodoxy, carefully vetted content and routinely censored speech and writing. Surveillance was formalized in 1709 with the establishment of the Board of Overseers, which kept almost all antislavery discussion out of print. Significant parts of that oral culture were refracted and preserved through *All Slave-Keepers . . . Apostates*.[24]

One of the most serious criticisms leveled against Benjamin in particular and those opposed to slavery in general was that they were trying to form a "party"—an antislavery faction, an organized "side" in a dispute—within Quaker meetings. Benjamin was seen as a leader of this effort: some "reflected on me, as if I wanted a Party, and to see what Numbers I could get on my side." Benjamin denied that he or others had any such intention, saying that the only party that interested him was the Lord's party, which was of course an artful evasion of the charge because in his view the Lord's party was inherently opposed to slavery. And that was his party no matter how small: "I must confess I rather chuse that Number, though but 5, then 500 that hold the Truth in unrighteousness and in unholiness." Yet by insistently drawing attention to unrighteous slave keeping, Benjamin was doing everything he could to make Quakers take sides on the issue, polarizing meeting after meeting through his dramatic agitation. When Robert

Jordan and others interpreted his actions as an effort to form a "party," they were not wrong.[25]

Benjamin actually explained how he sought to form a "party." He apparently kept in his head something of a map of the abolitionist movement in and around Philadelphia as he devised a strategy to expand it. He said to traveling Quaker ministers that "we will give thee a little Memorandum in thy Pocket of Places and Persons" who are members of the "heavenly Party," those who oppose the "hellish Practice" of slavery. This would assist the minister to find people who opposed slavery and perhaps to distribute abolitionist materials, even, after 1738, Benjamin's own book. He also coached such ministers about what to say when they spoke in Quaker meetings under heavenly inspiration—speech that could not be regulated by elders. When speaking to members of the congregation who owned slaves, his advice was, "thresh 'em going, spare' em not." If challenged by proslavery Quakers after the meeting about the propriety of including an antislavery message in the sermon, Benjamin advised the minister to say, "If the Coat fits thee, put it on; I had no Particular in View." He added that this practice had already borne fruit: "This is and has been the Practice of many worthy Friends, so they hide themselves, and strengthen our Party bravely." Benjamin probably referred to ministers such as his friend John Cadwallader, and of course he himself would do something similar, although without approval as a traveling minister. Together "worthy Friends" were building a regional antislavery "party" within and across Quaker meetings.[26]

Benjamin explained to his readers that slavery and abolitionism had deep roots in Pennsylvania, each dating back to the 1680s. He noted in 1738 that "Friends have been concerned in this Practice" of slave keeping some "50 Years and more," and during the same span of time "many dear tender Souls in our Society . . . have writ and bore Testimony against this Sin." Benjamin referred indirectly but quite precisely (he had a good memory and a sharp sense of historical time) to the introduction of slaves in the 1680s and to the Germantown petition against slavery in 1688, when for the first time Quakers declared themselves "against the traffick of men-body" and adumbrated—three times—the Golden Rule as the principal argument against it. Benjamin himself went on to invoke the argument six times in *All Slave-Keepers . . . Apostates*. The problem was not simply that Quakers owned slaves; it was their dishonesty about the practice, their tendency to minimize and rationalize it.[27]

Upon arrival in 1732 Benjamin made it his business to learn as much about the antislavery struggle in Philadelphia as he could, which is why he sought out Ralph Sandiford right away. As Brycchan Carey has demonstrated in his excellent study of Quaker antislavery rhetoric, a small, embattled, but resilient group of Quakers had, by the 1730s, established a core set of arguments against slavery. Debate among Quakers on the subject was serious and sustained although not always recorded in written documents. Benjamin talked to people, for example, about William Edmondson, one of the first to speak out against slavery, in the 1670s, and George Keith and his supporters, who published *An Exhortation & Caution to Friends Concerning Buying or Keeping of Negroes* in 1693. Benjamin seems to have known about the protests of Ralph Southeby and John Farmer, both of whom were silenced by the Quaker hierarchy. Farmer is an especially intriguing figure as he, like Benjamin, came from Essex. Benjamin's travels also put him in contact with William Burling in Long Island and no doubt other dissident Quakers, for example in Chester County, Pennsylvania, where several petitions against slavery originated between 1711 and 1730. And of course he knew Sandiford and his books intimately. Benjamin had been educated by enslaved people in Barbados between 1718 and 1720; he now absorbed the Pennsylvania experience and vowed to enlarge it.[28]

Benjamin repeated—and added new content to—three primary arguments against bondage. Like others who came before him, he emphasized the Golden Rule, saying to all Quakers "do unto all, as we would they should do unto us." But he gave the phrase a characteristically radical tilt, proposing a world turned upside down in which slave owners should be put in the place of the enslaved "in a very hard Service, that they might feel a little in themselves, of what they make so light of in other People." He also argued that the slave trade utterly violated the peace principle so central to Quaker identity: "We pretend not to love fighting with carnal Weapons, nor to carry Swords by our sides, but carry a worse thing in the Heart." In Benjamin's view there was no

> greater Hypocrisy, and plainer contradiction, than for us as a People, to refuse to bear Arms, or to pay them that do, and yet purchase the Plunder, the Captives, for Slaves at a very great Price, thereby justifying their selling of them, and the War, by which they were or are obtained.

Finally, he asked, how can Quakers support a diabolical "Engine" designed "to make Widows and Fatherless Children" of Africans? Such was the slave trade to a former sailor who knew the Atlantic slave system.[29]

Benjamin pushed beyond the familiar arguments. His originality lay in his utterly uncompromising attitude about slavery. Slave keeping was not merely a sin; it was a "filthy," "gross," "heinous," "Hellish" sin. It was a "soul Sin." Indeed it was "the greatest Sin in the World." He argued that "no Man or Woman, Lad or Lass ought to be suffered, to pretend to Preach Truth in our Meetings, while they live in that Practice [of slave keeping]; which is all a lie." The hypocrisy, in his view, was unbearable. Since slave keepers bore the "Mark of the Beast"—and therefore embodied Satan on earth—they must be cast out of the church: they should not be elders, ministers, or participants of any kind. No godly person should have anything to do with them. By arguing that slave traders and keepers were the spawn of the devil, and therefore evil in the purest possible way, Benjamin made compromise on the issue impossible, for himself and for others.[30]

And just when it appeared that Benjamin had pushed the indictment as far as it could go, he went further. Benjamin explained to any and all who would read or listen that slave keeping was not only a sin, as opponents of slavery had long maintained, but was also a crime, an "atrocious crime," as he announced in the advertisement of his book that appeared in the *American Weekly Mercury* on August 24, 1738. Slave traders, he insisted, were outright murderers. Slave-owning ministers committed a "double crime," against the enslaved and against their congregations. It followed that slave traders and keepers were not merely transgressors against God; they were also criminals, enemies of the social order, and therefore could be subject to prosecution. Benjamin, in short, helped to make slavery not only a matter of morality but a question of justice.[31]

Benjamin's antislavery chronicle also included the full pamphlet written by Samuel Sewell, a Puritan judge in Boston, entitled *The Selling of Joseph: A Memorial*, originally published in 1700 and widely regarded as the first antislavery publication in North America. Benjamin does not say why he reprinted the pamphlet in his book, but we may be sure that he liked Sewell's arguments that all the peoples of the earth were "of one blood" and that slave trading represented the Biblical crime of "man-stealing," for he makes both arguments himself. Benjamin wanted Quakers to know that the debate over slavery had been going on for decades, and in other American colonies.[32]

Benjamin also provides insight into the nature of the oral debate about slavery that took place in the meetings, especially what people said about him and his confrontational methods. Some said he was "too censorious about Trading in Slaves" or too harsh "against Traders in, and Keepers of Slavers." Benjamin made slave keeping too great a sin. He was too extreme, too rigid, in his views. Others added that "he is a troublesome Fellow, and has been so for many Years." (This allegation was true beyond any doubt, as Benjamin admitted when he called himself "a Man of Strife and Contention.") The conclusion many reached was "cast him out, cast him out, cast him out." But Benjamin saw his "sharp invectives" as necessary: the "Beast," meaning the devil, "is in those Men" and "the cause does require it." This, he said solemnly, "I believe in my very Soul."[33]

Following Sandiford's lead, Benjamin extended these arguments to ministers of other churches and to magistrates and elected officials in the colony of Pennsylvania. He added that "no Person whatsoever has any Right, or ought, according to Truths Discipline, to be suffered to have the Rule and Government, or any part of it, in the Church of God, which is the Kingdom of God, while he himself is in League with the Devil." The radicalism of the proposal was breathtaking in its sweep: Benjamin demanded that all persons involved with slavery in any way be stripped of both religious and political power. Since many wealthy Quakers—such as Israel Pemberton and John Kinsey—not only served in but led the Pennsylvania Assembly, Benjamin directly attacked ruling-class power.[34]

Benjamin called out specific "men of renown" for slave keeping—leaders in both church and state. They responded by flying into "a Rage, and such a Fury," attacking him and any who might support his ministry against "the Bondage and miserable Captivity of their poor Slaves." At other times they insulted Benjamin and his motives, saying that he and other "poor People" simply did not have the money to buy slaves so they "pretended" that slave owning was a matter of "Conscience." Probably the most common response was derision: they would "sit and stand and laugh . . . in as light and airy a manner as any Boy in the Town." The laughter was directed not only at Benjamin's cause but at him personally, in part because he was a little person. John Kinsey called him "a little whimsical fellow," a phrase that belied

Kinsey's determined efforts to crush his short but militant challenger. As it happened, Benjamin had a theory about how slave keepers and "men of renown" came into the world, and Kinsey himself played a leading part in it.[35]

PROPHECY

All Slave-Keepers . . . Apostates is a densely allusive, deeply religious work, written by someone who had studied the Bible for many years. Rare is the page that does not have a direct reference to the Bible. Many pages have several, and a few have twenty or more. Benjamin quotes at length from the Bible (especially the prophetic books of Isaiah and Jeremiah); he uses characters and parables from the Bible; he instructs his readers to read specific passages. The Bible functions as a code and an extra layer of meaning in his work. He assumes that his readers not only know the Bible but that they keep it close at hand as a way of illuminating other things they read. At times Benjamin does not even bother to state the point he wants to make: he just refers readers to a particular passage for instruction. He assumed common Biblical knowledge in his readers.

Benjamin ranged back and forth across the New and Old Testaments in writing *All Slave-Keepers . . . Apostates*, but his most important arguments centered on the Book of Revelation. He penned "Some Thoughts" on Revelation in September 1736, soon after he began writing the book. This mystical, vivid, surreal, chaotic, and, to some, incomprehensible part of the Bible was the foundation of Benjamin's book and his larger political philosophy. Again he reached back to the "primitive Quakers." James Nayler and George Fox had drawn heavily on the Book of Revelation at the very origin of the Quaker movement in the early 1650s. Benjamin wrote sixteen and a half detailed pages of exegesis on Revelation and returned to it repeatedly in *All Slave-Keepers . . . Apostates*, offering his own interpretation and showing how it illuminated his closely related themes of a "false ministry" and slavery. He also discussed Revelation in his correspondence with his friend the Quaker minister John Cadwallader and included the letters in the book. Benjamin's ruminations on this book of the Bible offer the key to his prophetic thought.[36]

Originally written, scholars believe, by John of Patmos, who was imprisoned by the Roman Empire for his Christian beliefs, Revelation offered a fierce critique of imperial power and a mystical affirmation that the late-first-century followers of Jesus Christ would triumph over persecution and repression. Revelation depicted a cosmic struggle between good and evil, between the archangel Michael and the Great Red Dragon, each leading an army of angels. The war between good and evil suited Benjamin's temperament, worldview, and aggrieved understanding of his circumstances in Pennsylvania. And like all apocalyptic accounts it required a prophet for proper interpretation. Benjamin was the man for the job. The Book of Revelation also allowed him to explain, within the same parable, the simultaneous origins of slave owners and false ministers, who in his experience were often one and the same person.[37]

Lay had special interest in the twelfth and thirteenth chapters of the Book of Revelation. So crucial are the ideas, imagery, and arguments he draws from them, I reproduce below the chapters in full, from the King James Version of the Bible, with brief summaries after each based on Lay's commentaries, to reveal his interpretation.

REVELATION 12

1. And there appeared a great wonder in heaven; a woman clothed with the sun, and the moon under her feet, and upon her head a crown of twelve stars:

2. And she being with child cried, travailing in birth, and pained to be delivered.

3. And there appeared another wonder in heaven; and behold a great red dragon, having seven heads and ten horns, and seven crowns upon his heads.

4. And his tail drew the third part of the stars of heaven, and did cast them to the earth: and the dragon stood before the woman which was ready to be delivered, for to devour her child as soon as it was born.

5. And she brought forth a man child, who was to rule all nations with a rod of iron: and her child was caught up unto God, and to his throne.

6. And the woman fled into the wilderness, where she hath a place prepared of God, that they should feed her there a thousand two hundred and threescore days.

7. And there was war in heaven: Michael and his angels fought against the dragon; and the dragon fought and his angels,

8. And prevailed not; neither was their place found any more in heaven.

9. And the great dragon was cast out, that old serpent, called the Devil, and Satan, which deceiveth the whole world: he was cast out into the earth, and his angels were cast out with him.

> *10. And I heard a loud voice saying in heaven, Now is come salvation, and strength, and the kingdom of our God, and the power of his Christ: for the accuser of our brethren is cast down, which accused them before our God day and night.*
>
> *11. And they overcame him by the blood of the Lamb, and by the word of their testimony; and they loved not their lives unto the death.*
>
> *12. Therefore rejoice, ye heavens, and ye that dwell in them. Woe to the inhabiters of the earth and of the sea! For the devil is come down unto you, having great wrath, because he knoweth that he hath but a short time.*
>
> *13. And when the dragon saw that he was cast unto the earth, he persecuted the woman which brought forth the man child.*
>
> *14. And to the woman were given two wings of a great eagle, that she might fly into the wilderness, into her place, where she is nourished for a time, and times, and half a time, from the face of the serpent.*
>
> *15. And the serpent cast out of his mouth water as a flood after the woman, that he might cause her to be carried away of the flood.*
>
> *16. And the earth helped the woman, and the earth opened her mouth, and swallowed up the flood which the dragon cast out of his mouth.*
>
> *17. And the dragon was wroth with the woman, and went to make war with the remnant of her seed, which keep the commandments of God, and have the testimony of Jesus Christ.*

According to Benjamin, the woman clothed in the sun is giving birth to the "true church," but the evil red dragon, "a Furious Beast, and Bloody Monster," is poised to devour it. The dragon gathers up a third of the stars of Heaven in its tail and casts them down to earth. This is a critical verse for Benjamin, for these fallen stars will produce "inlightened men," born of evil: slave keepers and false ministers will sprout from the soil where the stars were flung down. These men, to Benjamin, are "the greatest of Anti-Christs, and worst of Devils." They are motivated by greed; they "betray the Truth, for Gain." They become "wicked Spirits in high Places"—rich men, masters, elders, ministers, and magistrates. Benjamin thus uses the Book of Revelation to account for the formation not only of slave owners in particular but of an evil, covetous ruling class in general.[38]

Soon after the woman gives birth to a "Man-Child, begotten and Borne of the Truth," war breaks out in heaven: the archangel Michael and his angels battle the Great Red Dragon and his dark troops, the latter, according to Benjamin, fighting "for his Gain, to inslave the Bodies and Souls of Men." Spiritual and physical slaveries converge. In this apocalyptic battle, the forces of good triumph. The dragon, with his "worldly, covetous Spirit" is cast out of Heaven, where joy is proclaimed. But woe is now the portion of the earth. The message to Christians is that "the devil is come down unto you, having great wrath, because he knoweth that he hath but a short time." The devil operates through his own progeny, slave keepers and false ministers, his primary agents of evil. Meantime the woman who gave birth is given the wings of an eagle to fly into hiding in the wilderness, but she is followed and persecuted by the devil and his forces—just as Benjamin was harassed by slave keepers and false ministers. The devil launches all-out war against God's faithful, who must fight back waging "The Lamb's War," as Nayler famously called it. Benjamin concludes his exegesis of Revelation 12 by asking a pointed question: "What does our Slave-Keeping Preachers think of these Scriptures?"[39]

REVELATION 13

1. And I stood upon the sand of the sea, and saw a beast rise up out of the sea, having seven heads and ten horns, and upon his horns ten crowns, and upon his heads the name of blasphemy.

2. And the beast which I saw was like unto a leopard, and his feet were as the feet of a bear, and his mouth as the mouth of a lion: and the dragon gave him his power, and his seat, and great authority.

3. And I saw one of his heads as it were wounded to death; and his deadly wound was healed: and all the world wondered after the beast.

4. And they worshipped the dragon which gave power unto the beast: and they worshipped the beast, saying, Who is like unto the beast? who is able to make war with him?

5. And there was given unto him a mouth speaking great things and blasphemies; and power was given unto him to continue forty and two months.

6. And he opened his mouth in blasphemy against God, to blaspheme his name, and his tabernacle, and them that dwell in heaven.

7. And it was given unto him to make war with the saints, and to overcome them: and power was given him over all kindreds, and tongues, and nations.

8. And all that dwell upon the earth shall worship him, whose names are not written in the book of life of the Lamb slain from the foundation of the world.

9. If any man have an ear, let him hear.

10. He that leadeth into captivity shall go into captivity: he that killeth with the sword must be killed with the sword. Here is the patience and the faith of the saints.

11. And I beheld another beast coming up out of the earth; and he had two horns like a lamb, and he spake as a dragon.

12. And he exerciseth all the power of the first beast before him, and causeth the earth and them which dwell therein to worship the first beast, whose deadly wound was healed.

13. And he doeth great wonders, so that he maketh fire come down from heaven on the earth in the sight of men,

14. And deceiveth them that dwell on the earth by the means of those miracles which he had power to do in the sight of the beast; saying to them that dwell on the earth, that they should make an image to the beast, which had the wound by a sword, and did live.

15. And he had power to give life unto the image of the beast, that the image of the beast should both speak, and cause that as many as would not worship the image of the beast should be killed.

16. And he causeth all, both small and great, rich and poor, free and bond, to receive a mark in their right hand, or in their foreheads:

17. And that no man might buy or sell, save he that had the mark, or the name of the beast, or the number of his name.

18. Here is wisdom. Let him that hath understanding count the number of the beast: for it is the number of a man; and his number is Six hundred threescore and six.

In Revelation 13 a new many-headed beast, combining the feral features of leopard, bear, and lion, arises from the sea. The furious old dragon, says Benjamin, has given the "nasty" new beast "his Chair to sit in as Chief

Judge, and *great Authority*, to rule over almost all the Congregation in *America*." The congregation refers to all settlers and to Quakers in particular. The new creature had "a mouth speaking great things." Benjamin amplifies the point: it "could Preach so excellently as if he could almost make Slave-Keeping agreeable." The deluded people begin to worship the dragon and the beast, who continued their "war against the saints," overcoming, says Benjamin, "them that are not faithful." The beast gained power "over all kindreds, and tongues, and nations" and used it to harass and disown those like Benjamin who testified against its practice of slave keeping. Benjamin gives special emphasis to Revelation 13:10: "He that leadeth into captivity shall go into captivity: he that killeth with the sword must be killed with the sword." Quakers have blindly become "the worst of Villains, the worst of Robbers and Murtherers." They had embraced violence and they will perish by it.[40]

A second critical passage was the eleventh verse: "And I beheld another beast coming up out of the earth; and he had two horns like a lamb, and he spake as a dragon." The third beast "doeth great wonders" deceiving all "earthly minded Souls," appearing physically like Jesus (the lamb) to do the work of Satan. The clever new beast now "causeth all, both small and great, rich and poor, free and bond, to receive a mark in their right hand, or in their foreheads" to signify their allegiance. Only those with the mark "might buy or sell." Lay was sure this passage referred to the "buying & selling Slaves and Souls of Men." The "Mark of the Beast," the sign of the devil, deeply stamped upon the congregation, was "Slave-Keeping."[41]

Benjamin found in Revelation a story that encapsulated in dramatic form his concerns about slavery, false ministry, his own persecution, and the imperiled future of the Quaker faith. It even explained why most people could not detect the evil that stood before them, for the lamb-like beast, said Lay, was so "sweet in the Mouth." Revelation also allowed Benjamin to sound the warning that by keeping slaves, Quakers would themselves descend into captivity, and that by buying slaves taken through violent means, Quakers risked being killed in rebellion. Benjamin's brilliant exegesis of Revelation also affirmed his own importance as a prophet trying to save his people.[42]

Like all Old Testament prophets, Benjamin thundered condemnations, predicted ruin, self-righteously refused to compromise, and offered visions of a land of milk and honey should everyone follow his way and abolish slavery. He quoted not only the Book of Revelation but the prophets Isaiah, Jeremiah, and Ezekiel and their luminous, furious, poetic language of excoriation. Benjamin's use of prophetic language was one of the distinctive features of the book. As a man ahead of his time, without a social movement to support his radical views, he exercised the power of the dissident individual who challenged a regime of power. Benjamin liked the prophetic voice because it suited his temperament, angry and self-righteous. Quaker meetings did not make room for anger, so prophecy was an important outlet for thoughts and feelings he could not otherwise express.[43]

Benjamin's most spectacular prophetic performance, in which he ran a sword through a bladder with red berry juice and spattered "blood" all over the slave keepers at the Philadelphia Yearly Meeting in September 1738, just three weeks after the publication of his book, had a specific Biblical antecedent and meaning. Benjamin himself provided the key to his intentions when he asked in *All Slave-Keepers . . . Apostates*, "Will not the Lord *whet* his *glittering Sword*, and take *vengeance* on such *Enemies*, that pretend to preach Truth, and Practice a Lie, the greatest in the world"? He alluded to Deuteronomy 32:41–43, wherein God states to Moses and the Israelites, "If I whet my glittering sword, and mine hand take hold on judgment; I will render vengeance to mine enemies, and will reward them that hate me." Convinced that slave keepers, who practiced the greatest sin the world, were the mortal enemies of both himself and God, Benjamin threatened them with a divine, bloody vengeance: "my sword shall devour flesh; and that with the blood of the slain and of the captives, from the beginning of revenges upon the enemy." Here was the antinomian spirit of James Nayler, who acted the part of Jesus entering Jerusalem on a donkey in 1656; Benjamin trembled on the edge of playing God himself. Through him, the Almighty announced to "ye nations" that he will "avenge the blood of his servants, and will render vengeance to his adversaries," but will be merciful to the holy and the just. Benjamin's direct antinomian connection to God made him a fearsome messenger, if not an avenging angel.[44]

Benjamin did not leave the Revelation story at the level of ambiguous parable, especially when he wrote of the diabolical beast that would destroy the earth and the Quaker faith:

> *And the Beast that I saw was like a Leopard*, full of Spots, causes me to think of the first of *Isaiah; feet like a Bear*, to tear and rent, *Mouth like a*

> *Lyon*, roar against all that oppose 'em; and the furious Dragon gave the nasty Beast *his Power and his Seat*, his Chair to sit in as Chief Judge, and *great Authority*, to rule over almost all the Congregation in *America.*

Benjamin here alluded specifically to John Kinsey, who was, at the moment of the publication of *All Slave-Keepers . . . Apostates*, not only the clerk of the Philadelphia Yearly Meeting but soon to be the attorney general of Pennsylvania and the chief justice of the Pennsylvania Supreme Court. Such was Benjamin's prophecy about the man who would thrice be the "Chief Judge, and *great authority*," in religious, political, and legal institutions. Kinsey was, without question, the ruler of "almost all the Congregation in *America.*" A master of "political double-talk," he had "a mouth speaking great things."[45]

After the publication of Benjamin's book in August 1738, the "Chief Judge" would exercise his authority. As it happened, he had, in 1736, replaced Israel Pemberton Sr. as the head of the Board of Overseers, which would pass judgment on all publications by Quakers. Kinsey therefore wrote the official notice concerning Benjamin's book on behalf of the Philadelphia Yearly Meeting to the *Pennsylvania Gazette* and published it three times, on October 26, 1738, November 2, 1738, and November 16, 1738, in case anyone should miss the message. It represented the final official disavowal of Benjamin and his ideas.

> It is now some Months since a Book was published in this City, with the Title *All Slave-Keepers &c. Apostates.* In the Preface to which are these Words, viz. "These Things following are so far from offending or grieving my very dear, true and tender Friends called Quakers, who love the Truth more than all; that it is by their request and desire that They are made publick." From which Paragraph it is not improbable some Readers may be persuaded to believe the Author was one of the People called Quakers, and that his Book had been printed at their Request, especially, were they to be silent on this Occasion. Therefore, they have thought it fit, and hereby do give publick Notice, that the Book aforesaid contains gross Abuses, not only against some of their Members in particular, but against the whole Society: That the Author is not of their religious Community; that they disapprove of his Conduct, the Composition, and Printing of the Book; and therefore are not to be accountable for its Contents.

By Order of the Yearly-Meeting, held at BURLINGTON, for *New-Jersey* and *Pennsylvania*, the second day of the seventh Month last.

John Kinsey, Clerk.

As one of the members "in particular" who was "abused" in *All Slave-Keepers . . . Apostates*, Kinsey self-righteously denounced the book and cast Benjamin out, once and for all. One wonders what Benjamin thought when he saw that the official notice of repudiation had been written and signed by the "nasty beast," the devil incarnate.[46]

CHAPTER FIVE

BOOKS AND A NEW LIFE

AFTER THE DOUBLE EXPLOSION OF 1738, when Benjamin spattered the blood of God's vengeance on Quaker slave owners and, less than a month later, published his fierce prophetic attack on them, he entered a new phase of life. Although he had been disowned and denounced, he would remain involved with the Quaker community, attending worship services and arguing, through word and deed, about the evils of slavery. At the same time he turned his attention to building a new revolutionary way of life, which would fold his antislavery principles and practices into a broader, more radical vision of human possibility. He would build the New Jerusalem, on a small scale, and he would live there. He would embody his own hopes for the future. At fifty-six years of age, Benjamin decided that he would become more dangerous as he grew older.

Benjamin loved books, as autodidacts often do. He collected books and he read voraciously. Reading and reflection were his favorite pastimes. He carried books—probably his single most important possession—with him to Philadelphia in 1732. He worked as a bookseller, off and on, for much of his life. He participated in the print culture of the city, subscribing to the *Pennsylvania Gazette*, raising subscriptions to publish books he admired, and joining newspaper debate. He proudly built a personal library of two hundred volumes, some of which he loaned to friends. He had the fullest collection of early Quaker writings to be found in Pennsylvania, and probably in the Americas. His love of books connected to his love of children: "He took great pleasure in visiting schools, where he often preached to the youth. He frequently carried a basket of religious books with him, and distributed them as prizes, among the scholars." He wrote and published his own book, which few people of his class ever managed to do. Near the end of his life, when Deborah and Benjamin Franklin commissioned his portrait, the artists featured him holding his favorite book. Books were probably the only "worldly good" he cared about. Even though he called himself "illiterate," Benjamin Lay was very much a man of the book.[1]

As it happens, we know a great deal about Benjamin's books, and what he thought about them, from four sources. First, he published the list of books he thought it important to bring to Pennsylvania when he and Sarah migrated in 1732. Second, he included an extensive, thirty-page annotated bibliography of many of his books in *All Slave-Keepers . . . Apostates*, published in 1738. Third, various books he had read show up in other documents, for example an inventory taken in 1759 at his death and in the memoir about his life published by Roberts Vaux in 1815. Finally, a couple of books from Benjamin's personal library have survived. Taken together, these illuminate the reading and thinking of a self-made intellectual and prophet.

In imagining a new life Benjamin drew ideas and inspiration from many writers across a broad temporal and geographic expanse, from an English revolutionary of the 1640s and 1650s, to philosophers of ancient Greece and Rome, to an unconventional thinker, much like himself, whose ideas originated in places as diverse as India and Barbados. Benjamin translated the ideas he took from books into action, into concrete, practical ways of living. This chapter explores the reading of a common man as he rethought the ethical foundations of human life.

ANTINOMIANISM

Benjamin read and studied the work of William Dell, a militant chaplain of the New Model Army who was part of the occupying force in Colchester during the English Revolution. Dell was a man of "the light," although not a Quaker. We know that Benjamin admired Dell because he says so in *All Slave-Keepers . . . Apostates*. He approvingly mentions Dell's essay "The Right Reformation of Learning, Schools, and Universities, according to the State of the Gospel, and the True Light that Shines Therein," which appeared in a 650-page collection of Dell's works, *Several Sermons and Discourses of William Dell, Minister of the Gospel*, published in London by the Quaker printer J. Sowle in 1709. When Benjamin arrived in Philadelphia in 1732, he recommended and offered for sale "William Dell's Works," which might have referred to *Several Sermons and Discourses* or to a collection of individual books and pamphlets. In either case, he was thoroughly familiar with Dell's writings, and indeed he was in significant ways influenced by them.[2]

Benjamin's favorite work by Dell was *The Tryal of Spirits, Both in Teachers and Hearers, Wherein is held forth the clear Discovery and Downfal of the Carnal and Anti-Christian Clergy of these Nations, testified from the Word of God to the University Congregations in Cambridge*, originally published in London in 1653. Benjamin called it "an excellent book"—so excellent that he copied a sizable passage, about the "mark of the beast," into his own tome. We also know that Benjamin read the edition of the book published by the Quaker printer Thomas Sowle in London in 1699, and we know quite specifically what he thought about it, almost passage by passage, for his own personal copy of the book, amply annotated in his own somewhat crooked handwriting, has survived and is part of the collection at the Historical Society of Germantown, Pennsylvania, where Quaker protests against slavery began in 1688. Dell's book somehow made its way from the library in Benjamin's cave through at least three subsequent owners, over two and a half centuries, to its present location. Benjamin's dialogue with Dell spans two generations and the Atlantic Ocean.[3]

William Dell studied at Puritan-controlled Emmanuel College, Cambridge, where he received a bachelor of arts degree in 1628 and a master of arts degree in 1631, and afterward became a fellow. Radicalized during the 1640s and called by some a "Seeker," meaning someone who rejected formal religious organization and took a spiritual path toward the "pure" church, Dell became a chaplain in the revolutionary New Model Army at the very moment when the Levellers were ascendant. Neither he nor his fellow chaplain John Saltmarsh were formal members of the Leveller organization, but both held consistent radical ideas, several of which Dell expressed in a fast sermon delivered to the House of Commons on November 25, 1646. The chaplain spoke of the "turning and tumultuous times"; the world was "shaking." He recalled the era of the "primitive Christians," when Jesus bid his disciples to "*Go teach all Nations*," sending forth "*poor, illiterate, mechanick* men" who "turned the *world* upside down," just as the

New Model Army was doing as he spoke. Dell had recently preached to the soldiers: "the power is in you, the people; keep it, part not with it."[4]

This "key figure in the development of antinomian religion" in the 1640s and 1650s told members of Parliament that his sermon was "the Lord's *voyce* to you." Dell emphasized "spirit" over law and demanded the abolition of all "outward ordinances" that impinged upon individual conscience. He spoke mostly about the kingdom of God to the great men assembled, but he did make one demand—one might even call it a threat—about the kingdom of England:

> that you would regard the *oppression of the poor, and the sighing of the needy.* Never was there more injustice and oppression in the Nation than now; I have seen many oppressed and *crushed*, and *none to help them.* I *beseech* you *consider* this with *all* your *hearts*, for many who derive *power* from *you* are *great oppressors.* And therefore I *require you in the name of God, to discharge the trust* that *God hath put into your hands;* & so to *defend the poor and fatherlesse, to doe justice to the afflicted and needy, to deliver the poor and needy, and to rid them out of the hands of the wicked;* This is your business, discharge your duty: if you will not, then hear what the Lord saith, *Psal.* I, 12, 5. *For the oppression of the poor, for the sighing of the needy, now will I arise saith the Lord:* and Gods arising in this case would prove your ruine. If you will not doe Gods work in the *Kingdome* which he hath called you to, he will doe *it himself* without you, as it is written. *He shall deliver the needy when he cryeth, the poor also, and he that hath no helper,* he shall save *their soules* from *deceit and violence, the common evils* of the *times.* And this is all that I have to say for this Kingdome.

Many of the great men did not take kindly to Dell's self-assured, daunting instructions. They did not offer the class-conscious Dell official thanks for the sermon, nor did they have it printed for distribution, both customary practices. Dell spoke bluntly about the "*oppression of the poor.*" In 1645 he had written, "He that fears God is free from all other fear; he fears not men of high degree." Benjamin lived by this creed.[5]

In 1649, at the New Model Army's peak of power, Dell was, in a straightforward political appointment, "intruded" as master of Gonville and Caius College, Cambridge, thus creating a paradox: Dell was the era's leading radical critic of Cambridge and Oxford Universities. He attacked the elite monopoly on "humane learning" and spelled out a plan to democratize England's educational system. Benjamin too took a great interest in education; he called Dell's approach "a Method very excellent."[6]

Dell offered a radical plan for educating youth, to be undertaken not by the churches but by "civil power, or chief magistrates." He wanted schools to be built throughout the nation, in all cities, towns, and villages; they would be run by "godly and learned men," like himself. They would teach reading, so that all could know the Holy Scriptures, as well as grammar, rhetoric, logic, mathematics, and geography. Dell considered all of these subjects to be "very useful to human society, and the affairs of this present life." Cambridge and Oxford—where people loved private gain more than their brethren—would see their monopoly on humane learning broken as universities and colleges would be built in all the great towns and cities of England. In Dell's vision, education was geared both to a secular idea, improvement "in the use of reason," and to a republican idea, "the common good of the people." Benjamin affirmed the popular, democratic, and egalitarian values embodied in Dell's plan.[7]

Even more important for Benjamin was Dell's *The Tryal of Spirits*, which strongly influenced the Quaker's own antinomian thinking. It is impossible to know when Benjamin first read the book, but it may have been relatively early in his life. He acted on some of its central tenets in 1720 in criticizing Quaker ministers in London. He clearly drew heavily on Dell's book in formulating the arguments about "false prophets" that appeared in *All Slave-Keepers . . . Apostates*. Benjamin also wrote in the back of the book, "Benjamin Lay his Book borrowed by Jos ffowes this 21st day of May 1742." He thought the book important enough to recommend and loan to others.[8]

The Tryal of Spirits had two parts. The first was the printed version of a sermon Dell delivered to "the University Congregations at Cambridge," probably in 1653. The second was Dell's critical response to a sermon given around the same time by Sydrach Simpson, an Independent/Congregationalist minister, master of Pembroke Hall, and another Parliamentary appointment at Cambridge, entitled "A Plain and Necessary Confutation of divers Gross and Anti-christian Errors, delivered to the *University* Congregation." Judging by the number and range of his marginal comments, Benjamin took greater interest in the former than the latter.[9]

Benjamin respected Dell's learning, as well as his position as master of a Cambridge college. When Dell called himself a "bruised reed"—that is to say, a weak foundation for the heavy task of exposing anti-Christian ministers—Benjamin wrote in the margin that "if so great a Man as Wm Dell call himself a broused Reed which was Master of a Colledg in the University of Cambridg what may I call my self that was a poor common Sailer and no more." Benjamin had even greater respect for the humble, forthright, unpretentious ways Dell wore his learning. The very first comment Benjamin wrote in response to Dell's book was "If I desire to Live Let me desire to Live humble."[10]

Benjamin shared with Dell antinomian beliefs. Both men insisted on the primacy of the spirit over the letter, the word, and the law. When Dell wrote against those who use "the Outward letter of the Word" to serve "their own Worldly Ends and Advantages, and nothing else," Benjamin added, simply, "no spirit no life." At the end of the paragraph he penned that "if this be true what a sad condition is the World in." Dell was an outspoken advocate of "free grace," a code phrase for the antinomian spirit that elevated the believer above the authority of church and state. Benjamin quoted Dell on the power of grace to overcome the "mark of the beast," that is to say, slavery.[11]

Both authors were fiercely anticlerical, attacking the ministers of the Church of England and indeed all "false prophets"—the anti-Christian ministers who appear on the title pages of both *The Tryal of Spirits* and *All Slave-Keepers . . . Apostates.* Both Dell and Lay regarded the discernment and casting out of such ministers as crucial to building the pure church, the New Jerusalem, the kingdom of God on earth. Both warned against "dark powers": the snares, seductions, and delusions that would waylay the godly. Both emphasized the corrupting power of class. Dell told a story of dogs lying "at ease" on "a *rich Garment*, or *soft carpet*" until someone dared to speak against their privilege, whereupon these "*angry Dogs . . . bark* at them, and *rend* them, as much as they *can* or *dare.*" Benjamin declared his spiritual affinity with Dell by paying him the highest compliment, writing below the book's final published paragraph, "Pure reading I think Finis." Benjamin too was a Seeker after the pure church; he found a kindred spirit in William Dell.[12]

CYNIC PHILOSOPHY

On two occasions, someone who knew Benjamin well described him as a "Cynic" philosopher. The commentators did not mean that he had a skeptical view of human nature but rather something both deeper and more specific. The first comment appeared in the *Pennsylvania Gazette* March 25, 1742, in an article about a protest Benjamin had conducted in the Philadelphia marketplace regarding the "vanity of Tea-drinking." The author of the article was in all likelihood the printer of the newspaper, Benjamin Franklin, who had published Lay's book three and a half years earlier and knew him well. He called Benjamin a "Pythagorean-cynical-christian Philosopher." The second comment was recorded four years later by a Pennsylvania/New Jersey Quaker politician named John Smith, who wrote in his diary, "Had part of the Evening in the Comp[an]y of B. Lay, the Comi-Cynic Philosopher." It is not clear what the prefix "Comi-" was meant to imply—perhaps that Benjamin used humor in his conversation or, condescendingly, that he himself was somehow "comical," an attitude many adopted toward little people. In either case Smith suggested that the ideas of Cynic philosophy had been part of the evening's conversation. These remarks reveal a significant influence on the formation and character of Benjamin's thought and activism.[13]

Benjamin was a serious reader of ancient philosophy. He had read the single greatest survey of ancient Greek and Roman thought published in English during his time, Thomas Stanley's *History of Philosophy: Containing the Lives, Opinions, Actions and Discourses of the Philosophers of Every Sect*, which appeared in three volumes between 1655 and 1661. (Benjamin had probably read the combined, single-volume edition published in 1701.) Here Benjamin learned about many thinkers, most notably "the Cynick Philosophers," including the founder of the group, Diogenes of Sinope. Benjamin had also read the work of the Stoic philosopher Epictetus, who admired Diogenes and considered Cynicism to be "the highest, and hardest, human calling." Among the books Benjamin brought from London was *Epictetus his Morals, Done from the Original Greek, by a Doctor of Physick*, published in 1702. He also brought the work of the Roman Stoic philosopher Seneca the Younger. Lay used the ideas of these thinkers and others as he fashioned his critique of slavery and the social order in Pennsylvania.[14]

Scholars agree that the Cynics, founded by Diogenes (c. 412–323 BCE) in Athens in the fourth century BCE, carried on a more or less coherent line of philosophical thought over nine hundred years, stretching to Rome in the fifth century CE. Diogenes, the original Cynic, was described as

Lay studied the ideas of ancient Greek philosophers and had a special interest in Diogenes and his fellow Cynics. Lay followed the example of Diogenes by acting out his radical ideas in public confrontations.

"Socrates gone mad." Like Socrates he believed that philosophical ideas had to be embodied in public action—and he carried the point to extremes. Seeking to shock and provoke, Diogenes walked the streets of Athens dressed in simple clothes, carrying a walking stick, engaging anyone and everyone he met in philosophical conversation. He attacked all received wisdom, all prevailing custom, all long-standing taboos; one of his many mottoes was "Deface the currency." He was said to have masturbated and defecated in public. Diogenes challenged people high and low with one subversive act after another. He lived outdoors, slept in a large ceramic jar, walked everywhere, ate only vegetables, drank only water, and in all respects affirmed the simple life as a matter of principle. He rejected Greek nationality and insisted on a new kind of citizenship: he declared himself a "cosmopolitan"—a citizen of the cosmos—inventing a new word that has lasted down to the present.[15]

Much can be learned of Diogenes through an anecdote Benjamin read in Stanley's *History of Philosophy*: The philosopher had become so famous that King Alexander the Great sought out his company and came upon him one day as he lay in repose, sunning himself. Alexander offered to grant Diogenes any wish, any wish at all: "Ask of me what thou wilt." Diogenes looked up at the great man and answered that there was one thing he could do: "*Do not stand between me and the Sun.*" Such was the legendary scorn that Diogenes, a former slave, poured upon the rich and the high-born. Combining wit, color, imagination, and serious moral message, he practiced philosophy from below.[16]

Other philosophers—from Crates to Lucian—carried on and expanded the corpus of Cynic ideas, evolving a set of fundamental virtues, values, and principles. At the center of it all was the notion of *parrhesia*: free, frank, blunt, candid speech, uttered with indifference to worldly authority, just as Diogenes had spoken to Alexander. Cynics were known above all else for fearless speech. A second value was *autarkeia*, the ideal of self-sufficiency, the freedom to enjoy nature's gifts without the interference of material goods and the false needs they created. Next came the related virtues of *askêsis*—rigorous training in asceticism, endurance, and physical toughness—and *karteria*: the practice of patient self-control that leads to moral toughness. A fifth and final value was *tuphos:* commitment to an unrelenting attack on wealth, prestige, appearance, luxury, and social standing. Cynics sought to live "life in agreement with nature." They chose a simple, natural existence over and against the artificialities of "civilization," affirming a pantheistic vision of interconnected life, which included an affinity with animals. The ideal Cynic society was antinomian: it would have no law, no courts, no money, no war, and no slavery. All would be based on love, which would be freely given to friends, citizens, foreigners, even barbarians.[17]

As part of his commitment to *askêsis* and *karteria*, the strict training that led to physical and moral toughness, and in honor and imitation of Jesus, Benjamin took an example from Matthew 4:1 and, in February 1738, began a forty-day fast. He resolved to drink only spring water several times a day. For the first few days, he kept up his normal routine, rising at daybreak, gardening, and making "his usual excursions in the neighbourhood." On the ninth day of the fast he observed, I "am as well in health, as ever, since I came to Pennsylvania, which is six Years this Spring." One morning he walked eight miles to Philadelphia, where he met with Benjamin Franklin, who later remarked that Benjamin's "breath was so acrid as to produce a suffusion of water in his eyes, which was extremely painful." By the third week of the fast his strength began to fail. He was soon confined to his cave and eventually to his bed. Yet he would not give up. He asked a friend to place a large loaf of bread on a nearby table. Although weak of voice he continued to test his will by saying repeatedly, "Benjamin thou seest it, but thou shalt not eat it." His friends at this point grew alarmed, explaining that if he did not eat "he would certainly perish." After three weeks his "mental faculties began to fail," whereupon his friends began to feed him, slowly bringing him back to life. He discovered his own physical limits but he retained a strong commitment to "resolute self-denial" and an austere, virtuous way of life.[18]

Benjamin adapted Cynic ideals to the dictates of radical Christianity, but part of that adaptation had already taken place hundreds of years before he was born. Many scholars think the Cynics had a significant impact on the early Christians, shaping their practices of asceticism, voluntary poverty, the sharing of material goods, and the gospel of universal love. A few even see Jesus himself as a Cynic philosopher, especially when he said, "I have come into the world to be a witness to truth" (John 18:37). It is also noteworthy that the famous Biblical phrase (1 Timothy 6:10) "The love of money is the root of all evil" was not only a Cynic idea but a specific historical phrase the philosophers used. Benjamin wrote in the margins of a book, "Mammon—cursed love of mammon—mammon surfeits and corrupts the mind, and darkens the understanding—Oh the blessed doctrine and practice of the first christians, which kept out luxury, pride, and cursed covetousness." Benjamin admired both the Cynics and the "primitive Christians" as described in the Book of Acts.[19]

Benjamin patterned significant parts of his new revolutionary life on the ideas and practices of the Cynics. Like Diogenes he wore a long beard and simple clothes, ate only fruits and vegetables, drank only water, and traveled long distances on foot using his walking stick—the very characteristics of Benjamin emphasized by artists in their portraits during the late 1750s and early 1760s. Benjamin practiced philosophy in public and generated endless discussion of his actions. In group discussions, wrote

This portrait, by William Williams and his apprentice, the soon-to-be-famous Benjamin West, depicted Lay in front of his cave but made no reference to his deep commitment to the cause of abolitionism.

These details of the Williams-West portrait show Lay's distinctive appearance, his vegetarian habits, and his love of Thomas Tryon's book *The Way to Health, Long Life and Happiness, or, A Discourse of Temperance and the Particular Nature of all Things Requisit for the Life of Man* (1683).

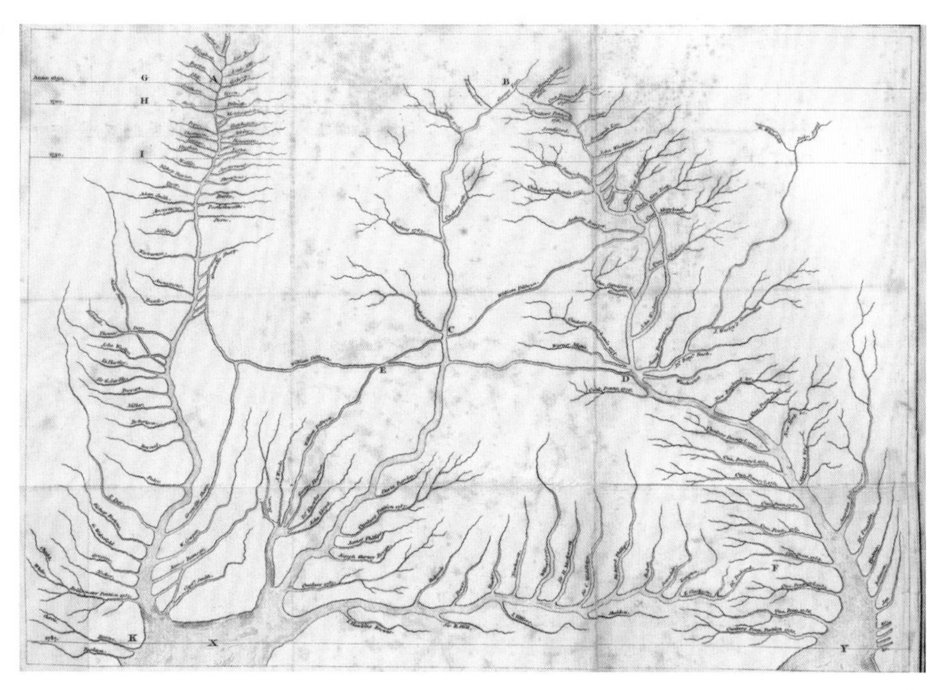

After the British parliament abolished the slave trade in 1808, Thomas Clarkson created this riverine genealogy of the triumphant antislavery movement, giving great credit to American Quakers. Clarkson labeled one of the tributaries in his map "Benjamin Lay."

Lay lived in London and worked along the Thames (above) as a sailor for a dozen years in the early 1700s. His wife, Sarah, also came from a maritime background, living in Deptford, England, site of the British Royal Navy's first shipyard, where vessels such as the *Cambridge* were launched (below).

Two views of the Philadelphia waterfront, where Benjamin and Sarah arrived in 1732. Peter Cooper shows (above, 1720) Anthony Morris's brewery at left (#4); below an artist named G. Wood provides a view across the Delaware River, 1735.

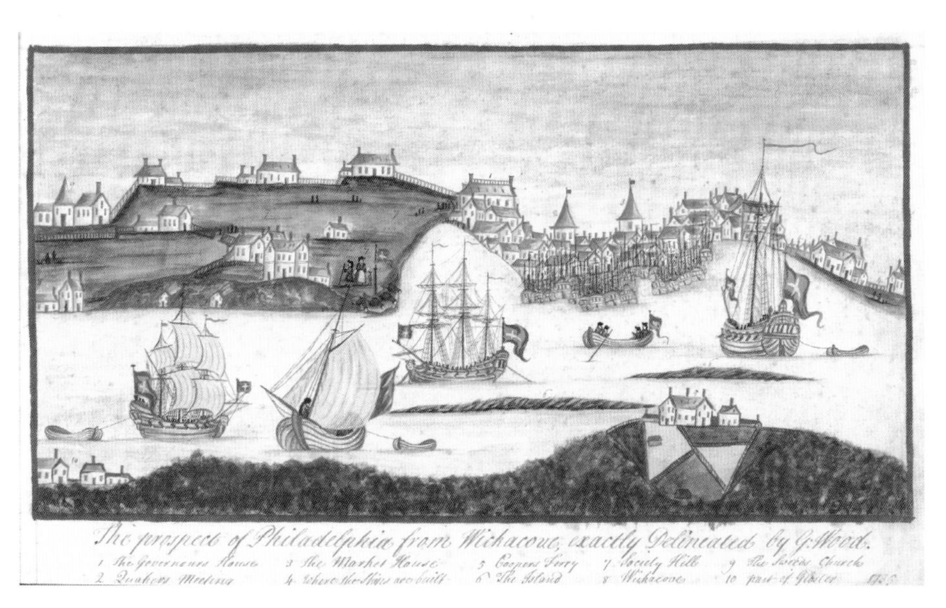

This image of a Quaker meeting, painted by an unknown artist most likely in the late eighteenth century, shows a man standing and addressing his fellow Quakers, men and women with covered heads, as the spirit of the "inward light" moved him. Lay thundered his denunciation of slavery at such meetings dozens of times.

The Quaker meetinghouse in Burlington, New Jersey, where Lay used a sword to pierce an animal bladder full of bright-red pokeberry juice, spattering the symbolic blood on the bodies of Quaker slave owners.

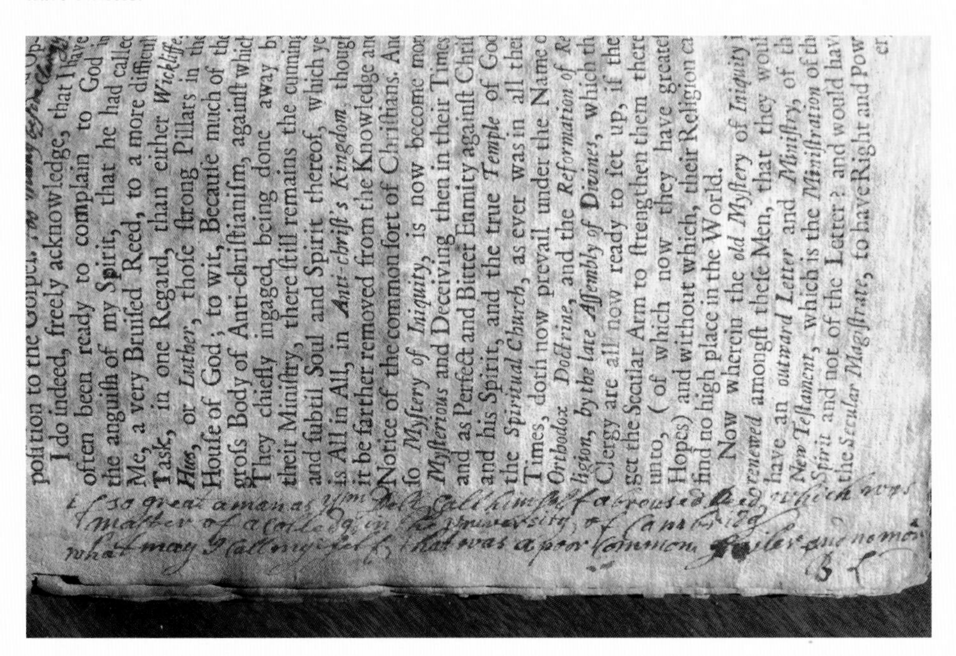

position to the Gospel. ... Op-
I do indeed, freely acknowledge, that I have often been ready to complain to God in the anguish of my Spirit, that he had called Me, a very Bruised Reed, to a more difficult Task, in one Regard, than either *Wickliffe*, *Hus*, or *Luther*, those strong Pillars in the House of God; to wit, Because much of the gross Body of Anti-christianism, against which They chiefly ingaged, being done away by their Ministry, there still remains the cunning and subtil Soul and Spirit thereof, which yet is All in All, in *Anti-christ's Kingdom*, though it be farther removed from the Knowledge and Notice of the common sort of Christians. And so *Mystery of Iniquity*, is now become more *Mysterious* and Deceiving then in their Times, and as Perfect and Bitter Enmity against Christ and his Spirit, and the true *Temple* of God the *Spiritual Church*, as ever was in all their Times, doth now prevail under the Name of *Orthodox Doctrine*, and the *Reformation of Religion, by the late Assembly of Divines*, which the Clergy are all now ready to set up, if they get the Secular Arm to strengthen them thereunto, (of which now they have greatest Hopes) and without which, their Religion can find no high place in the World.
Now wherein the *old Mystery of Iniquity* is *renewed* amongst these Men, that they would have an *outward Letter* and *Ministry*, of the *New Testament*, which is the *Ministration* of the Spirit and not of the Letter? and would have the *Secular Magistrate*, to have Right and Power,

A book from Lay's library by the English revolutionary William Dell, with a handwritten marginal comment about his past as a "common sailer."

Benjamin Franklin was a friend of Lay and, in 1738, published his book, *All Slave-Keepers That Keep the Innocent in Bondage, Apostates*. Franklin himself had an ambivalent attitude about slavery, but later in life he took pride in having published Lay's early, uncompromising attack on the institution and those who upheld it.

Benjamin Rush—Philadelphia physician, abolitionist, social reformer, and signer of the Declaration of Independence—was Lay's first biographer. He wrote an admiring account of the life of the controversial antislavery activist in 1790, just as the abolitionist movement was gaining strength.

The oil portrait of Lay standing in front of his cave, commissioned by Benjamin and Deborah Franklin, c. 1758, was painted by William Williams (above) and Benjamin West (below) almost certainly without Lay's permission.

The great English poet and artist William Blake shared with Lay a fascination with the Book of Revelation. The "Great Red Dragon" depicted here represented the satanic forces of oppression militantly opposed by Lay and Blake.

Commissioned by Lay's friends to create a memorial soon after his death, Henry Dawkins engraved this portrait, based on the Williams-West portrait, c. 1760. The print circulated widely among abolitionists on both sides of the Atlantic.

Roberts Vaux, "he would often make observations and remarks, calculated to provoke argument, with a view to fathom the minds of those with whom he conversed; and the estimate of their characters was formed with astonishing facility and correctness." He may have copied Diogenes, who refused to eat with tyrants, when he walked out on an acquaintance whose slave served breakfast. Both Benjamin and Diogenes were better known by their actions, and by the huge folklore that grew up around them, than by their writings. In his post-1738 life Benjamin practiced *parrhesia* (fearless speech), *autarkeia* (self-sufficiency), *askêsis* (physical toughness), *karteria* (moral toughness), and *tuphos* (attacks on wealth and standing). He wrote in the margins of another book, "Money—the love of money,—the destruction of nations—the fountain of evil." He railed against the "custom" that made the sin of slavery "familiar, easy and sweet." He even adapted part of the Cynic critique of slavery, that the institution was deforming and horrible for both the enslaved and the master, who grows "lazy, arrogant, and peevish." Benjamin reiterated this argument in *All Slave-Keepers . . . Apostates*, in which he called all masters "proud, Dainty, Lazy, Scornful, [and] Tyrannical." Finally, Benjamin, like the Cynics, was mocked for his ideas and way of life. Like Crates, who was also a hunchback, he was ridiculed for his appearance.[20]

Like Diogenes, Benjamin excelled in wit and public exchanges, as John MacPherson, captain of a Philadelphia privateer, learned the hard way. He spotted Benjamin and sought to provide "diversion" for his traveling party of friends by engaging the little man in repartee. MacPherson approached Benjamin using deferential gentlemanly language, declaring himself to be "his most humble servant." As a crowd gathered 'round, Benjamin asked in response, "Art thou my servant?" MacPherson answered, "Yes, I am." Benjamin then raised up his foot toward the captain and demanded, "Then clean my shoe." The crowd roared in laughter as insincere speech got what it deserved: mockery. Seeking to redeem himself, Captain MacPherson asked if Benjamin could please instruct him as to the direct route to heaven. Benjamin asked, "Dost thou indeed wish to be taught?" MacPherson insisted that he did. Benjamin then replied in a more serious way, quoting the prophet Micah: "Do justice, love mercy, and walk humbly with thy God." Embarrassed, MacPherson and his friends mounted their horses and quickly rode away, having become the object of "merriment" rather than its authors.[21]

The public action that prompted Franklin to call Benjamin a "Cynic" philosopher took place in the open-air market of Philadelphia in March 1742. Benjamin set up a table and arranged on it a set of fine China teacups and saucers. (These had apparently belonged to Sarah, who had died seven years earlier.) As a crowd gathered, Benjamin took out a hammer and smashed one teacup after another to protest the mistreatment of those who harvested the tea in Asia and those who produced the sugar in the Americas that sweetened it. The crowd was shocked, some screaming that Benjamin must not destroy the beautiful teacups—Give them to me! was the cry. Others offered to buy them, but Benjamin refused to listen. Smash! His iconoclastic attitude toward fine private property caused pandemonium to erupt. A growing mob finally rushed Benjamin and threw him to the ground. When he got up, "a stout youth" stepped up behind him, "adroitly slipped his head between his legs, and suddenly rising, lifted him up, and carried him off." The lad's mates then "saved the balance of the tea-set from destruction" and "carry'd off as much of it as they could get." But Benjamin had made his point.[22]

Again, like Diogenes, Benjamin had a knack for commanding the attention of powerful people. He wrote in *All Slave-Keepers . . . Apostates* that he had two meetings with English royalty: on the first occasion with King George I, probably during the time he lived in London, working as a sailor, and on the second with both King George II and Queen Caroline, in the late 1720s or early 1730s, before he left England for Philadelphia. How he arranged these meetings is unknown. If, however, the kings and queen thought they were meeting a "royal dwarf," full of aristocratic flattery and deference, they were soon disabused of the stereotype. On both occasions Benjamin brought a gift, indeed the same gift each time: John Milton's pamphlet *Considerations touching the likeliest Means to Remove Hirelings out of the Church, Wherein is also Discours'd of Tythes, Church-fees, Church-revenues; and whether any Maintenance of Ministers can be settl'd by Law*, first published in 1659. Benjamin gave a classic anticlerical text to the kings and queen, hoping, as he put it, that "they might see what a Company of destructive Vermin they had about them." Like Milton, Benjamin thought that "worldly Interest" among Anglican ministers was profoundly corrupting and that the monarchs needed to understand this. Benjamin, in short, used his audience to attack the very institution over which the kings were the titular head as "Supreme Governor of the Church of England." The Quaker Diogenes spoke truth to power.[23]

LIBERTY OF THE PRESS

Benjamin took an interest not only in books but in other parts of print culture, especially newspapers. He seems to have spent a good bit of time in the print shops of Benjamin Franklin and Andrew Bradford, selling his own books there and occasionally raising subscriptions to republish books he liked. Here he engaged with the world beyond the debates among Quakers about slavery, as Roberts Vaux pointed out in his biography of Benjamin published in 1815: "Benjamin Lay's mind was not exclusively directed to the subject of the trade in human flesh, and the shocking train of evils by which it was attended; it observed, and investigated, other objects connected with the interests of civil society and the welfare of man."[24]

Of special interest in this regard was an exchange in the *Pennsylvania Gazette* in April 1738. Franklin republished an article that had appeared three months earlier in the *Craftsman* in London, a ringing defense of John Peter Zenger, a printer and journalist with the *New York Weekly Journal* who had criticized New York governor William Cosby, who in turn sued for libel and locked Zenger in jail for eight months in 1733–1734. Defended by the distinguished Philadelphia attorney Andrew Hamilton, Zenger won his case, establishing a crucial legal milestone and precedent for an independent press.[25]

The author of the first article framed the Zenger case as a struggle for the "*Rights* and *Privileges* of *Englishmen*," highlighting the courtroom drama. Attorney Hamilton begged presiding royalist judge James DeLancey: "I hope to be pardon'd, *Sir*, for my Zeal upon this Occasion." Governor Cosby had abused his authority by harassing the printer "in an *extra-judicial* and *arbitrary Manner*"; he, like all "*Leaders of the People*," must be called to account. In his closing argument to the jury Hamilton explained, "Many injure and oppress the People under their Administration, provoke them to cry out and complain, and then make that very Complaint the Foundation for *new Oppressions* and *Prosecutions*." The people must therefore oppose "*arbitrary Power* . . . by *speaking* and *writing* TRUTH." He concluded that the case "may in its Consequence, affect every Freeman that lives under a

British Government on the Main of *America.* It is the best Cause. It is the Cause of Liberty." Hamilton's speech moved the jury to return a not-guilty verdict after a brief deliberation. Upon the announcement, "*Three great Huzzas*" rang out through the hall of justice.

An anonymous gentleman in Philadelphia responded to the reprinted article with ridicule, suggesting that Hamilton was a hypocrite—merely playing popular politics, seeking "veneration among the vulgar" and lacking any principled commitment to "Liberty of the Press." The hypocrite, he went on, "of all Creatures is generally agreed to be the most detestable and destructive to Society." He made his point through a double appeal to prejudice. The author of the Zenger defense merits "Shame and Contempt" when he tries "to persuade us, that an Æthiopian is as Fair as a Helen or that *Ben Lay* is the tallest and straightest Man in *America.*"

Benjamin responded immediately, not only to the personal insult but to the larger argument, which interested him in several ways. He had his own concerns about censorship and freedom of expression as the Quaker Board of Overseers in Pennsylvania was busy denying publication to all critics of slavery. They had refused to publish the work of John Farmer and Ralph Sandiford, and they would have denied the book Benjamin was at that very moment working on. Benjamin too opposed the "*Leaders of the People*" and their "*arbitrary Power* . . . by *speaking* and *writing* TRUTH." This was *parrhesia*, the creed of the Cynic philosophers, which Benjamin embraced and practiced. He responded to the anonymous writer in the very next issue of the *Pennsylvania Gazette.*

> *To the Man that mentioned me in his idle Paper*, THESE.
>
> THEE has taken the Freedom to publish to the World, that I am neither tall nor strait in Body.—Friend,—we neither made our own Bodies, nor can we mend them. But our bad Lives and Manners we *may* mend; and our foolish and ignorant Conduct and Behaviour we *may* mend; wherefore take it not amiss that I admonish *thee* a little.

Benjamin then praised Attorney Hamilton for "the Pains he hath taken in defending that Liberty," which his anonymous critic "makes such large tho' ill Use of." He added that the gentleman was wrong to circulate "silly Books, said to come from *Barbadoes*, written against the *Liberty of the Press*, and against its Defender, for the Speeches he made at the Tryal of the said

New York Printer." He also objected to the attacks on Hamilton's character, which anyone acquainted with the man knew to be false, and to the "vain Desire of being thought learned," which caused the writer to pilfer lines from Aesop's fables and dabble in Latin. Benjamin concluded by saying,

> And now let me advise thee to regulate thy Diet, and live henceforth on the innocent Fruits of the Earth.—Friend,—clean Foods make a clean Body, which has a sympathetic Effect upon the Mind: And I perceive by the many Impurities that flow from thee, that thee feeds foully. Indeed, by thy spitting Venom round thee, by thy being swollen black with Envy, and by the low groveling dirty Malice that appears in all thy Papers, I do strongly suspect thee has eaten Toads lately. *Fare thee well.*

Benjamin demonstrated, in his brief response, his attitude toward a variety of topics: his own dwarf body; elite learning; and colonial politics. He also showed considerable rhetorical skill; command of the ideas of the Cynic philosophers and of his favorite writer, Thomas Tryon; and a sharp sense of humor.

Speaking in the familiar Quaker idiom of "thee" and "thou," Benjamin addressed before all else the condescending comment about his height and shape, offering, in his own voice, the only direct comment on the subject to be found in surviving historical evidence. He had, of course, encountered ridicule many times throughout his life, so his response was surely well chosen and tested through experience. He embraced the statement that "I am neither tall nor strait in Body" and quickly added that he had no control over the matter: "we neither made our own Bodies, nor can we mend them." He then pivoted to what can be controlled—and what he considered more important: "Lives and Manners" and "Conduct and Behaviour." Here his "Friend" failed, as Benjamin would show in careful detail.

Clearly Benjamin knew the person who wrote the objectionable article. He referred to "thee and thy Friends," to "thy last Paper," indeed to "all thy Papers," which presumably were also published in the *Pennsylvania Gazette*. He links the writer to Barbados and therefore likely to slavery: his friend's friends were likely slave owners. It is also clear that Benjamin knew and respected Andrew Hamilton, the attorney who won the Zenger case. This exchange was part of a continuing debate about liberty in Philadelphia, Barbados, and London, which is to say, around the Atlantic.

Part of Benjamin's purpose was to expose the writer's vanity, expressed in a florid, patrician style of writing. Benjamin demonstrates his own knowledge of Aesop's fables, specifically the "crow with borrowed feathers," who strutted about pretending to be something other than what he was. Benjamin even slipped in a classical low-church Protestant dagger, accusing the writer of reading "Latin Prayers from a Book, to be admired of the Ignorant." Benjamin bestowed one of his greatest insults in saying that the man had written an "idle Paper," by which he meant worthless.

Benjamin concluded by offering advice, premised on his own principles of "life in agreement with nature." He urged the writer to live "on the innocent Fruits of the Earth"—food that required no human or animal exploitation—and thereby to cleanse his body and mind. Benjamin's body was suddenly not the only one under discussion! His opponent's body was neither short nor crooked but "foul," full of impurities; his ways were "foolish and ignorant." Indeed, wrote Benjamin, "I do strongly suspect thee has eaten Toads lately." After this clever, humorous flourish, Benjamin signed off with literal advice: "*Fare thee well.*"

THE WAY TO HAPPINESS

Benjamin considered William Dell "pure reading" and thought so highly of the Cynic philosophers as to live some of their ideas. But there was another author he loved even more: a then popular but now little-known late-seventeenth-century English Atlantic writer named Thomas Tryon. As it happened, the two men lived parallel lives: Tryon was, like Benjamin, a former shepherd who came out of the radical Protestant movement in England, became a craftsman (a hatter), and lived in Barbados for a time. He too was appalled by slavery and came to oppose it. When artists created images of Benjamin between 1758 and 1760, they pictured the Quaker holding a book, on which was visibly written *Trion on Happiness*. The reference is to Tryon's 1683 *The Way to Health, Long Life and Happiness, or, A Discourse of Temperance and the Particular Nature of all Things Requisit for the Life of Man*. Benjamin loved this book so much, noted biographer Benjamin Rush, "he frequently carried [it] with him, in his excursions from home."[26]

Benjamin may have been drawn to Tryon's angry denunciation of slavery in another book, *Friendly Advice to the Gentlemen-Planters of the East and*

West Indies, published in 1684. Here Tryon imagined a conversation between an "Ethiopian or Negro Slave" and his Christian master, the former offering a withering critique of the cruelty and terror of the ruling class of Barbados. But Benjamin found more in Tryon to like than his opposition to slavery. Tryon opposed violence and embraced other Quaker ideals such as simplicity and temperance. (Tryon was never a Quaker himself, but many of his books were published by Quaker printers.) Like the Greek philosopher Pythagoras, Tryon believed that war had its origins in the cruelty human beings practiced against animals. In *All Slave-Keepers . . . Apostates*, Benjamin repeated a key phrase from Tryon: "the merciful Man is merciful to his Beast." Benjamin's comments about food, body, and mind in the Zenger debate restated Tryon's most fundamental idea.[27]

Tryon combined German mysticism (Heinrich Cornelius Agrippa and Jacob Böhme), neo-Platonism (Pythagoras), and Indian Hinduism into an argument that vegetarianism promoted human "health, long life, and happiness." He followed the Ranter shoemaker Jacob Bauthumley, who wrote, "I see that God is in all Creatures, Man and Beast, Fish and Fowle, and every green thing." Tryon saw enclosed lands as "the effects of Violence" and relatedly observed that cattle and other animals were being industrially produced and turned into "a grand Commodity, and (as it were) a Manufacture." Tryon called animals "Fellow Citizens of the World"; they possessed natural rights. Profoundly influenced by the Brahmin philosophers of India, he wrote a different kind of history from below—"The Horses Complaint against their Masters"—as well as a different kind of history from above: "The Complaints of Birds and Fowls of Heaven to their Creator, for the Oppressions and Violences Most Nations on Earth do offer unto them, particularly the People called *Christians*, lately settled in several Provinces in *America*." Tryon narrated these complaints in the animal voice: "We [horses] with great Toil and Labour draw their [master's] Luggage in Carts and Wains, and their fat lazy Paunches in Charriots and Coaches."[28]

Tryon and Lay were both fond of the phrase "fellow creature," which was to English revolutionaries of the 1640s and 1650s what "citizen" was later to the French—a means of expressing equality, solidarity, and unity within the movement. Long after the restoration of monarchy in 1660, "fellow creature" survived as a mark of radicalism, a red thread that would thicken over time and stand out in the weave of abolitionism in the nineteenth century. Benjamin used the phrase repeatedly to refuse division and

Roger Crab, a Leveller soldier in the English Revolution who in the 1650s became a vegetarian and ate only "herbs and roots," may have been a model for Lay.

to express kinship with fellow Quakers, indentured servants, slaves—and animals. All creatures were fellow creatures. "Are not we the work of the great *Creators* hands," asked Tryon. Were we, he wondered, not all endowed with the same spark of divinity?[29]

Benjamin encountered Pythagoras (c. 570–495 BCE) through Tryon, but he had also read him on his own; he cites him in *All Slave-Keeper's . . . Apostates.* In the seventeenth and eighteenth centuries, Pythagoras was known not only for his famous theorem in geometry ($a^2 + b^2 = c^2$) but also for his vegetarianism and his opposition to the killing of animals. Pythagoras had said, "As long as Man continues to be the ruthless destroyer of lower living beings, he will never know health or peace. For as long as men massacre animals, they will kill each other. Indeed, he who sows the seed of murder and pain cannot reap joy and love." Here were the ancient origins of ideas Benjamin held dear.[30]

Vegetarianism thus had classical roots, but it sprouted anew in the churned-up soil of the English Revolution. Tristram Stuart writes that many radicals "used vegetarianism to articulate their dissent from the luxurious mainstream, and called for a bloodless revolution to institute a slaughter-free society of equality."[31] Benjamin may have been inspired by the cave-dwelling vegetarian Thomas Bushell or the Ranter-like vegetarian prophet John Robins. Most intriguing—and brimming with parallels—was the life of Roger Crab, a former soldier denounced as a Leveller "Agitator" and, he claimed, sentenced to death by Cromwell, perhaps after the great Leveller mutiny at Burford in 1649. Somehow reprieved (several were executed), Crab retired to the countryside to live a "strange reserved and unparallel'd kind of life," much like Lay did two generations later. He thought himself the "Wonder of this Age," as he announced in a pamphlet entitled *The English Hermite*. Crab considered it "a sin against his body and soule to eate any sort of flesh, fish, or living creature, or to drinke any wine, ale, or beere." Instead, like Benjamin, he ate "roots and hearbs, as cabbage, turneps, carrets, dock-leaves, and grasse"; his clothing was "sack-cloath." He practiced pacifism, proclaimed "universal love," and, like any good antinomian, considered himself "above ordinances."[32]

Benjamin used Tryon's ideas just as he used the similar ideas of the Cynic philosophers: he acted on them. Tryon in many ways offered a Christianized version of Cynic ideals, living not just "life according to nature" but according to "God's Law in Nature," that is to say, a higher law. The goal was to live without violence, in "innocency," in a state, wrote Tryon, where people neither "oppresseth nor hurteth nothing." To kill animals was to break the Golden Rule. Water was the best drink, wrote Tryon, because it is simple and endowed "with such Equality." Benjamin dressed in simple, undyed clothes as Tryon suggested. He embraced self-denial and temperance; like Benjamin Franklin, he thought "a little is sufficient." He even retired to the countryside, described by Tryon as the place where "all is *sedate* and *serene, still* as the Voice of *good Spirits*, and *quiet* as the Birth of *Flowers*; no noise to be heard but the ravishing Harmony of the *Wood-Musitians*, and the innocent Lowings of *Cows*, and Neighings of *Horses*, and Bleating of the pretty *Lambs*." Doing all of these things, wrote Benjamin, would enable "Mankind" to live the "sweet comfortable and happy Life."[33]

As Benjamin built a new way of life after 1738, he combined the ideas of William Dell, the Cynic philosophers, Pythagoras, and Thomas Tryon, none of whom, it must be emphasized, were Quakers. Many were not even Christians. The free-thinking Benjamin decided that he must do something new. Armed with fresh ideas and a wealth of worldly experience, he withdrew from the culture and economy of slavery, violence, and capitalism. He returned to the commons with Sarah in 1734 and expanded his commitment to a new way of life in the years after her death in 1735.

BACK TO THE LAND

Benjamin and Sarah's new home, Abington, was eight miles north of Philadelphia. The colony had gained the eastern half of the township by treaty with the Lenni Lenape Indians in 1683, the western half in 1687. Always interested in history, Benjamin took pride in the nonviolent way William Penn acquired the land from the indigenous leader Tamanend, and taught children about the famous Elm tree at Shackamaxon, where the first treaty was thought to have been agreed to. Voltaire would later remark that this was only treaty Christians ever made with Indians that was not broken. Benjamin West would memorialize the event in a famous painting of 1771–1772.[34]

Benjamin and Sarah joined Quakers who had begun to settle in Abington in the 1690s. The quality of the land was excellent and in 1693 the colony began to construct "York Road," a vital artery of commerce, northeast toward New York. A list of landowners in Abington drawn up in 1734—the very year Benjamin and Sarah moved there—contains the names of forty-two people, thirty-eight of whom owned between fifty and five hundred acres each. The median was a hundred acres, suggesting that this was a settlement of smallholders who slowly cleared the land for agriculture. Benjamin and Sarah did not buy land themselves, choosing instead to live on a small piece of property owned by fellow Quakers John and Ann Phipps, on Old York Road, about a quarter mile from the Friends Meeting House in Abington.[35]

Here Benjamin decided to reorganize his life outside the increasingly global market economy. He built his own abode, selecting a spot for habitation "near a fine spring of water" and erecting a small cottage into a "natural excavation in the earth . . . to afford himself a commodious apartment." He lined the entrance with stone and created a roof with sprigs of evergreen. The interior of the cave was apparently quite spacious, with room for a spinning jenny. He made his own clothes in order to avoid the exploitation of the labor of others, animals included: "he would not even use the wool of sheep in his clothing and never wore any but flax-made garments." His sitting room in the cave was festooned with "skains of thread, spun entirely by himself." The cave also contained a large library. This was where he lived a life of the mind: "he reflected, read, and wrote." Nearby he planted apple, peach, and walnut trees and tended a massive bee colony—an apiary a hundred feet long. He made honey a staple of his diet, never killing the bees. He also cultivated potatoes, squash, radishes, and melons. He essentially built a commons for himself.[36]

Benjamin conducted his life in full keeping with his evolving democratic, egalitarian, and antinomian principles. He lived simply and unostentatiously, in "plain" style as was the Quaker way, but he went further: he ate only fruits and vegetables, drank only milk and water; he was a strict vegetarian and very nearly a vegan two centuries before the word was invented. Because of the divine pantheistic presence of God he perceived in all living things, he refused to eat "flesh." Animals too were "God's creatures." He opposed the death penalty in all instances, even for animals. Most tellingly, Benjamin consciously boycotted all commodities produced by slave labor. He understood the dark secrets of the marketplace: he saw the violent conditions under which the commodity sugar was produced and the suffering of the producers, all of which he first grasped in Barbados, where "sugar was made with blood." Benjamin expanded the boycott into a positive idea: people had to learn to live on the "innocent fruits of the earth," such as those he grew in his garden. He lived "life in agreement with nature," embodying a new ecological consciousness.[37]

Benjamin's unusual way of life attracted the curious, who wanted to see how he translated his ideas into practice. Visits generated an expansive folklore as people will talk—and write. When Governor Richard Penn, Benjamin Franklin, and "some other gentlemen" showed up at his cave, he received them "with his usual politeness" and engaged them in his always witty, starkly honest conversation. He then spread a table for dinner and covered it plentifully with the fruits and vegetables he had grown. He announced to his visitors, "This is not the kind of fare you have at home, but it is good enough for you or me—and such as it is, you are welcome to eat of it." His own favorite meal was "Turnips boiled, and afterwards roasted." His favorite drink was "pure water." He produced his own nutritious food and did not depend on the money economy for subsistence.[38]

Part of Benjamin's refusal to eat meat was philosophical, but part of it was personal and temperamental: he had a sensitive soul and could not abide cruelty, even when it was his own. He once encountered a groundhog that repeatedly ravaged his garden. He caught and killed the troublesome creature, dissected it, and nailed its parts to the four corners of the garden, perhaps unconsciously replicating the practices of the English ruling class, which drew and quartered criminals, and displayed their body parts to terrorize others. Lay was immediately stricken with remorse over the cruel act, and soon thereafter, under the tutelage of Tryon, he renounced killing and eating animals and declared himself a vegetarian. Tryon had recommended the virtues of a quiet, simple, rural life, based on "Harmony and Unity" with the world. In the last phase of his life, Lay followed Tryon in rethinking humanity's most fundamental relationship to nature.[39]

THE NEW JERUSALEM

The final and indeed the core element of Benjamin's "life in accordance with nature" was Christian asceticism. He was part of a long line of devout people who sought spiritual strength through self-denial and a humble, secluded life. The prophet Jeremiah had lived in a cave, as had monks of many kinds over the centuries. Francis Daniel Pastorius, who drafted the Germantown petition against slavery in 1688, had lived in a cave at Front and Spruce Streets in the early years of Philadelphia's settlement. German pietists such as Johannes Kelpius and his followers lived in caves not far from Benjamin's own. The common effort was to recapture the lost innocence of man before the Fall—before Adam and Eve were expelled from the Garden of Eden. Benjamin shared this hope and consciously expanded it to include an ethical relationship to all of nature, to other human beings, to animals, and to the "innocent Fruits of the Earth." Benjamin's greatest challenge to humanity was not merely to abolish slavery but to eradicate all forms of exploitation and oppression. This he attempted to exemplify in his own way of life. He built the inward and outward New Jerusalem, in his own soul and on a small patch of land. This was an embodied prophecy about the future.[40]

In the end Benjamin's ideal society was one in which all people could visit the "sweetly refreshing Streams of the River of Life for Drink, and the Tree of Life for Food," where "they may have a proper right to partake of the Fruit daily, without Money or Price, all free as was the *Hebrews* Manna." Subsistence would not be mediated by money and restricted to those who had it. He continued in rapture, "Oh! Holy Pleasure indeed, to eat of such Food, and drink of such Drink." His fondest hope, and ultimate political goal, was that "the Earth might become a *Paradise* again, to all People, as it is to some."[41]

CHAPTER SIX

DEATH, MEMORY, IMPACT

IN 1757, AT AGE SEVENTY-FIVE, Benjamin's health began to deteriorate. He had complained of being "weakly in body" years earlier, but somehow he never slowed down. His mind remained clear and his spirit as fiery as ever, but now his long travels by foot ceased. He stayed at home, in his Abington cave and, ever the enemy to idleness, tended his garden, spun flax, and engaged in other "domestic occupations." He took special pleasure in watching the labors of his bees in their massive, bustling hive. He read in his treasured library. He had outlived wife, Sarah, by more than two decades.[1]

Benjamin continued to receive visitors in his cave. To one of them he made a startling request, offering one hundred pounds if he would perform a favor after his death: "burn his body, and throw the ashes into the sea." Cremation was not yet the accepted practice it would become in the late nineteenth century, and to Christians this was at the time nothing but a barbarous act of paganism. Benjamin offered no explanation for the request to the astonished visitor, but no doubt his formative years of life at sea had something to do with it. Benjamin's biographer, Roberts Vaux, speculated that he may also have wanted to follow the example of Lycurgus, the legendary leader of ancient Sparta who epitomized the virtues of equality, bodily fitness, and self-denying austerity, all values the Quaker held dear.

In any case, the visitor refused the favor and Benjamin apparently "never after mentioned it."[2]

Another visitor, a friend and fellow Quaker who shared the hope of abolition, arrived at Benjamin's cave in 1758, in the middle of the Seven Years War, which could have been seen as the bloody catastrophe Benjamin had prophesied two decades earlier. Since 1754, a group of Quaker reformers had undertaken an internal "purification" campaign, calling for a return to simpler ways of living, stricter church discipline, and a gradual end to slavery, all to appease an angry God. Through the carnage and the chaos of war, the visitor brought news that may have been the best of Benjamin's entire life: in 1758 the Philadelphia Yearly Meeting, after much agitation from below, initiated a process to discipline and eventually disown Quakers who traded slaves. Slave holding itself was still permitted (and would be for eighteen more years), but the first big step toward abolition had been taken. When the friend relayed this news, Benjamin fell silent. After "a few moments reflection," he rose from his chair and "in an attitude of devotional reverence" stated, "Thanksgiving and praise be rendered unto the Lord God." A few moments later he added, "I can now die in peace." His labors had borne fruit and his prophecy had been partially fulfilled, which gave him "joyful anticipation." He would end his time on earth "in tranquillity." His dear fellow Quakers had finally begun to see the light.[3]

Not long after this meeting, Benjamin's health took a serious turn for the worse. The specific causes are unknown. His friends, led by Joshua Morris, convened to discuss what could be done for him. Benjamin requested that he be taken to Joshua's home in Abington and indeed he was. According to Vaux, who heard the story of Benjamin's death from several who knew him, "The continued violence of his disease convinced those around him that it would terminate his life, and Lay himself was fully sensible of his danger." He lived ten days longer and on February 3, 1759, "peacefully surrendered his life to him who gave it." Thus ended forty-one years of "zealous testimony against African slavery."[4]

Like most Quakers of his time, Benjamin opposed carrying distinctions of class into the afterlife; he was buried in an unmarked grave, near his cherished Sarah, in the Quaker burial ground in Abington. In the book of "Burials at Abington" for the year 1759 is a simple notation: "Benjamin Lay of Abington died 2 Mo. 7th Inter'd 9th, Aged 80 Years." The scribe made an error in the age, which was off by three years. Other entries in the book of the Quaker dead had in the margin by the name an "E" for "elder," an "M" for minister, and a notation of whether the person was a member of the congregation. Benjamin's name had none of these alongside, which would have been a source of pain and sadness to him. He was buried as a stranger to the faith he loved.[5]

Benjamin had made out a will in 1731, before he left Colchester for Philadelphia. It was still in force twenty-eight years later. He had originally bequeathed "my Goods Chattels Moneys and personal Estate" to his long-deceased wife, Sarah. They had no children. More of the estate now went to other family members, especially the children of his late half-brother John and to several relatives on his mother's side. Yet he left the bulk of his money to "poor Friends"—and both words in that designation were crucial. He helped fellow workers: wool combers, gardeners, sawyers, thatchers, millers, and weavers. He even left money to Cyrus Scott, the grave digger in the Colchester Quaker burial ground and the sergeant of arms who threw him out of meetings! Benjamin bore no hard feelings. Widows were the largest social group of recipients in his will, and more than half of the named recipients were women. He illustrated his bottom-up approach to giving when he stipulated that if any money happened to be left over after paying out the bequest to all the people he had named, the remainder should go to the "next poorest person belonging to the Meeting"—as long as that person were of "good Life & Conversation and sound in the principle." (Many would have considered this clause ironic as they doubted the soundness of Benjamin's principles. He himself did not.) He also specified that his money should go to "the service of poor Friends of Colchester monthly Meeting" who "take no collection" from the congregation—in other words, those who had no other means. He reserved the largest single amount of money (one hundred pounds) to be awarded, five pounds per person, to poor Quakers who wanted "to Transport themselves to America." This would allow poor people to migrate without having to indenture themselves as servants.[6]

Benjamin continued his "preferential option for the poor" in the verbal will he gave on his deathbed at Joshua Morris's farm. The man who thought so little of worldly goods made arrangements to dispose of his own. Being of "sound Mind Memory and Understanding" to the end, Benjamin expressed to his friends his wish to leave forty pounds to the school of the Abington Monthly Meeting—the very meeting that had last disowned him—"to be applied towards the education of poor Children belonging to the sd Society." His final wish answered the destructive power of class.[7]

The "Inventory of the Estate late of Benjamin Lay decd" was a curious collection of goods. How did a man who, like the "primitive Christians," disdained worldly goods have an estate worth £586 ($117,000 in 2016 dollars) at his death? Over the course of his life Benjamin made money—as a sailor, a glover, and a petty merchant—and probably never spent much of it because of his austere way of life. Quakerism demanded of its adherents "plain" lifeways and Benjamin, with his usual zeal, carried the point to extremes. Moreover, during the last years of his life, he produced his own food and clothes, which meant that he probably had no living expenses, except perhaps books. Benjamin, in his own way, illustrated Max Weber's famous thesis about the abstemious, hard-working Protestant who made but never spent money, resulting in unanticipated savings.[8]

Eighty percent of the value of Benjamin's estate consisted of bonds and bills—loans he had made, at interest, even though he worried about what he called "Extortion, in paying or receiving Interest for Money." He justified the practice saying that he was "weakly in Body, and pretty well [on] in Years" and might therefore need "something else to live on but the Labour of my Hands." The loans were, therefore, a kind of security, but we have no evidence that he ever intended to collect them or that the executors of his estate ever did. It seems likely that the money owed to Benjamin was like the money he bequeathed in his will: small sums involving lots of poor people. As a philanthropist, Benjamin routinely gave away money. For example, in 1757 he contributed twenty pounds to support additional construction at the Pennsylvania Hospital, first established in 1751 "for the reception and cure of the sick poor . . . free of charge." He once gave several pieces of silver through a third party to a poor woman in his neighborhood, instructing the person to "lay this out for her, but don't let it be known where it came from."[9]

Benjamin's surviving worldly goods were the residue of a long and ever-changing life, an agglomeration of items he had probably dumped in a barn or shed owned by fellow Quaker John Phipps, on whose land he lived. Many of the goods were "damnified," including several that belonged to Sarah, who had died almost a quarter of a century earlier. One entry was for "Sundry wearing Cloaths Belonging to his Late Wife much Damaged," of little or no value. Several "Delph" (Delft) plates, bowls, and dishes, as well as "Chinea" saucers and cups, also appear on the list, so apparently Benjamin did not destroy all of Sarah's fine wares in his protest against tea and sugar in 1742. A few more valuable things—silver spoons, pewter dishes—may also have belonged to Sarah.

The largest number of items were likely leftovers from his time running a general store in Barbados—fabrics (muslin, cambric, silk), handkerchiefs, cups, candlesticks, knives, forks, the goods of everyday life. (If he operated a retail shop for anything other than books in or around Philadelphia, there is no documentary record of it.) Gloves, shears, and goods made of leather, buckskin, or sheepskin echoed his working life as a glover, even though he would not have used or produced such commodities after his conversion to vegetarianism and animal rights during the 1730s. More reflective of his later life were the "Earthen Jars" full of honey and the eleven yards of tow linen, spun from flax by his own hands and used for clothing because no animal had been harmed in their manufacture.

Probably the most treasured part of Benjamin's estate were "2 Large Bibles," no doubt well worn from use, twenty books in folio (largest size), nineteen books in quarto (smaller), fifty-nine books in octavo (smaller still), thirty-nine books in "twelves" (smallest of all), and "Sundry paper Books." These included *Plutarch's Lives* and a broad variety of works in philosophy, theology, and history. He also had a "Looking Glass," always valuable for a reader his age, and he had "a frame to hold a book." Benjamin the writer also had on hand "2 Quire of Paper" and valonia (acorn cups) used for making ink. He left behind unpublished writings—on which subjects we cannot know. His papers were left to John Phipps but were apparently destroyed by the British army during the occupation of Abington and the surrounding area in late 1778, during the American Revolution.[10]

THE PROPHET DISARMED

In spring 1758, as Benjamin's health deteriorated, Deborah Franklin decided to make a gift to her husband, Benjamin Franklin, who was in London representing the American colonies before the British government at the time. She commissioned a local artist, William Williams, to paint a portrait of Benjamin Lay. The relationship between the two Benjamins went back twenty years, to the publication of *All Slave-Keepers . . . Apostates* in 1738. Deborah probably thought this would be a pleasant keepsake about a memorable and perhaps likely to be historic figure, a commemoration of sorts before his death. When Benjamin Franklin found out about the portrait, he wrote his wife, saying, "I wonder how you came by Ben. Lay's Picture." The artist later made clear, in a comprehensive list of his works dated 1791, that he had painted a "small portrait of Benjamin Lay for Dr. Benjamin Franklin," apparently at Deborah's request.[11]

Franklin asked his wife the question because he knew that Benjamin would never have agreed to sit for the portrait. In his refusal Lay would have been like the austere, pious, plain-living, founding generation of Quakers, who fiercely rejected portraiture. (This is why no reliable portraits survive of George Fox or James Nayler.) Indeed, as Franklin himself explained two years later, "the primitive Quakers us'd to declare against Pictures as a vain Expence; a Man's suffering his Portrait to be taken was condemn'd as Pride; and I think to this day it is very little practis'd among them." The abolitionist Thomas Clarkson, who published a three-volume *Portrait of Quakerism* in 1806, added, "Friends belonging to the first generation of Quakerism consistently refused to have their portraits drawn or painted." As a counterculture of "plain people," the early Quakers regarded portrait painting as a frivolous, vain, ungodly upper-class indulgence.[12]

Benjamin, of course, did not belong to the first generation, but he strongly identified with it, railing against vanity and pride, and urging throughout his life a return to founding principles and ways of living. Even though portraits, especially silhouettes, had become more common among Quakers in America by the middle of the eighteenth century, especially among wealthy merchants who regarded them as symbols of success, there can be little doubt that Lay would have seen the practice as a betrayal of proper Quaker values. Indeed as recently as 1746 the Philadelphia Yearly Meeting had urged Quakers to live in "the primitive plainness & simplicity of the Gospel" and "to testify against the vain Spirit of the World, in all its Appearances." Benjamin would have seen a portrait as one such appearance.[13]

How then did Williams paint the portrait if Lay did not sit for it? In all likelihood he had seen Lay numerous times in and around Philadelphia, perhaps at Franklin's own print shop, and took in the details of his appearance (face and body) that way. He also would have heard stories about Benjamin—his cave and his vegetarian habits especially—and added details to the portrait accordingly. The landscape in the background of the painting appears to be generic and invented, suggesting that Williams probably had not actually visited Benjamin in Abington. We do know, however, that the painter did not make the whole thing up. London abolitionist William Dillwyn, who grew up in Philadelphia and as a youth knew Benjamin, wrote Roberts Vaux in 1815, what "thou has considered generally as a caracature is certainly a faithful Resemblance of the Man."[14]

It also appears that Williams did not do all of the painting. Working as an apprentice to Williams at the time was a third Benjamin, Benjamin West, the soon-to-be-famous prodigy of an artist who grew up in what is now Swarthmore, near Philadelphia, in a household with a Quaker father. Born in the year of the "bladder-of-blood" spectacle (1738), West would have heard stories about the notorious Lay and probably took a special interest in the portrait. Dillwyn later referred to "the Portrait which I remember Benj. West painting."[15]

Painted in oil on a mahogany panel roughly fourteen by fifteen inches, the small portrait is unsigned and undated. The painting was known in the eighteenth century and served as a basis for several subsequent engravings, but it disappeared from view in the nineteenth century until it was rediscovered, in near-ruined condition, by antique dealer Edwin C. Hild at an auction in Buckingham, Pennsylvania, in 1977 and purchased for four dollars. Conservators Joyce Stoner and Mervin Martin of the Winterthur Museum restored the painting, which was eventually purchased by the National Portrait Gallery in Washington, DC, where it is currently on display.[16]

Benjamin Lay would likely have approved of Williams if not his trade. Born in humble circumstances and apprenticed to a line of work he disliked, he, like Benjamin, escaped to the sea as a youth. In writing one of America's first novels, entitled *Mr. Penrose, The Journal of Penrose, Seaman*, Williams called himself "an illiterate sailor." He too had traveled the world and proudly proclaimed his cosmopolitan experience. Williams also used his time among motley crews to develop antislavery ideas. If the two met, they would have had much to talk about.[17]

The painting itself features Benjamin standing in front of a stone-lined entrance to his cave, edged with sprigs of evergreen. (See insert.) A brook lies in the immediate foreground and green rolling hills at the left in the background. In the near foreground at the left are the signs of Benjamin's self-sufficient vegetarianism: two kinds of melons, one slit open by a nearby knife, and a basket of fruit and vegetables (pears, apples, squash). At the right, on the ground, are a cluster of green grapes and two turnips; the latter was Benjamin's favorite food. Close by is a red clay bowl, and near the mouth of the cave sits an urn for Benjamin's "pure water."

Benjamin himself is depicted with a deeply furrowed brow and brown eyes, the left one appearing to wander slightly. He has circles under his eyes and a gray-white beard of medium length. (Beards were uncommon in portraits of the era.) A small, rounded mouth suggests a hint of surprise or perhaps disapproval, both of which he would certainly have expressed had he seen the portrait. What appears to be longish hair creeps out from under a floppy cream-colored hat.

Benjamin holds in his right hand both a walking cane and one of his favorite books, *Trion on Happiness* (i.e., Thomas Tryon's *A Way to Health, Long Life and Happiness*, 1683), which was something of a Bible for Benjamin's simple way of life. (Williams was probably instructed to label the book but did not know how to spell the author's name or accurately give the title.) Benjamin's left hand is held just above his waist in a peculiar gesture, as if commanding attention as he prepares to speak. His body appears to be unusual, but it would have been hard to tell from the painting that he was either a dwarf or a hunchback, even though the chest does protrude forward and upward. His lower body looks unnaturally thin, making it clear why Vaux wrote later that "his legs were so slender as to appear almost unequal to the purpose of supporting him."[18]

Benjamin's dress in the portrait is surprising because he was known at the time to wear only undyed "light-coloured plain clothes," which he had made, and often repaired, himself. One who knew him said he "used to go barefoot, wore tow trowsers, and a tow coat, very much darned." (Coming from a textile region and having repaired sails at sea, Benjamin knew his way with needle and thread.) Here he appears in tailored, not self-made, fully respectable "Quaker drab," the unostentatious dress for which Friends were known. Neither the overcoat nor the waistcoat has pockets, which was unusual for the day but standard among Quakers. The style of the suit is ordinary for the middle of the eighteenth century. The waistcoat has a slit in the back, the purpose of which would have been to facilitate the riding of horses, which Benjamin did not do. (Williams probably did not know this.) The stockings are bright white, which suggests high-quality material, probably cotton, perhaps even silk. The boots appear to be leather, which is doubly surprising given Benjamin's attitude toward killing animals and his preference for going barefoot. The boots do not appear to have soles or heels. Indeed they are nonspecific—not painted in a realistic way. The whiteness of the shirt also suggests the quality of the fabric, but the absence of a cravat and ruffled sleeves—like the rest of the outfit—speaks "plainness." The portrait presents someone neither rich nor poor but decidedly of modest middle rank and most respectable, indeed rather too respectable given Benjamin's rejection of class convention. An authentic article is the wide-brimmed hat, which could be felt or wool: it is the dress of a working man. It seems likely that Williams and West imagined Benjamin in the finer clothing they had routinely seen on Philadelphia's prosperous Quaker merchants around the city.[19]

What is perhaps most remarkable about the Williams-West portrait is what *it does not include*: any reference to the cause for which Benjamin was best known, his unbending opposition to slavery. The omission must have been occasioned by the controversy that surrounded Benjamin's ideas and methods. As historian David Waldstreicher has made clear, Benjamin Franklin was ambivalent about slavery throughout his life. He had left his name as printer off the title page of *All Slave-Keepers . . . Apostates* in 1738, but half a century later he would take pride in having published it. Before that, though, Benjamin Lay, even in death, was such a dangerous man that a commemorative portrait would have to disarm him of the central idea of his life.[20]

After Benjamin's death in February 1759, a group of his "Friends," Anthony Benezet probably among them, asked Philadelphia engraver Henry Dawkins to create a print based on the Williams-West portrait. (See insert.) Dawkins credited the original artist for the image by adding at the lower left "W Williams Pinxt." The engraving follows the Williams-West painting closely, featuring Benjamin in front of his cave, in similar dress, holding a cane and the Tryon book in his right hand, his left in the same unusual gesture. The tree at Benjamin's right is more prominent and leafier, the landscape behind it less verdant. In the lower left foreground are what appear to be two beehives, an apt and accurate addition. Another open book lies immediately below, its pages illegible. The basket of fruit and the knife have been moved from the left foreground to the right, as has the brook or creek.[21]

Dawkins changed the image of Benjamin in significant ways: his beard is longer and scragglier; he looks a few years older. The other change is that his clothing seems to have been lightened in color, especially on the surviving hand-colored versions of the engraving. It is no longer Quaker dark and drab. Dawkins's greatest innovation was the addition of text below the image:

> Benjamin Lay. Lived to the Age of 80, in the Latter Part of Which, he observ'd extreem Temperance in his Eating and Drinking, his Fondness for a particularity in Dress and Customs at times Subjected Him to the Ridicule of the Ignorant, but his Friends who were Intimate with Him thought Him an Honest Religious man.

The "Friends" probably included the Franklins, who would have known Dawkins within the artisan and print cultures of Philadelphia. Other friends, likely dissident Quakers, also probably played a part. Dawkins too would likely have known Lay.

Once again a portrait of Benjamin says nothing directly about abolitionism, which is especially odd given its timing. If the image was engraved soon after Lay's death, around 1760, as seems likely, it came into being shortly after the Philadelphia Yearly Meeting had taken a big step to ban Quaker participation in the slave trade but had not yet made slave owning a disownable offense. (This would finally happen after several more rounds of debate, in 1776.) Benjamin's "Friends" apparently did not wish their memorial to stir up the deep and bitter feelings that Benjamin himself so often occasioned through his confrontational guerrilla theater.

They therefore emphasized instead Benjamin's temperance (a theme dear to Franklin, who was also influenced by Thomas Tryon) and his "particularity" (read: *peculiarity*) of "Dress and Customs." And they added another important point: he was subjected to "the Ridicule of the Ignorant." Unspecified people made fun of Benjamin's "Dress and Customs," which would have included his beliefs about slavery. Slave keepers led the chorus of ridicule—and the successful effort to disown Benjamin. The issue of antislavery is therefore discreetly alluded to, as anyone who knew Benjamin would have understood. This ridicule also likely referred to Benjamin's physical appearance, the prejudice he encountered as a little person.

The engraving proved to be popular. It went through several printings and according to Benjamin Rush, writing in 1790, it was to be "seen in many houses in Philadelphia." The reproductions increased with the

This image of Lay, holding a book entitled *African Emancipation*, was engraved by William Kneass for Vaux's biography of Lay, published in 1815.

growth of the abolition movement in general and the Society for the Relief of Free Negroes Unlawfully Held in Bondage (soon to be the Pennsylvania Abolition Society), founded in 1775, in particular. When William Kneass engraved a version of the portrait for Roberts Vaux's *Memoirs of the Lives of Benjamin Lay and Ralph Sandiford*, published in 1815, Benjamin's role in opposing slavery was finally given visual acknowledgment: the book he held in his right hand was no longer labeled *Trion on Happiness*. It now read *African Emancipation*.[22]

Both the painting and the engraving had transatlantic lives, like Benjamin himself. After more than half a century of no documentation of its whereabouts, the Williams-West painting turned up in Bristol, England, in the possession of a Quaker physician, social reformer, and amateur painter named Thomas Pole, who made a copy of it in 1817–1818. This we know because Pole wrote four letters about the painting to Roberts Vaux. In the first, dated November 8, 1817, he said,

> Lay lived before my remembrance or knowledge. . . . I have an oil painting of him which I have employed some of my leisure hours before breakfast to copy in order to present to thee, but the mornings have now become so dark, from the awakening of the days, that I have not been able to compleat it to send by a Vessel this Autumn, as the Baltic, in which this letter is to go, is the last expected to sail and she does not sail for Philad. a Philadelpha Vessel may be going in the Spring, when I hope to forward it immediately to your City, but I almost doubt its being worth thy acceptance from the hand of so imperfect an artist.

Pole's copy is now located in the Bristol Museum and Art Gallery in Bristol, England. The original painting thus went from Philadelphia to London, to Bristol, and back to the Philadelphia area, where it would be found in 1977. The engraving appeared in a London edition of Vaux's *Memoirs* published in 1816. Both painting and print moved within the transatlantic networks of Quakers, to whom Benjamin Lay, in the age of abolition, was an increasingly important figure. It took more than half a century after his death, but finally Benjamin's portrait would make clear his lifelong militancy against human bondage.[23]

"MEN OF RENOWN" REVISITED

Benjamin's battle with the "men of renown" lasted until death and beyond. Minister Robert Jordan died relatively young, at the age of forty-nine, in 1742. Politician and Philadelphia Yearly Meeting clerk John Kinsey suffered a fatal "apoplectic fit" in May 1750. Israel Pemberton Sr., merchant and clerk of the PMM, passed away after a ten-year stretch of poor health, he too of a stroke, in 1754. When Benjamin died, in 1759, only merchant and brewer Anthony Morris Jr. was left; he would live four more years. Thus ended the lives of those "three or four Men" who, according to Benjamin, possessed "the whole Rule of Discipline, and Govern contrary to all Justice and Equity" among both Quakers and the Pennsylvania population at large.[24]

Benjamin had written in *All Slave-Keepers . . . Apostates* that these men had "the Mark of the Beast, and the Number of his Name, Slave-Keepers, upon them in their Foreheads." What, in his mind, would have been the signs of apostasy at their deaths? The slave owners Pemberton and Morris died extremely wealthy men. Pemberton's vast estate, valued at more than £25,000 ($4.9 million in 2016 dollars), was divided among his sons in a "meticulously crafted will." He had grown rich in the first instance by trading with the slave keepers of the Caribbean. He enhanced that original accumulation later in life by intensive land speculation. Part of Pemberton's bequest was to care for his slave Betty. Morris found himself in the awkward position of running a big brewery and several taverns at a time when Quakers decreed against alcohol and the drunkenness it occasioned. The influential elder was apparently allowed to keep his drinking establishments, but one wonders how he felt when, as mayor of Philadelphia in 1738, he tried to quell public drunkenness on Sundays. The Slave Code he helped to draft in 1725–1726 remained the law of the land, and in his will of 1760 he did not free his slaves. At his death his landed property alone was worth £11,000 ($2 million in 2016 dollars). Both the Pemberton and Morris families retired to the countryside, which, according to Gary B. Nash, "provided a better rooting bed for lineally descended oligarchies."[25]

John Kinsey was even more powerful than Pemberton and Morris, serving as speaker of the Pennsylvania General Assembly, chief justice of the colony's Supreme Court, trustee of the General Loan Office of the province, and clerk of the Philadelphia Yearly Meeting. Despite his lofty position at the top of the Quaker hierarchy, Kinsey had been backsliding for several years. He had become wealthy and ostentatious, known for his "extravagant style of living." He owned not one but two stately homes: one at Fifth and High Streets in downtown Philadelphia, the other an elegant brick mansion he built across the Schuylkill River, named Plantation House. According to his political opponent Richard Peters, Kinsey possessed a "lust for prestige and influence" and "an Extream desire after Popularity." He was considered both proud and vain, even by non-Quakers. In 1747 Peters wrote that "his Conduct is to be sure unbecoming a man in his Station; he is quite gay, affects young company, . . . is perpetually gallanting the Ladies, lives in the utmost profusion at home, his Children, at least the Eldest, is full of Money & extravagant." Quaker simplicity no longer suited Kinsey, and after a series of deaths in his family, he became a heavy drinker. Quakers began to shun him.[26]

Kinsey's high living and prestigious career came to a sudden end May 11, 1750, when he suffered a stroke while arguing a case before the New Jersey Supreme Court in Burlington, where Benjamin had spattered blood on slave owners, perhaps including Kinsey himself, a dozen years earlier. At his death Kinsey was hailed as a great man of "unshaken Integrity"—until it became clear that as trustee of the Loan Office he had been embezzling money, most likely to fund his own speculation in land. Israel Pemberton's son, Israel Jr., took charge of Kinsey's estate and did his best to cover up what Quakers considered to be deeply shameful behavior, especially since Kinsey himself had presided over a new entry in the Book of Discipline in 1746 warning Quakers against "worldly engagements" and encouraging their own "plain and moderate way of living." In any case, the younger Pemberton could not hide the corruption, which became a public scandal. The embezzled amount was £3,600 (a little more than $728,000 in 2016 dollars), a sum fifteen times Kinsey's annual salary as chief justice of the Pennsylvania Supreme Court and Speaker of the House. Once the word got out, Richard Peters wrote that "all mens Mouths open upon him," much to the horror of the Quakers.[27]

It was entirely fitting that Benjamin the antinomian would find his greatest adversary in a man who was not only an attorney but one who took it upon himself to collect and codify the laws of both New Jersey (1732) and Pennsylvania (1741). The man of spirit and the man of law were bound to clash. Kinsey embodied everything Benjamin thought wrong about Quakerism in America during the 1730s and 1740s—the embrace of wealth, property, and "worldly affairs," and the resulting vanity, pride, and corruption. We have no record of what Benjamin thought of Kinsey's ignominious end. If he felt satisfaction that "All the Congregation in America" would finally see "the mark of the beast" on his enemy, he probably suppressed it as a sinful expression of pride.[28]

It was no coincidence that the deaths of Kinsey and Pemberton in 1750 and 1754, respectively, coincided with renewed discussion and progress among the Quakers on the issue of antislavery. As elders and as the clerks of the Philadelphia Monthly and Yearly Meetings, as well as leading members of the Board of Overseers, which routinely prohibited publications on slavery until 1754, Kinsey and Pemberton wielded enormous power among Friends, even as attitudes toward slavery were changing from below. Benjamin had written back in 1738 that it was time to put away the "rusty old candlesticks"—the old leaders—and replace them with the lights of a new generation. This began to happen in the early 1750s. Some of the new leaders were Pembertons—John, James, and Israel Jr., who would be called "King of the Quakers"—all of whom eventually supported abolition. Benjamin seems to have been friendly with John, who assisted him in 1754 in sending money to an ailing relative back in Essex. John campaigned against the slave trade, and James became president of the Pennsylvania Abolition Society in 1790. In the struggle over abolition, Benjamin lost the battle with the father but won the war with the sons.[29]

IMPACT

It is not easy to evaluate Benjamin's impact on the development of an antislavery movement, for two reasons, one historical and one historiographical. First, his contemporary enemies suppressed his activism and tried to limit the circulation of his subversive ideas. The "men of renown" forced him to publish his book without approval, then denounced it, and at the same time expelled him unjustly from both the Philadelphia and Abington Monthly Meetings. They could not abide his confrontational antislavery "preaching." Even though Benjamin exerted influence within the evolving debate, Quakers leaders would never acknowledge it, nor would the official documentation of Quaker meetings reflect it.

Even later abolitionists sometimes had a hard time giving Benjamin proper credit for his role in the struggle. A quarter century after Benjamin's death, Ann Emlen, wife of the devoted antislavery campaigner Warner Mifflin, was still put off by his provocative, polarizing methods. Benjamin, she wrote in a letter of 1785, was "fiery" and "zealous," a "Trumpit" against slavery. He was "quite noisy & talkative in Meetings of Publick Worship" and eventually "got himself disowned." (She blamed the victim.)

His manner, she concluded, "was by no means acceptable to Friends," even though many acknowledged that "what he said in a great many expressions" was "the truth."[30]

A second difficulty stems from the ways in which historians have written about Quaker antislavery thought. For many years they marginalized the more radical voices of Sandiford and Lay while exalting Anthony Benezet and especially John Woolman, who led the next generation of Quaker activists. In 1754 the recently changed Board of Overseers approved publication of Woolman's *Considerations on the Keeping of Negroes*, and the Philadelphia Yearly Meeting published *An Epistle of Caution and Advice, concerning the Buying and Keeping of Slaves*, probably written by Benezet. The movement from below broke through to enable Quaker abolition from above. Benezet and Woolman have been depicted not only as the "effective" abolitionists but essentially as saints. At the same time Benjamin was banished to the background as someone who was variously overzealous, misguided, deranged, and therefore much less instrumental to the development of an antislavery movement.[31]

This broad interpretation began to change in 1985, when Jean R. Soderlund emphasized in *Quakers and Slavery* that the crucial period for the change in rank-and-file Quaker attitudes toward slavery was not the 1750s, as historians had long maintained, but rather the 1730s and 1740s, when slave trading and ownership were declining significantly in both the monthly meetings and the PYM. Antislavery ideals, wrote Soderlund, were gaining "substantial support" during these years. Her history of Quaker antislavery "from below" suggested that early abolitionists such as Benjamin had a more forceful impact than previously realized.[32]

Brycchan Carey takes the argument further in *From Peace to Freedom*, showing that the breakthroughs of the 1750s happened precisely *because* antislavery activists had won the debates of the 1730s and 1740s. Based on a close reading of the minutes of the PYM, Carey concludes that the years 1735–1743—when Benjamin's antislavery protests were at their peak—mark "a profound shift in the attitudes of Philadelphia Quakers toward buying imported slaves." This was the moment when Quakers incorporated antislavery ideas into their "queries," a group ritual in which Quaker meetings read questions aloud to the congregation, effectively pressuring—and shaming—any member who continued to do business with slave traders. By the time Woolman published *Considerations on the Keeping of Negroes* in 1754, Carey suggests, the day had been won: "It was almost certainly Ralph Sandiford and Benjamin Lay, alongside less vocal supporters, who had changed the hearts and minds of a younger generation in the 1730s and 1740s."[33]

Benjamin's impact can even be discerned at the very moment when the "men of renown" were doing everything they could to expel him from the congregation. At the end of the Philadelphia Yearly Meeting of September 1738, after Benjamin had pierced the bladder of blood and spattered the Quaker slave holders, and after which both he and his book would be denounced at the highest level of Quaker authority, "Divers Friends in this Meeting exprest their Satisfaction" that "there is so little occasion of offence given by Friends concerning encouraging the importing of Negroes." This official minute of the PYM noted that Quaker involvement in the slave trade was declining—and there can be no doubt that Benjamin's endless agitation over the previous six years on the issue was a major reason why. The PYM, presided over by John Kinsey, officially desired that "this particular may be continued." Benjamin had even begun to convince some of his enemies of the righteousness of his cause.[34]

The question remains: how, in the face of extreme opposition from the most powerful men in the colony of Pennsylvania, was Benjamin able to exert influence? He transmitted his truth in four ways: through his book, *All Slave-Keepers . . . Apostates*; through the engraving of him by Henry Dawkins; through his actions, which generated stories that recounted and spread his ideas; and relatedly through the symbolism of his life, how he chose to live. Each medium had its own means of circulation and impact, in the near term and the long. The first, third, and fourth were of his own doing—conscious, willed actions meant to have specific effects—while the second was not. Let us evaluate them in turn.

Benjamin's book was the fourth major antislavery publication in North America, after Samuel Sewell's pamphlet *The Selling of Joseph* (1700), John Hepburn's *The American Defence of the Golden Rule* (1715), and Ralph Sandiford's *A Brief Examination of the Practice of the Times* (1729), revised and republished as *The Mystery of Iniquity* (1730). Benjamin's book was the longest and the most radical of the four. It was also the most difficult to read, which helps to explain why it was not republished until 1969. Benjamin wrote the book for a "General Service" but more specifically for Quakers, the generation younger than himself in particular. He published the book at his own expense and, as Roberts Vaux explained, freely distributed it "among those who were about to succeed the generation which was then passing away." He focused on Benezet, Woolman, and their cohort. The elderly Friends interviewed by Vaux attested to the value and impact of the book: "there can be no doubt that his conscientious efforts made a deep and useful impression upon most persons who perused what he had written, with the attention which it certainly merited." A generation later, Benjamin Rush and Thomas Clarkson had read the book, and it seems likely that other abolitionists had done so as well.[35]

The image engraved by Henry Dawkins soon after Benjamin's death in 1759 went through several reprints as suggested above, in tandem with the rise of the abolitionist movement in Pennsylvania in the late eighteenth century. Rush noted in 1790 that the print was displayed in private homes, surely by those who identified with the cause of antislavery and considered Benjamin something of a founding father. Rush augmented the power of the image by publishing an adoring biography of Benjamin on March 1, 1790, the very moment when the first federal Congress was fiercely debating the petitions of abolitionist organizations against slavery and the slave trade. The engraving took on broader significance in the abolition movement after Benjamin Lundy and Lydia Maria Child included it in their biographies of Benjamin, published in 1830 and 1842, respectively, and after the *American Anti-Slavery Almanac* reproduced Child's account in 1843. The print can now be found in archives and libraries up and down the east coast of the United States and in England, suggesting wide circulation, again, surely among abolitionists.[36]

Benjamin's influence was probably most strongly felt through the endless stories people told about him. Indeed most of what is known about the last twenty years of his life has come down to us through personal reminiscence. Some stories showed up in newspapers, while others were gathered by biographers Rush, Vaux, and Child. Rush noted that in his own day and after, Benjamin was to many "an object of admiration, and to all, the subject of conversation." His guerrilla theater caused endless discussion and of course Benjamin had taken action with this outcome in mind. Like Diogenes, he approached philosophy through public activism: he thought himself both a preacher—albeit an unapproved one to the Quaker hierarchy—and a teacher. He wanted to provoke, to unsettle, even to confound—all to wake up those who were "fast asleep," to make them sit up, think, and act. Even if his Quaker modesty would not permit him to say so, Benjamin sought to ignite public debate about his ideas, which, he genuinely believed, were God's ideas. He succeeded. As Rush noted, there was a time when Benjamin was the best-known person in the colony of Pennsylvania.[37]

The symbolism of Benjamin's life also had a potent impact on younger activists, especially John Woolman and Anthony Benezet, who would help to carry Quakers to full abolition in 1776. Both men would adopt kinder, gentler methods of persuasion in the antislavery struggle, no doubt because they saw how much opposition Benjamin's zeal and fury provoked. But both agreed with Benjamin that abolition should be but one part of an entirely new way of life. They followed his example by embodying their own hope for a new kind of social order. This was precisely the point of Benjamin's decision to "live" Cynic philosophy: he expressed the truth, as praxis, through his dwarf body.[38]

Little is known about the relationship between Woolman and Lay, mostly because the latter did not write about his experiences in the antislavery struggle after 1738, while the former apparently never made a reference to Benjamin in his written work. Woolman would have known Benjamin or at the very least known a lot about him. Woolman was in all likelihood present for the bladder-of-blood spectacle that took place in Burlington, New Jersey, not far from his home in Mount Holly, in September 1738. The nineteenth-century poet John Greenleaf Whittier speculated that the act "must have made a deep impression on his sensitive spirit." And even if Woolman was not present, he had heard stories about Benjamin, who attended many Quaker meetings in New Jersey. As historian Geoffrey Plank has pointed out, Woolman was extremely careful about his public image and would have understood how a direct connection to the controversial Benjamin might damage it. But there can be no doubt that the connection was there and that Benjamin significantly influenced his younger, milder brother—and not only on the issue of slavery.[39]

In the spirit of the "primitive Quakers," especially James Nayler, both Lay and Woolman wanted their lives to be, as the latter put it, "a sign to the People." An old Quaker motto was "Let your lives speak." Woolman therefore refused to consume any commodity such as sugar or tobacco that had been produced by slave labor. He expressed a tender concern for animals, which included walking in order to avoid the exploitation of horses.

He wore simple, undyed clothing: blue dyes were made from indigo, often produced by slaves; red dyes from cochineal beetles. He criticized the destructive power of money, greed, and materialism, and he tried to dissociate himself from aspects of the growing international capitalist economy. Many Quakers remarked on Woolman's "singularities," but as it happened, his practices were not singular at all. Benjamin had pioneered every single one of them and, as everyone knew, had been doing so from the time Woolman was a teenager. Woolman followed Benjamin in making antislavery principles part of a new, more deeply ethical way of life.[40]

Benjamin's impact on Benezet was similar—and it grew from friendship. Roberts Vaux, who wrote biographies of both men, noted in 1815: "The most cordial attachment subsisted between [Lay] and the truly honourable Anthony Benezet." It may have been Benjamin the sailor who tipped off Benezet to study seafaring accounts as he wrote against slavery, which, according to Maurice Jackson, allowed him to construct an alternative vision of Africa and to contest the vicious, racist, self-serving accounts of slave traders. Benezet continued and carried to a higher level Benjamin's critique of covetousness, making the "Gains of Oppression" a major theme in early American antislavery in the 1760s and after. Benezet, like Woolman, also embraced the antinomian idea of "universal love" and indeed made it central to the PYM's first major initiative against slavery in 1754. Perhaps most significantly of all, Benezet lived simply, wore undyed clothing, rejected materialism, refused to consume slave-produced commodities, and became a vegetarian. He was known to feed rats in his backyard, and when once asked by his brother to dine on poultry, he asked, "What, would you have me eat my neighbors?"[41]

In rethinking the relationships among the early abolitionists, it is important to remember that Benjamin's extreme tactics may have made the later successes by Benezet and Woolman possible, as Benjamin Rush suggested when he wrote of Benjamin in 1790: "Perhaps the turbulence and severity of his temper were necessary to rouse the torpor of the human mind" during the early phase of struggle. He continued, "The meekness and gentleness of Anthony Benezet, who completed what Mr. Lay began, would probably have been as insufficient [but] for the work performed by Mr. Lay." The thundering prophet and the gentle saints worked hand in dedicated hand.[42]

Benjamin was the keeper of the sacred flame of abolition between the years 1733 and 1753, the very years when Quaker attitudes toward slavery were changing dramatically. He was the most famous—and infamous—speaker and actor on the subject. He made himself central to endless discussions, whether he was present or not; he was a tireless agent of education on the subject. His greatest power, indeed his genius, lay in his gift as an agitator. In every meeting he attended, public or private, he drew a line over the issue of slavery. He asked everyone he met, Which side are you on? For Benjamin, slavery admitted no neutrality, no middle ground. One of his mottoes was "He that is not with me is against me." To be sure, a great many Quakers grew utterly exasperated by Benjamin's endless agitation. He was a difficult man, to say the least. But he consistently tried to force Quakers out of their complacency, out of any comfortable "business as usual."[43]

The great nineteenth-century militant abolitionist Frederick Douglass, a former runaway slave, understood the necessity and the power of agitation. He explained, in 1857,

> Those who profess to favor freedom and yet depreciate agitation, are people who want crops without ploughing the ground; they want rain without thunder and lightning; they want the ocean without the roar of its many waters. The struggle may be a moral one, or it may be a physical one, or it may be both. But it must be a struggle. Power concedes nothing without a demand. It never did and it never will.

Benjamin was the supreme agitator—ploughman, thunder, lightning, and roaring ocean all rolled in one. He confronted power fearlessly with radical demands, and eventually he forced it to concede. He paid a heavy price for his principled opposition—ridicule, repression, and expulsion from the community of faith he loved. He deserves to be remembered as a leader, even if a lonely one, in the struggle. He was the prophet whose torch of pure fire showed the way out of darkness.[44]

CONCLUSION

THE GIANT OAK

BENJAMIN LAY WAS the first revolutionary abolitionist. He demanded an end to slavery and therefore radical change in all societies where it had a significant presence, and he anchored abolition in a new way of life, without human and animal exploitation, based on the "innocent Fruits of the Earth." The first person to call him a revolutionary was Benjamin Rush, in his biography of 1790, published at the beginning of a decade that would see the Atlantic in flames, from Paris to Belfast to Port-au-Prince. Rush explained that Benjamin sowed "the seeds of a principle which bids fair to produce a revolution in morals,—commerce,—and government, in the new, and in the old world." Benjamin the commoner would have liked the planting metaphor, and Benjamin the sailor would have liked the transatlantic reach.[1]

How did Benjamin break through the conventional wisdom of his day? How did he plant revolutionary seeds of principle in the barren soil of almost universally accepted slavery? How did he resist the pressure, ridicule, and repression he faced from the majority who supported slavery? How did he imagine a better future? The answer to these questions lies in his creative combination of experience, personality, and belief.

Born to a Quaker farm family in a small rural village, Benjamin moved as a young man to London and went to sea, relocated to Barbados at age thirty-six, and moved to Philadelphia at age fifty. He entered an urban trade and then a global seafaring culture between roughly 1700 and 1714, became a convinced abolitionist after his encounter with slavery between 1718 and 1720, and devoted himself to a new kind of commoning radicalism from the 1730s through the late 1750s. To a foundation of Quaker antinomianism he added the egalitarianism and cosmopolitanism of seafaring culture, the life-and-death struggles of African America, and the environmentally friendly ways of commoning and vegetarianism. He talked with and learned from enslaved people in Barbados. He fed the hungry and preached an end to slavery, earning the wrath of the master class. He denounced ministers—Quakers and others—who did not live up to his standards. He spoke truth to power, shaming and defying slave traders and keepers. He dared to live in a new way based on an ethical relationship to all living things. He applied evolving radical principles to all aspects of his life, changing himself as he changed the world. Benjamin's radicalism combined Quakerism, ancient philosophy, seafaring culture, abolitionism, and commonism. He chose what he considered the best practices from multiple social worlds as he tried to create a new one. He wrote and lived an eighteenth-century "theology of liberation."[2]

Benjamin's broad experience mattered hugely to the breakthrough to a new way of life, but so did his personality. The word that Quakers used most often to describe him was "zeal"—he was always said to be full of passion, fervor, or what in his era was called "enthusiasm," a politically charged term for exuberant and potentially subversive emotion. Like many a prophet, Benjamin was possessed by his ideas, utterly convinced of his own righteousness. He could be humorous and charming, but his strength of conviction also made him aggressive, difficult, and stubborn. Moreover, he had a temper that often flamed beyond his control. Verbally skilled, sure of his principles, and never given to back down, he was a formidable opponent in discussion and debate.[3]

At the same time Benjamin professed endless love—to those who agreed with him. He celebrated love, a practice central to Quaker theology, writing about it more than a hundred times in *All Slave-Keepers . . . Apostates*. He had love for his wife, Sarah; for his fellow Quakers; for his "fellow creatures"; and finally for "Truth" and for God, which were, in his view, one and the same. He proudly noted "the Love and Zeal I bear to the *TRUTH* and Honour of God." Of special importance to him was the old antinomian idea of "the universal Love of God to all People." His combination of zeal, love, and fearlessness was suited for the task and the times.[4]

Benjamin's dwarf body also shaped his radicalism. For someone "not much above four feet" tall, life was a struggle to be considered equal, even to be taken seriously in many situations. Benjamin had to fight. He had to prove himself by going to sea. He had to insist on the Quaker community's commitment to equality, an ideal he saw as besieged on all sides by covetousness and corrupting wealth. He had to speak freely, achieve self-sufficiency, and cultivate toughness. He waged a politics of the body every day of his life—with compassion and empathy. He was profoundly moved by his experience of slavery in Barbados and again in Pennsylvania. He expressed concern for the poor throughout his life. Benjamin was thrice an outsider to mainstream society, as a religious radical, an abolitionist, and a dwarf. His experience as a little person, coupled with his commitment of universal love to all peoples, turned compassion into active solidarity. Benjamin's life as a dwarf was thus another key to his radicalism—a deep source of his empathy with enslaved and other poor people, with animals, and with all of the natural world.

Benjamin planted seeds he had harvested from the English Revolution of the 1640s and 1650s. He had steeped himself in the books and culture of the original "primitive Friends." He drew freely on the heritage of "the world turned upside down": He was part Leveller, concerned with democratic and egalitarian principles that would curb the powers of the "men of renown." He was part Seeker, like William Dell, after the pure church. He was part Ranter, who believed that those who "are born of God Sin not, neither can they, for his Seed remaineth in them; they cannot Sin, because they are Born of God." He was part Digger, who returned to the commons, what Gerrard Winstanley called the "Earthly Treasury." And he was all Quaker, of the early revolutionary sort.[5]

Benjamin held a special place in his heart for the great poet of the English Revolution, John Milton. He gave copies of Milton's *Considerations Touching the Likeliest Means to Remove Hirelings out of the Church* (1659) to King George I, King George II, and Queen Caroline. He quoted Milton's words, "Religion brought forth Wealth, and the Daughter devoured the Mother," to explain what was happening in Pennsylvania. Perhaps most significantly of all, Benjamin chose to end *All Slave-Keepers . . . Apostates* with a long passage from *Paradise Lost*, expressing his own belief that the Quaker paradise in Pennsylvania had been lost to slave traders and owners, and that this reflected an even greater loss of faith itself. The lines selected echo Benjamin's own main themes—the danger of false ministers and teachers, the corrupting power of "lucre and ambition." Benjamin also included an antinomian passage on the eternal struggle between law and spirit:

> *Spiritual laws by carnal power shall force*
> *On every conscience; laws which none shall find*
> *Left them inrolled, or what the Spirit within*
> *Shall on the heart engrave. What will they then*
> *But force the Spirit of Grace itself, and bind*
> *His consort Liberty?*

That someone like Benjamin would carry on the ideals of the "good old cause" was foreseen by the Ranter-influenced Quaker Edward Burrough, whose writings Benjamin studied and admired. At the moment of the English Revolution's defeat, Burrough spoke to the Restoration Parliament in 1659 of the coming execution of the regicides and the long-term nature of the struggle: you may "destroy these vessels . . . yet our principles you can never extinguish, but they will live for ever, and enter into other bodies to live and speak and act." Benjamin was one such body, one such Atlantic vessel. Through him flowed the resistance of the early Quakers, deep-sea sailors, ancient philosophers, hardy commoners, and enslaved Africans. Through him lived on democratic and egalitarian principles into the modern age. Benjamin was, in many ways, the last radical of the English Revolution.[6]

Benjamin would reinvent and expand the legacy, not least by attaching the uncompromising spirit of antinomianism to the antislavery cause, effectively linking the English Revolution to a broader struggle over slavery and freedom. As Peter Linebaugh and I argued in *The Many Headed Hydra*, the radical ideas and practices of the English Revolution would migrate across the Atlantic, then return to Europe to help ignite the "age of revolution" in the late eighteenth century. Benjamin was a vector of connection and causation in this process.[7]

As Benjamin Rush understood, many of the seeds Benjamin planted would eventually bear fruit. He militantly demanded immediate emancipation for enslaved Africans everywhere. Historians have emphasized the importance of "immediatism" in nineteenth-century debates about abolition, but few know that the debate was going on among Quakers a century earlier. Previous critics of slavery, from George Fox to Morgan Godwyn, to Thomas Tryon, all advised slave owners to treat their slaves better. Of course Benjamin always preached compassion to all creatures, but he had better advice: *free all enslaved people now.* He steadfastly refused to compromise with those who advocated gradual emancipation. When moderate Quakers tried to convince him that abolition must "be a gradual work," he responded that slavery was "an offence in the sight of Divine Purity" and was therefore completely unacceptable for any duration of time. When other Quakers "made their Wills," arranging "to set their Negroes free at such an Age, 30 or 40, after their Death," Benjamin was furious. He announced that such an act "will not salve the Sore, it is too deep and rotten." More importantly, "God will not be mocked so, nor Wise Men neither."[8]

Another revolutionary seed was the use of direct action to accomplish emancipation. Benjamin always embodied his antislavery ideas in public action. The Quaker pacifist was, in paradoxical ways, a lineal ancestor of the great nineteenth-century radical abolitionist John Brown. Benjamin dressed as a soldier, wielded a sword, refused compromise, and used the violent language of war as he opposed bondage. His antinomian spirit channeled the will of God: right-minded people could, indeed must, tear down Babylon and build the "New Jerusalem." His nonviolent activism was every bit as militant as those who later demanded physical force.[9]

Benjamin was also one of the first practical abolitionists, grounded in the real day-to-day struggles of enslaved peoples of African descent. His radicalism was driven by close personal proximity to slavery and its attendant horrors, as the French revolutionary Jacques Pierre Brissot de Warville observed in 1792. Noting that abolitionists were frequently criticized for "having not been witnesses of the sufferings which they describe" in their writings about slavery, he was quick to add, "This reproach cannot be made against Benjamin Lay." Benjamin's experience in Barbados, where he saw the "horror inspired by the frightful terrors of slavery" and where he developed personal relationships with enslaved people, caused him "to preach and write for the abolition of slavery." He engaged in "profound meditations," showed "an indefatigable zeal for humanity," and created "a life without a stain."[10]

Sources are lacking to explore Benjamin's personal involvement in the lives of enslaved people in and around Philadelphia. We do not know, for example, whether he helped bondmen and bondwomen to escape to freedom through what would have been a forerunner of the Underground Railroad, which developed a century later with the growth of a national abolitionist network. Such action would have been consistent with everything Benjamin believed and preached. We do know, however, that he advocated incessantly for emancipation, in some cases on behalf of specific individuals he knew.[11]

One such person was a "negro girl"—her name has not survived in the evidence—who was owned by Quaker neighbors in Abington. Benjamin argued repeatedly with the man and woman about the iniquity of keeping slaves, insisting that the girl be freed, but to no avail. The couple not only kept her in bondage; they justified the practice. One day Benjamin explained to them the "wickedness" of the slave trade, emphasizing how it separated children from their parents. Soon after, Benjamin encountered the six-year-old son of the couple a short distance from their farm. He invited him to his cave about a mile away and entertained the boy all day inside, out of view.

When evening came on, Benjamin observed the boy's father and mother running toward his dwelling. He advanced and met them, "enquiring in a feeling manner, '*what is the matter?*'" The parents replied in anguish, 'Oh Benjamin, Benjamin! our child is gone, he has been missing all day.'" Benjamin listened with sympathy, paused, and said, "Your child is safe in my house." Then he explained why he was there: "You may now conceive of the sorrow you inflict upon the parents of the negroe girl you hold in slavery, for she was torn from them by avarice." Once again Benjamin expressed a simple, profound message: do unto others as you would have them do unto you. In this case the other was a particular human unjustly held in bondage.[12]

How can it be that a man of such important and humane ideas is unknown today? Why have most people never heard of the fearless Benjamin Lay? The reasons are essentially two. The first is that he did not fit the dominant, long-told "story" about the history of the abolitionist movement. He was not a "gentleman saint." He was neither properly educated nor "enlightened." He came from the wrong class. He was too wild, too confrontational, too lacking in gentility. Even Roberts Vaux, who helped to restore Benjamin to abolitionist and popular memory, shared some of these misleading assumptions:

> his intellectual powers were not expanded by an education founded upon the basis of sound and liberal learning, nor was his mind polished and refined by the embellishments of ornamental literature. His knowledge of mankind was extensive, but to the polite accomplishments of the world, he paid little regard.

What Vaux did not mention is that in Benjamin's era, men of education, literature, and polite accomplishment were often the *supporters* of slavery, and sometimes, like the "enlightened" Thomas Jefferson, actual slave masters themselves. Benjamin's class background, self-education, and antinomian free thinking actually *helped* him to break through the profound proslavery consensus.[13]

Benjamin calls attention to a point rarely appreciated by historians: the earliest published critics of slavery in the seventeenth and eighteenth centuries were almost all working people of humble origins. George Fox was a shoemaker's apprentice. Thomas Tryon herded sheep and made hats. William Edmondson and Elihu Coleman were carpenters. John Hepburn came to New Jersey as an indentured servant. William Southeby built boats. Ralph Sandiford sailed the high seas, and John Woolman tailored clothing. A few of these men experienced upward mobility in their lives, becoming independent farmers or merchants, but all of them, crucially, had personally experienced a plebeian world of hard work, which would be a basis for sympathetic identification with enslaved people. This is yet another way in which abolitionism was not simply a middle-class movement. As a shepherd, sailor, and glover, Benjamin embodied the class composition of early Atlantic antislavery.[14]

A second reason why Benjamin is unknown was because he has long been considered "deformed"—in both body and mind. As a little person and as a man thought eccentric at best and more commonly deranged or insane, he was ridiculed and dismissed, in his own day and in subsequent histories. Writers and historians marginalized him as "the little hunchback" or a "deviant personality," even as they grudgingly acknowledged his contribution to the struggle against slavery. No one understood that his actions, placed in the long-term contexts of radical Quakerism and the English Revolution, had a specific history and clear rationality.[15]

No one grasped that Benjamin experienced a different kind of enlightenment, which allowed him to rise above the conventions of his day. He was "enlightened," not in the salons of Paris or London but on the decks of a ship and the waterfront of the world's leading slave society, where the "inward light" of Quakerism met the dark outer reaches of the Atlantic. His was an "enlightenment from below." It occurred while he was working "all the World over," among "all Colours, and Nations."[16]

In late 1728 or early 1729, enlightenment from above and below may have met in person in the Quaker meetinghouse on Gracechurch Street in London. The very embodiment of the traditional enlightenment, Voltaire, was in exile in London at the time and took an interest in Quakerism. He went to worship services at a meeting Benjamin was known to attend. Whether they met is unknown but they certainly came close: Voltaire's English language tutor, Quaker John Kuweidt, signed Benjamin's marriage certificate. Voltaire developed respect for the Quakers he met, but he could not resist having a little fun at their expense: he asked whether it was "possible for mankind to respect virtue when revealed in a ridiculous light." Had the two "enlightened" men met, Benjamin would no doubt have thought Voltaire's aristocratic ways equally ridiculous. But they would have found common ground in their interest in slavery.[17]

Benjamin's revolutionary abolitionism suggests a new genealogy of antislavery, the history of which has long been associated with elites such as Voltaire and the late eighteenth-century Enlightenment. Benjamin belongs to a history of abolition "from below," which has a longer trajectory. His were the ideas and practices of an ordinary working man—shepherd, sailor, glover, petty merchant, commoner. He challenges a history that has long emphasized middle- and upper-class abolitionist "saints," from William Wilberforce to Lewis Tappan. Benjamin also shifts the origin of the abolitionist movement back to the radical ideas of the English Revolution as a constituent source of liberal enlightenment in the late eighteenth-century. Historian John Donoghue has emphasized how the radicals of the English Revolution developed their own critique of slavery in a time before "slavery" was fully racialized. Benjamin carried many of their ideas into the eighteenth century, planting the seed of antinomianism in what would be the world's first modern social movement.[18]

Benjamin's ideas, images, and prophecies anticipated those of another antinomian radical more than a generation later: William Blake (1757–1827). As E. P. Thompson has shown, the visionary poet and artist also drew inspiration from the religious radicalism of the English Revolution, particularly a group called the Muggletonians, who split off from the Ranters in 1651. Lay and Blake also shared a deep fascination with the Book of Revelation, which Blake illustrated in a series of watercolors between 1805 and 1810, depicting the Great Red Dragon in a vivid, poetic, even hallucinogenic way that echoes the same qualities to be found in Lay's writings. The antinomian prophets both "witnessed against the beast" and passionately opposed New World slavery. Almost a century before Blake wrote about the "dark Satanic mills" of industrial England, Benjamin had discovered its necessary predecessor: the "Hellish Iron Furnace" of Caribbean sugar production.[19]

Benjamin's prophecy speaks to our time. He predicted that for Quakers and for America, slave keeping would be a long, destructive burden. It "will be as the poison of Dragons, and the cruel Venom of Asps, in the end, or I am mistaken." As it happens, the poison and the venom have had long lives indeed, down to the present, as we still live with the consequences of slavery: prejudice, poverty, deep structural inequality, and premature death. Just as tellingly, Benjamin counseled his readers to beware rich men who "poison the World for Gain." Despite his prophecy, Earth has grown much sicker since Benjamin's day, which makes it easier now to hear his message. It may have taken more than two and a half centuries, but it seems that the world is finally beginning to catch up with the prophet's radical, far-reaching ideas through a growing, if far from universal, environmental consciousness.[20]

Benjamin Lay was, in sum, a class-conscious, gender-conscious, race-conscious, environmentally conscious vegetarian ultraradical. Most readers of this book would think this combination of beliefs possible only since the 1960s, two full centuries after Lay's remarkable life ended. He lived the principles that today animate a global movement against sweatshops, whose logo-adorned clothing and shoes disguise the horrific conditions under which workers produce them. As the first person to boycott slave-produced commodities, Benjamin pioneered the politics of consumption and initiated a tactic that would become central to the ultimate success of abolition in the nineteenth century. In his time Benjamin may have been the most radical person on the planet. He helps us to understand what was thinkable and what was politically and morally possible in the first half of the eighteenth century—and what may be possible now. It was more than we thought.[21]

Let us return to Benjamin Rush, who foresaw the revolutionary implications of Benjamin's philosophy. Writing after an abolitionist movement had burst into existence during the "age of revolution," Rush was acutely conscious that Benjamin had been a lonely fighter against slavery for forty long years, suffering endless persecution, ridicule, and repression, without a movement to support and sustain him. Rush saw that his very survival took rare strength, confidence, certitude, and character. He sought to turn the experience into an object lesson for activists of his own time. The "benefactors of mankind," he continued, must not "despair, if they do not see the fruits of their benevolent proportions, or undertakings, during their lives." Wherever the "seed of truth or virtue" is planted, it will "preserve and carry with it the principle of life." Some seeds bear fruit quickly, Rush explained, but the "most valuable of them, like the venerable oak, are centuries in growing." Like the fearless Benjamin Lay, these giant oaks do not wither. "They exist and bloom for ever."[22]

AUTHOR'S NOTE

I FIRST ENCOUNTERED Benjamin Lay as Peter Linebaugh and I researched and wrote our book *The Many-Headed Hydra: Sailors, Slaves, Commoners, and the Hidden History of the Revolutionary Atlantic* (Boston: Beacon Press, 2000). We were interested in an Atlantic cycle of rebellion during the 1730s, when enslaved Africans and indentured Europeans organized dozens of conspiracies and rebellions that challenged the slave societies of the western Atlantic. Benjamin's book, *All Slave-Keepers That Keep the Innocent in Bondage, Apostates* (Philadelphia, 1738), was a product of this wave of struggle. I was intrigued by his early opposition to slavery and by his fearless guerrilla theater. I made a mental note to myself that he deserved a study all his own. Twenty years later, he got it.

I seek in this book to treat Benjamin with the respect he deserves. I hope to illuminate and overcome once and for all the condescension, opposition, and isolation he received from his contemporaries and from some who have written about him since his death. Showing respect required that I figure out how to write about his dwarfism, kyphosis, and alleged derangement. In these pages Benjamin is not referred to by the insulting epithet "midget." The terms "dwarf" and "little person" are used instead, in keeping with the preferences of the organization Little People of America (www.lpaonline.org) and many others who to this day suffer discrimination based on size and an often tyrannical normative image of the human body.

It was my pleasure as I worked on this book to give lectures to various audiences about Benjamin and his ideas. The single most meaningful of these followed an invitation to speak in February 2016 to the Abington (PA) Friends Monthly Meeting—to which Benjamin once belonged. In the beautiful old stone and oak meetinghouse, with Benjamin's body buried only a few feet from where I was speaking, I recounted my findings about this illustrious former member of the congregation. At the end of the talk I encouraged the Quaker audience to reinstate Benjamin. Everyone in the room knew he was right about slavery. Benjamin dearly loved his fellow Quakers (at least those who did not own slaves), and there is no doubt in my mind that he would have wanted to be readmitted to the fold. I am happy to report that discussion of this matter has begun in Abington. It is my fondest hope that the Meeting will once again embrace its unfairly disowned brother. This would be an act of retrospective justice.

Another just act would be for all of us to make a prominent place for Benjamin in the larger drama of American history. We live in a time when many traditional historical heroes are wobbling on their pedestals. The British imperialist and white supremacist Cecil Rhodes has been toppled in South Africa and challenged in Oxford. America's founding fathers, so many of whom were slave owners, now fit awkwardly with our sensibilities about slavery and its legacy in the present. Thomas Jefferson was undeniably a brilliant man but at the same time one of the leading racists of his era, arguing fiercely in international debate against the intellectual capabilities of peoples of African descent. These pages suggest that Benjamin Lay embodies a higher set of American ideals and is a more suitable hero for a society that values democracy, diversity, and equality.

It is a time-tested truth that biographers develop strong imaginary ties to the people they study. I am no different. Benjamin spoke to me across the centuries. I have learned a lot from him and I have enormous respect for the way he chose to live his life. In writing the book I have even tried to act on advice he gave. In the margin of one of the two hundred tomes he kept in his cave, Benjamin wrote, "Dear souls, be tender hearted." He loved tender-hearted people and always tried to be one himself in order to feel compassion for all living creatures. When he described someone as "tender-hearted," he was paying that person his highest compliment, invoking his most cherished ideal. In these pages I have offered what I hope is a "tender-hearted" history of a deeply principled and often impossible man.

ACKNOWLEDGMENTS

THIS BOOK WAS MADE possible by the helpful staffs of many research institutions. I wish to thank Chris Densmore and Pat O'Donnell (Friends Historical Library, Swarthmore); Ann Upton and Mary Craudereuff (Quaker and Special Collections, Haverford Libraries); Alexander Bartlett (Germantown Historical Society Library); Daniel M. Rolfe (Historical Society of Pennsylvania); Richard Newman and James Green (Library Company of Philadelphia); Kathy Ludwig (David Library of the American Revolution); Kate LeMay and Brandon Fortune (National Portrait Gallery); and Ken Grossi (Oberlin College Library). In the United Kingdom I was assisted by Allyson Lewis (Essex Record Office); Jennifer Milligan and Josef Stein (Library of the Society of Friends, London); Nigel Cochrane and Sandy Macmillen (Special Collections, University of Essex); Trevor Coombs and Jenny Gaschke (Bristol City Museum and Galleries); and the staff at the National Archives of the United Kingdom.

Two excellent scholars of Quakerism, Larry Gragg and Jean R. Soderlund, kindly shared with me their research on the Quaker communities of Barbados and Pennsylvania. I was fortunate to have the help of James E. Hazard, a superb Quaker genealogist, and two research assistants, my student Alexandra Krongel and Ann Upton, a specialist in the Quaker archives of the Philadelphia region. Sophie White and Kirk Savage gave me expert advice on the portraits of Benjamin Lay. Charles Neimeyer and Wayne Bodle taught me about the military history of the American Revolution as I searched for Benjamin Lay's papers, which were apparently confiscated (and destroyed) by the British army in late 1778. Jonathan Sassi, Adrian Davies, and A. Glenn Crothers kindly discussed the history of Quakerism with me. Nicole Joniec (Library Company), Susan Newton (Winterthur Museum), Pat O'Donnell, and Anne A. Verplanck assisted me in the search for illustrations. Warm thanks to all.

I wish to express my gratitude to a talented, hard-working group of University of Pittsburgh students with whom I studied "The Origins of Antislavery" in spring 2015: Stan Averin, Jacob Craig, Kiran Feinstein, Julia Gitelman, Andrew Gryskewicz, Kane Karsteter-McKernan, Max Kenney, Brett Morgan, and Ian Sames. Their exuberance as we read the "kick-ass Benjamin Lay," as one of them called him, was a special encouragement.

Jules Lobel discussed this book with me on many a searching long walk, while Rob Ruck engaged me about the meaning of Benjamin Lay's life dozens of times over several years. Peter Linebaugh and Staughton Lynd helped me to understand Benjamin's radicalism and its larger antinomian tradition. I also wish to thank Dr. David S. Friedland, who has been a generous and enthusiastic reader of my books for more than a decade now.

I thank the following people for organizing talks and useful discussions: Anthony Bogues and Neil Safier (Brown University); Linda Colley (Princeton University); Steven Pincus (Yale University); Costas Douzinas and Oscar Guardiola-Rivera (Birkbeck College, University of London); Lynne Siqueland and Rosie Bothwell (Abington Friends Meeting); Françoise Vergés (Collège d'études mondiales/Fondation Maison des sciences de l'homme, Paris); John Donoghue (Loyola University/Newberry Library); Staughton and Alice Lynd (Trumbull Correctional Institute, Ohio); and Kirk Savage and Jonathan Arac (University of Pittsburgh).

It was, once again, a tremendous pleasure to work with my editor at Beacon Press, Gayatri Patnaik, whose intelligence and wise judgment suffuse these pages. Thanks too to Tom Hallock, Rachael Marks, Marcy Barnes, Bob Kosturko, Susan Lumenello, and the rest of the Beacon gang. My agent, Sandy Dijkstra, believed in this project and helped it to find the perfect publishing home.

Three friends, two of them former students, read the entire manuscript and gave me the benefit of their deep learning: Maurice Jackson, who has written on Quaker abolitionist Anthony Benezet; John Donoghue, who has discovered the origins of abolitionism in the English Revolution; and Gary B. Nash, who has been studying Quakers and American society (and much else) for more than half a century. All three gave me inspiration as well as concrete help. It was a special pleasure to work alongside Gary, whose personal warmth and extraordinary scholarship have meant a lot to me over many years, as we both wrote biographies of Quaker abolitionists. I would also like to remember a departed friend, Christopher Hill, whose towering work on the English Revolution inspired me many years ago to become a historian and inspires me still, in this very book.

Final thanks are reserved for the members of my family, who have lived the book with me, listening with good cheer to an endless array of stories about an unusual man from a distant time. Wendy was, as always, my first reader and my most challenging and helpful. My children—Eva, Zeke, and Greer—encouraged me warmly as I wrote the book. Zeke was one of the first to urge me to write the book, and Eva shared her knowledge of special education in valuable ways. I dedicate the book to them, with love and hope.

ABBREVIATIONS

AMM	Abington Monthly Meeting
BL	British Library, London
Child, *Memoir*	Lydia Maria Child, *Memoir of Benjamin Lay: Compiled from Various Sources* (New York: American Anti-Slavery Society, 1842)
CMM	Colchester Monthly Meeting
CPRW	City of Philadelphia Registry of Wills, Philadelphia
CTWM	Colchester Two Weeks Meeting
DHMM	Devonshire House Monthly Meeting
DMM	Deptford Monthly Meeting
EQM	Essex Quarterly Meeting
ERO	Essex Record Office, Chelmsford, England
FHL-SCL	Friends Historical Library, Swarthmore College Library
Fitch, *Colchester Quakers*	Stanley Henry Glass Fitch, *Colchester Quakers* (Colchester: Stanley G. Johnson, n.d.)
HSP	Historical Society of Pennsylvania
Hunt, "Notices of Lay"	John Hunt, "Notices of Benjamin Lay," *Friends' Miscellany, Being a Collection of Essays and Fragments, Biographical, Religious, Epistolary, Narrative and Historical* (Philadelphia: J. Richards, 1833)
Kite, "Account"	Nathan Kite, "Account of the Life of Benjamin Lay, One of the Early Anti-Slavery Advocates," *The Friend: A Religious, Literary and Miscellaneous Journal* 29 (1856)
Lay, *All Slave-Keepers*	Benjamin Lay, *All Slave-Keepers That Keep the Innocent in Bondage, Apostates* (Philadelphia), 1738

LSF	Library of the Society of Friends, London
LTWM	London Two Weeks Meeting
LYM	London Yearly Meeting
NA	The National Archives of the United Kingdom, Kew Gardens
PMM	Philadelphia Monthly Meeting
PQM	Philadelphia Quarterly Meeting
PYM	Philadelphia Yearly Meeting
QC-HCL	Quaker Collection, Haverford College Library
Rush, "Account"	Benjamin Rush, "An Account of Benjamin Lay," *The Universal Asylum, and Columbian Magazine*, March 1790
SFC-UE	Society of Friends Collection, Special Collections, University of Essex, Colchester, England
Vaux, *Memoirs*	Roberts Vaux, *Memoirs of the Lives of Benjamin Lay and Ralph Sandiford, Two of the Earliest Public Advocates for the Emancipation of the Enslaved Africans* (Philadelphia: Solomon W. Conrad, 1815)

A NOTE ON DATES

BEFORE 1752 BRITISH PEOPLES used the Julian (Old Style) calendar in which the new year began March 25. With the advent of the Gregorian calendar the new year began January 1. Quakers referred to weekdays and months by numbers and numerals rather than use their "heathen" names (Sunday, Monday, January, February, etc.). Prior to 1752 Quakers therefore considered the "first month" to be March and the twelfth month to be February. Sunday was "first day" and so on throughout the week. I have chosen to give Quaker meeting dates as they appeared in the original sources: the day as a number, the month as a numeral, and the year. A meeting held September 19, 1738, is rendered (according to the Julian calendar) as 19.vii.1738. September 19, 1753, is 19.ix.1753.

NOTES

INTRODUCTION

1. This and the next three paragraphs draw on the four primary source accounts of Lay's action at the Burlington meeting: a note by John Kinsey dated September 19, 1738, PYM Minutes, 1681–1746, MRPh469, FHL-SCL; interview with John Forman, 1785, in Hunt, "Notices of Lay," 274–76; Rush, "Account"; and Vaux, *Memoirs*. The yearly meeting was the highest in the hierarchy of Quaker meetings, which ascended from preparative to monthly, quarterly, and yearly, each one routing members and representatives to the one above. Most business was conducted in the monthly meetings, usually one for men and one for women: discipline was dispensed, certificates for travel awarded, and proposed marriages evaluated. The quarterly and yearly meetings, which met four times and once a year as their names implied, handled the larger issues of policy.

2. Rush, "Account." Mario Caricchio refers to the "spectacular prophetic performances" of the Ranter Abiezer Coppe during the English Revolution. See his "News from the New Jerusalem: Giles Calvert and the Radical Experience," in *Varieties of Seventeenth- and Early Eighteenth-Century Radicalism in Context*, ed. Ariel Hessayon and David Finnegan (Farnham, Surrey, UK: Ashgate, 2011), 71.

3. Lay, *All Slave-Keepers*. It is not clear why the publication date on the title page is listed as 1737 when several entries in the book are dated 1738. Lay also took out a notice in the *American Weekly Mercury* to announce the recent appearance of the book on August 24, 1738.

4. *Semi-Weekly Eagle*, July 16, 1849 (Brattleboro, VT). Jean R. Soderlund has shown that between 1731 and 1751, two-thirds of the members of the Board of Overseers owned slaves. See her *Quakers and Slavery: A Divided Spirit* (Princeton, NJ: Princeton University Press, 1985), 34.

5. Rush, "Account"; Vaux, *Memoirs*, 20–21. Rush's estimate of Lay's height ("not much above four feet") is to be preferred to that of Vaux ("four feet seven inches

in height") because Rush gathered information twenty-five years earlier, when many more people who knew Benjamin were still alive. It should also be noted that Benjamin may have used his small stature to advance his ideas. Christopher Hill wrote that, during the English Revolution, many radicals "deliberately exaggerated their eccentricities in order to get a hearing." This was especially true of many of the early Quakers. See Christopher Hill, *The World Turned Upside Down: Radical Ideas in the English Revolution* (orig. publ. 1972; Harmondsworth, UK: Penguin, 1984), 16.

6. Lay, *All Slave-Keepers*, 38. This study of Lay's life seeks to contribute to the relatively new and rapidly growing field of history known as disability studies. For an overview and a synthesis, see Kim E. Nielsen, *A Disability History of the United States* (Boston: Beacon Press, 2014). See also Nathaniel Smith Kogan, "Aberrations in the Body and in the Body Politic: The Eighteenth-Century Life of Benjamin Lay, Disabled Abolitionist," *Disability Studies Quarterly* 36 (2016), http://dsq-sds.org/article/view/5135/4410.

7. Quotations: Vaux, *Memoirs*, 24; *Semi-Weekly Eagle*, July 16, 1849; David Brion Davis, *The Problem of Slavery in Western Culture* (Ithaca, NY: Cornell University Press, 1966), 324. See also Hunt, "Notices of Lay"; C. Brightwen Rountree, "Benjamin Lay (1681–1759)," *Journal of the Friends Historical Society* 33 (1936): 3–19; Thomas E. Drake, *Quakers and Slavery in America* (Gloucester, MA: Peter Smith, 1950), 44–48. Among the best works on Quakers and slavery are Soderlund, *Quakers and Slavery*; Thomas P. Slaughter, *The Beautiful Soul of John Woolman, Apostle of Abolition* (New York: Hill and Wang, 2009); Maurice Jackson, *Let This Voice Be Heard: Anthony Benezet, Father of Atlantic Abolitionism* (Philadelphia: University of Pennsylvania Press, 2010); Geoffrey Plank, *John Woolman's Path to the Peaceable Kingdom: A Quaker in the British Empire* (Philadelphia: University of Pennsylvania Press, 2012); and Brycchan Carey, *From Peace to Freedom: Quaker Rhetoric and the Birth of American Anti-Slavery, 1657–1761* (New Haven, CT: Yale University Press, 2012). I would also mention three important collections of essays: Richard Newman and James Mueller, eds., *Antislavery and Abolition in Philadelphia: Emancipation and the Long Struggle for Racial Justice on the City of Brotherly Love* (Baton Rouge: Louisiana State University Press, 2011); Brycchan Carey and Geoffrey Plank, eds., *Quakers and Abolition* (Urbana: University of Illinois Press, 2014); and Maurice Jackson and Susan Kozel, eds., *Quakers and Their Allies in the Abolitionist Cause, 1754–1808* (London: Routledge, 2015).

8. J. P. Brissot de Warville, *New Travels in the United States of America, performed in 1788* (Dublin: W. Corbet, 1792), 267; Thomas Clarkson, *The History of the Rise, Progress, and Accomplishment of the Abolition of the African Slave-Trade, by the British Parliament* (London, 1808), 84–85; [Benjamin Lundy], "Biographical

Sketches: Benjamin Lay," *Genius of Universal Emancipation, A Monthly Periodical Work Containing Original Essays, Documents, and Facts Relative to the Subject of African Slavery* 1 (1830): 38–40; Child, *Memoir*. On Garrison, see Henry Mayer, *All on Fire: William Lloyd Garrison and the Abolition of Slavery* (New York: W. W. Norton, 2008). Three outstanding histories of the abolition movement in Britain and America are Adam Hochschild, *Bury the Chains: Prophets and Rebels in the Fight to Free an Empire's Slaves* (Boston: Houghton Mifflin, 2005); Christopher Leslie Brown, *Moral Capital: Foundations of British Abolitionism* (Chapel Hill: University of North Carolina Press, 2006); and Manisha Sinha, *The Slave's Cause: A History of Abolition* (New Haven, CT: Yale University Press, 2016).

9. Lay, *All Slave-Keepers*, 151. Exemplary "biographies from below" have been written by Carlo Ginzburg, *The Cheese and the Worms: The Cosmos of a Sixteenth-Century Miller* (Baltimore: Johns Hopkins University Press, 1976); Natalie Zemon Davis, *Women on the Margins: Three Seventeenth-Century Lives* (Cambridge, MA: Harvard University Press, 1997); Natalie Zemon Davis, *Trickster Travels: A Sixteenth-Century Muslim Between Worlds* (New York: Hill and Wang, 2007); Alfred F. Young, *The Shoemaker and the Tea Party: Memory and the American Revolution* (Boston: Beacon Press, 2000); and Linda Colley, *The Ordeal of Elizabeth Marsh: A Woman in World History* (New York: Pantheon, 2007).

10. Vaux interviewed ten people who averaged eighty-two years of age. See *Memoirs*, viii. For Fox's reforms, see chapter 1.

11. Ephraim Pagitt, *Heresiography, or, A Description of the Hereticks and Sectaries of these latter Times* (London, 1647); Hill, *The World Turned Upside Down*; Christopher Hill, "Antinomianism in 17th-Century England," in his *Collected Essays of Christopher Hill*, vol. II, *Religion and Politics in 17th-Century England* (Amherst: University of Massachusetts Press, 1986), 179. Frederick B. Tolles mistakenly claimed that by 1739 "no trace" of antinomianism remained in Quakerism. See his "Quietism Versus Enthusiasm: The Philadelphia Quakers and the Great Awakening," *Pennsylvania Magazine of History and Biography* 69 (1945): 27.

12. *Pennsylvania Packet*, February 7, 1774; Ann Emlen to John Pemberton, 15.1.1785, Pemberton Family Papers, vol. 42, 162, HSP. I thank Gary B. Nash for the Emlen reference.

13. Vaux, *Memoirs*, v, vi, 20, 22, 25.

14. Meeting of 24.iv.1737, PMM Minutes, 1715–1744, MRPh383, fo. 285–86, FHL-SCL. See chapters 2 and 3 for accounts of Benjamin's disownments from various Quaker meetings.

15. Hunt, "Notices of Lay," 274.

16. Here is the original Latin version of the poem quoted by Vaux (18): *Justum, et tenacem propositi virum, / Non civium ardor prava jubentium / Non vultus instantis tyranni / Mente quatit solida.*

CHAPTER ONE: EARLY LIFE

1. David Ross, "Copford, St Michael and All Angels Church," *Britain Express*, http://www.britainexpress.com/counties/essex/churches/copford.htm, accessed April 25, 2016.

2. Janet Cooper, ed., *A History of the County of Essex*, vol. X, *Lexden Hundred (Part) Including Dedham, Earls Colne and Wivenhoe* (London: Victoria County History, 2001), 139–43; Harold C. Greenwood, "Quaker Digest of Essex Births, Index, 1613–1837," 1997, SFC-UE; Catherine Ferguson, Christopher Thornton, and Andrew Wareham, eds., *Essex Hearth Tax Returns: Michelmas 1670* (London: The British Record Society, 2012), based on Q/RTh 5, ERO.

3. Presentments by hundreds of Ongar, Harlow, and Waltham, 1667, Q/SR 412/40, ERO; CMM Minutes, 1672–1718, meetings of 5.ii.1672 (fo. 3) and 7.iv.1672 (fo. 3), SFC-UE. It seems unlikely that the William Lay mentioned in the Quaker records was Benjamin's father, who would have been only eighteen years old in 1672. On the distances that members lived from the CMM meeting, see John Heveningham, "Williamson Loyd," "Richard Freshfield," "Benjamin Dikes," John Layswell, James Catchpool, John Kendall, and "Thomas Kendall" to PMM, 27.vi.1732, ff. 84–85, SFC-UE.

4. CMM Minutes, 1672–1718, meetings of 3.xi.1679 (fo. 38), 6.iii.1687 (fo. 74), 3.iv.1687 (fo. 75), and 2.iii.1712 (fo. 258), SFC-UE.

5. Will of William Lay, Husbandman of Copford, Essex, 30 October 1684, PROB 11/377/453, NA; Will of William Lay of Fordham, yeoman, 17 October 1722, D/ABW 84/2/75, ERO; Will of John Lay of Copford, yeoman, 24 August 1735, D/ABW 89/1/113, ERO. While copyhold and freehold differed in the medieval period, by the late seventeenth and eighteenth centuries both conveyed a right of ownership. For background, see A. W. B. Simpson, *An Introduction to the History of Land Law* (Oxford, UK: Oxford University Press, 1961), 135–62. Thanks to Janelle Greenberg on this point.

6. J. H. Round, ed., *Register of the Scholars Admitted to Colchester School, 1637–1740* (Colchester, UK: Wiles and Son, 1897); Vaux, *Memoirs*, 13, 44.

7. Philip Morant, *The History and Antiquities of the County of Essex* (London, 1768), xxv; Thomas Cromwell, *History and Description of the Ancient Town and Borough of Colchester, in Essex* (London: Robert Jennings, 1825), 83; "To be SOLD," *American Weekly Mercury*, October 12–19, 1732. Two of the people mentioned in Benjamin's will of 1731 were bay makers; four more were weavers. See "A Copy of Benjamin Lay's Will, Dated ye 9: 1 month 1731," folder 56, SFC-UE. On Benjamin's spinning, see Rush, "Account."

8. John Walter, *Understanding Popular Violence in the English Revolution: The Colchester Plunderers* (Cambridge, UK: Cambridge University Press, 1999); Christopher Hill, "From Lollards to Levellers," in *Rebels and Their Causes: Essays in*

Honour of A. L. Morton, ed. Maurice Cornforth (Atlantic Highlands, NJ: Humanities Press, 1978), 52–61.

9. Shannon McSheffrey, *Gender and Heresy: Women and Men in Lollard Communities, 1420–1530* (Philadelphia: University of Pennsylvania Press, 1995), 78–79. See also Hill, "From Lollards to Levellers," for discussion of the "direct links in ideas from Lollards through Familists and Anabaptists to the Levellers, Diggers, Ranters, and Quakers of the mid-seventeenth century," 63.

10. Adrian Davies, *The Quakers in English Society, 1655–1725* (Oxford, UK: Clarendon Press, 2000), ch. 10: "From Lollards to Quakers."

11. Pagitt, *Heresiography*. For a comprehensive, first-rate study of the "antinomian underground," from the Grindletonians in the early seventeenth century up to the outbreak of the English Revolution, see David R. Como, *Blown by the Spirit: Puritanism and the Emergence of an Antinomian Underground in Pre-Civil-War England* (Stanford, CA: Stanford University Press, 2004).

12. Rosemary Moore, *The Light in Their Consciences: The Early Quakers in Britain, 1646–1660* (University Park: Pennsylvania State University Press, 2000), 69; Barry Reay, *The Quakers and the English Revolution* (New York: St. Martin's Press, 1985), 14. On Fox and Nayler, see H. Larry Ingle, *First Among Friends: George Fox and the Creation of Quakerism* (Oxford, UK: Oxford University Press, 1996); Leo Damrosch, *The Sorrows of the Quaker Jesus: James Nayler and the Puritan Crackdown on the Free Spirit* (Cambridge, MA: Harvard University Press, 1996); and David Neelon, *James Nayler: Revolutionary to Prophet* (Becket, MA: Leadings Press, 2009). Christopher Hill noted in *The World Turned Upside Down*, 232: "The whole early Quaker movement was far closer to Ranters in spirit than its leaders later liked to recall, after they had spent many weary hours differentiating themselves from Ranters and ex-Ranters." See also Robert Barclay, *The Anarchy of the Ranters, and Other Libertines* (London, 1676).

13. Davies, *Quakers in English Society*, 26; Parnell quoted in Reay, *The Quakers and the English Revolution*, 36. Phyllis Mack offers a vivid portrait of Martha Simmonds in her *Visionary Women: Ecstatic Prophecy in Seventeenth-Century England* (Berkeley: University of California Press, 1992), 197–208.

14. Reay, *The Quakers and the English Revolution*, 26, 44, 53; Davies, *Quakers in English Society*, 13, 27, 182; Hill, *The World Turned Upside Down*, 25; Damrosch, *The Sorrows of the Quaker Jesus*, 43. Melvin B. Endy Jr. emphasizes the "spiritualist" origins and genealogy of Quakers among the Seekers and Ranters, who were "anti-clerical Antinomians." See his essay "Puritanism, Spiritualism, and Quakerism: An Historiographical Essay," in *The World of William Penn*, ed. Richard S. Dunn and Mary Maples Dunn (Philadelphia: University of Pennsylvania Press, 1986), 281–301. Endy also sums up the antinomianism that lay at the heart of Quakerism: "saints were free from all human authorities, which were all corrupt,

and could submit only to the witness of God within them." Everyone, including rulers, were, according to the apostle Paul (Roman 13:1), "subject to the Higher Power" of God, which was beyond all man-made law. See his *William Penn and Early Quakerism* (Princeton, NJ: Princeton University Press, 1973), 86–87.

15. Fitch, *Colchester Quakers*, 37–38; Kenneth L. Carroll, *John Perrot: Early Quaker Schismatic* (London: Friends Historical Society, 1971), vii; Moore, *The Light in Their Consciences*, 193–203; Davies, *Quakers in English Society*, 67, 131.

16. Damrosch, *Sorrows of the Quaker Jesus*, 29, 244; Davies, *Quakers in English Society*, 17.

17. Simmonds quoted in Patricia Crawford, *Women and Religion in England, 1500–1720* (London: Routledge, 1993), 170, 178; Kenneth L. Carroll, "Sackcloth and Ashes and Other Signs and Wonders," *Journal of Friends Historical Society* 63 (1975): 314–25; Kenneth L. Carroll, "Early Quakers and 'Going Naked as a Sign,'" *Quaker History* 67 (1978): 69–87; Damrosch, *Sorrows of the Quaker Jesus*, 5, 7; Moore, *The Light in Their Consciences*, ch. 3.

18. Reay, *The Quakers and the English Revolution*, 111, 113–14; Moore, *The Light in Their Consciences*, 214–28; Davies, *Quakers in English Society*, 189; Hill, *The World Turned Upside Down*, 254–56; Clare J. L. Martin, "Tradition Versus Innovation: The Hat, Wilkinson-Story and Keithian Controversies," *Quaker Studies* 8 (2003), available at http://digitalcommons.georgefox.edu/quakerstudies/vol8/iss1/1.

19. Lay announced his commitment to Protestant radicalism soon after he arrived in Philadelphia in 1732 with an advertisement in the *American Weekly Mercury* listing books for sale, the very first of which was John Foxe's *Book of Martyrs* (1563), the classic account of Protestant sufferings at the hands of the Catholic Church. See "To be SOLD, by Benjamin Lay," *American Weekly Mercury*, October 12–19, 1732. Lay also studied the writings of the founding generation of Quakers—George Fox, Edward Burrough, Richard Hubberthorne, William Dewsbury, Francis Howgill, and George Whitehead, all members of the Quaker "Valiant Sixty"—as well as the leading figures of the second generation, William Penn and Robert Barclay. He knew William Sewel's *The History of the Rise, Increase, and Progress of the Christian People Called Quakers* (1722). He had also read extensively about the persecution of the "Quaker lambs" by Puritans in seventeenth-century Boston; indeed he had visited the very spot where their executions had taken place.

20. Lay, *All Slave-Keepers*, 131–33; "A Copy of Benjamin Lay's Will, Dated ye 9: 1 month 1731," SFC-UE, folder 56.

21. Sheep were valuable to farmers like Benjamin's brother for their wool, for mutton when sold to butchers, and for manure that fertilized fallow fields, as Swedish naturalist Peter Kalm wrote during his tour through eastern England,

including Essex, in 1748. See *Kalm's Account of his Visit to England in his Way to America in 1748* (London: Macmillan and Company, 1892), 301–2.

22. Lay, *All Slave-Keepers*, 28, 265.

23. James Nayler, *The Lamb's War* (London, 1657), reprinted in James Nayler, *A Collection of Sundry Books, Epistles, and Papers written by James Nayler, some of which were never before Printed: with an Impartial Relation of the most Remarkable Transactions relating to his Life* (London, 1716). For an excellent analysis of Fox's radical early use of the Book of Revelation, see David Loewenstein, "The War of the Lamb: George Fox and the Apocalyptic Discourse of Revolutionary Quakerism," in *The Emergence of Quaker Writing: Dissenting Literature in Seventeenth-Century England*, ed. Thomas N. Corns and David Loewenstein (London: Frank Cass, 1995), 25–41. For a succinct summary of "The Lamb's War," see Meredith Baldwin Weddle, *Walking in the Way of Peace: Quaker Pacifism in the Seventeenth Century* (Oxford, UK: Oxford University Press, 2001), 70–71.

24. This and the following two paragraphs draw from R. Campbell, *The London Tradesman, being a Compendious View of All the Trades, Professions, Arts, both Liberal and Mechanic, now Practiced in the Cities of London and Westminster* (London: T. Gardner, 1747), 223; Inventory of the Estate late of Benjamin Lay decd, Exhbitd 12 March 1759, File A-55-1759, CPRW; Amelia Mott Gummere, *The Quaker: A Study in Costume* (Philadelphia: Ferris & Leech, 1901), 43–46.

25. Vaux, *Memoirs*, 14 (emphasis added). This section draws on research presented in Marcus Rediker, *Between the Devil and the Deep Blue Sea: Merchant Seamen, Pirates, and the Anglo-American Maritime World, 1700–1750* (New York: Cambridge University Press, 1987), and *Outlaws of the Atlantic: Sailors, Pirates, and Motley Crews in the Age of Sail* (Boston: Beacon Press, 2014).

26. Daniel Defoe, *The Storm: or, a Collection of the most remarkable Casualties and Disasters which happen'd in the late dreadful Tempest, both by Sea and Land* (London, 1704).

27. Basil Lubbock, ed., *Barlow's Journal of His Life at Sea in King's Ships, East & West Indiamen, & Other Merchant Men from 1659 to 1703* (London, 1934), 553.

28. Benjamin likely disdained parts of seafaring culture, especially the profanity and drinking of rum. It is hard to imagine how, at his height, he would have been able to turn the capstan, a mechanical gearing device operated by the physical strength of the crew. Perhaps he did other work.

29. "Curious Cave Dweller Once Made Home Here," *Philadelphia Inquirer*, April 1, 1901. The hammock appears in the "Inventory of the goods & Chattals of Benjamin Lay of the Town of Abington in the County of Philadelphia Deceasd as appraised by us the Subscribers this twenty first and twenty third Days of the Second mo 1759," file A-55-1759, CPRW.

30. Lay, *All Slave-Keepers*, 145–46.

31. Ibid., 230–31. "Picaresque proletarian" comes from Peter Linebaugh, *The London Hanged: Crime and Civil Society in the Eighteenth Century* (London: Allen Lane, 1991), ch. 4.

32. Barnaby Slush, *The Navy Royal; or, a Sea-Cook Turn'd Projector* (London, 1709); DHMM Minutes, vol. III, 1707–1727; London and Middlesex Quarterly Meeting Book, vol. III (1713–1724); London Two Week Meeting, Book of Certificates, A1716–67; London and Middlesex Quarterly Meeting, Digest Register of Marriages, vol. I (1657–1719); all in the LSF. On October 16, 1717, Cotton Mather complained of a "furious, venomous, rancorous Man" who, "for no Reason in the world, insulted me." This may have been Lay, who was in Boston at the time. See *The Diary of Cotton Mather, 1681–1724* (New York: Ungar, 1957), vol. II, 480. I am grateful to Steven Pitt for this reference.

33. Meeting of 3.i.1732, CMM Minutes, 1718–1756, shelf 6, no. 2, SFC-UE.

34. Lay, *All Slave-Keepers*, 17.

35. Ibid., 161.

36. Ibid., 55–56.

37. Ibid., 6; Philippe Rosenberg, "Thomas Tryon and the Seventeenth-Century Dimensions of Antislavery," *William and Mary Quarterly*, Third Series, 61 (2004): 609–42; Rediker, *Between the Devil and the Deep Blue Sea*, ch. 4. Here is the passage from the King James Version of the Bible, which Lay apparently quoted from memory: "Woe unto him that buildeth his house by unrighteousness, and his chambers by wrong; that useth his neighbour's service without wages, and giveth him not for his work."

38. Frederick Engels, *The Condition of the Working Class in England* (London, 1845), 168, 184. Benjamin's friend and fellow Quaker activist Anthony Benezet was not a sailor, but he too used maritime knowledge, especially sea-going travel accounts, to attack slavery. See the outstanding biography by Jackson, *Let This Voice Be Heard*, 80–88.

39. See the Transatlantic Slave Trade Database at www.slavevoyages.org and Marcus Rediker, "History from Below (the Water Line): Sharks and the Atlantic Slave Trade," *Atlantic Studies* 5 (2008): 285–97.

CHAPTER TWO: "A MAN OF STRIFE & CONTENTION"

1. Benjamin Lay's Certificate, LTWM Minutes, Book of Certificates A (1716–1767), FHL-SCL. Benjamin might have attended Quaker meetings prior to 1714, but his presence would likely have been fitful because of long voyages at sea. Given his personality and antinomian beliefs, it is hard to believe that he would not have left some kind of documentary trace had he been attending services regularly.

2. Ibid.

3. "Sarah Lay," entry in John Smith, "Lives of Ministers Among Friends," unpublished manuscript, 975A, three volumes, QC-HCL; DMM Minutes, vol. I (1694–1726); London and Middlesex Quarterly Meeting, Digest Register of Marriages, vol. I (1657–1719), book 835, pg. 554, both in LSF. See also the excellent article by Andreas Mielke, "'What's Here to Do?' An Inquiry Concerning Sarah and Benjamin Lay, Abolitionists," *Quaker History* 86 (1997): 22–44.

4. Miles Walker (DHMM) to CTWM, 7.ix.1722, fo. 24, SFC-UE.

5. Meeting of 4.x.1717, fo. 247, DHMM Minutes, vol. III, 1707–1727, LSF; Lay, *All Slave-Keepers*, 255–56.

6. Meeting of 18.xi.1717, fo. 250, DHMM Minutes.

7. Meetings of 5.i.1718 and 9.ii.1718, ff. 253, 260, DHMM Minutes.

8. Meetings of 12.iii.1718 and 4.iv.1718, ff. 263, 265–266, DHMM Minutes; London and Middlesex Quarterly Meeting, Digest Register of Marriages, vol. I (1657–1719), book 835, pg. 554. See also meetings of 15.iv.1718 and 7.vii.1718, DMM Minutes, vol. I (1694–1726), LSF.

9. See Larry Gragg, "The Making of an Abolitionist: Benjamin Lay on Barbados, 1718–1720," *Journal of the Barbados Museum and Historical Society* 47 (2001): 166–84, and the same author's *The Quaker Community on Barbados: Challenging the Culture of the Planter Class* (Columbia: University of Missouri Press, 2009). On the broader history of Barbados, see Richard S. Dunn, *Sugar and Slaves: The Rise of the Planter Class in the English West Indies, 1624–1713* (Chapel Hill: University of North Carolina Press, 1972), and Hilary McD. Beckles, *White Servitude and Black Slavery in Barbados, 1627–1715* (Knoxville: University of Tennessee Press, 1989).

10. This and the following two paragraphs are based on Thomas Walduck, Letters on Barbados, to James Petiver: 1710–1712, Sloane MS 2302, BL.

11. Lay, *All Slave-Keepers*, 40, 45. By the time Benjamin and Sarah arrived Morgan Godwyn and Thomas Tryon had written critiques of the slave system of Barbados: Godwyn, *The Negroes' and Indians' Advocate, suing for their Admission into the Church, or a Persuasive to the Instructing and Baptizing in the Negroes and Indians on our Plantations, with a brief Account of Religion in Virginia* (London, 1680), and Tryon, *Friendly Advice to the Gentlemen-Planters of the East and West Indies* (London, 1684).

12. Lay, *All Slave-Keepers*, 45.

13. Ibid., 44. See also Mielke, "'What's Here to Do,?'" 22–44.

14. Lay, *All Slave-Keepers*, 34.

15. Ibid., 36, 38, 39; Vaux, *Memoirs*, 19.

16. Lay, *All Slave-Keepers*, 44, 80.

17. Meeting of 2.ix.1720, ff. 306–307, DHMM Minutes.

18. Meeting of 4.xi.1720, ff. 311, DHMM Minutes.

19. Meetings of 1.i.1721 and 5.ii.1721, ff. 315, 316, DHMM Minutes; Meeting of 20.vi.1722, fo. 338, "Mens Meeting Book for ye frnds of Colchester Comencing ye 6th, 6 mo., 1705–1725," box 6, no. 6, SFC-UE.

20. Fitch, *Colchester Quakers*, 11, 59–60. Daniel Defoe noted the lasting impact of the siege during his visit to Colchester in 1722. See his *A Tour Through the Whole Island of Great Britain* (orig. publ. in three volumes, 1724–1727; rpt. Harmondsworth, UK: Penguin, 1971), 57–58.

21. Meetings of 20.vi.1722 and 3.vii.1722, CTWM Minutes, 338, 339; Peter Jarvis Jr. to the Meeting for Sufferings in London, 20.vi.1722, "Copys of Letters & Certificates & Papers of Condemnation," CMM, 1720, Item #1102, fo. 19. For the charges against Lay to setting up shop while not a "Freeman of the City," see Essex Quarter Session Roll, Mich. 1723, D/B5 ST136, ERO. Uninspired preaching was a lifelong concern to Benjamin, who condemned not only the speakers who had nothing to say but the "Elders and Ministers" who countenanced "such filthy Stuff." See Lay, *All Slave-Keepers*, 131.

22. Meetings of 10.x.1722, 24.x.1722, 7.xi.1722, and 12.xi.1722, CTWM Minutes, 348, 350, 351, 354.

23. Fitch, *Colchester Quakers*, 19; Meeting of 6.xi.1692, CMM Minutes, 1672–1718, ff. 93–94, SFC-UE. On the formation of the separate women's meeting among the Quakers, see Phyllis Mack, *Visionary Women: Ecstatic Prophecy in Seventeenth-Century England* (Berkeley: University of California Press, 1992), 265–304.

24. Meeting 6.ix.1724, CMM Minutes, 1718–1756, shelf 6, no. 2, fo. 78: Fitch, *Colchester Quakers*, 17–18.

25. Meetings of 1.iii.1723, 5.iii.1723, 15.iii.1723, 27.iii.1723, 14.iv.1723, and 17.iv.1723, CTWM Minutes, 363–68.

26. Meeting of 22.v.1723, CTWM Minutes, 373–74.

27. Meeting of 5.vi.1723, CTWM Minutes, 375. John Locke credited New Model Army chaplain John Saltmarsh as the original source of keeping the hat on as protest during the English Revolution. Indeed, when Saltmarsh arose from his death bed in December 1647 to travel to London to upbraid Oliver Cromwell after the imprisonment of Levellers at Corkbush Field, he refused to take off his hat. See Roger Pooley, "Saltmarsh, John (d. 1647)," *Oxford Dictionary of National Biography*, Oxford University Press online, 2004, http://www.oxforddnb.com.pitt.idm.oclc.org/view/article/24578, accessed January 30, 2016.

28. Meeting of 29.ii.1724, CTWM Minutes, fo. 400.

29. Meeting of 13.iii.1724, CTWM Minutes, fo. 403.

30. Meeting of 24.iv.1724, CTWM Minutes, 409–10; Stanley Fitch noted the "intransigent spirit" of the CTWM in the 1720s. See *Colchester Quakers*, 14.

31. Meetings of 26.viii.1724, 9.ix.1724, 23.ix.1724, and 26.x.1724, CTWM Minutes, 423, 427–28, 431, 436–37; Benjamin Lay to the CTWM, 7 December 1724, Letters of Condemnation, fo. 35. As critic Francis Bugg wrote in *Quakerism Drooping* (1704), Quakers used to "go naked for a sign" and call no man master, but by the early eighteenth century they "walked Cloathed" and gave up "*Levelling*." See Davies, *The Quakers in English Society*, 220–21.

32. Meeting of 1.xii.1724, CTWM Minutes, ff. 439–40. Division among the committee spilled over into the final report when several members said they could not remember Benjamin making the "acknowledgments" that appeared in the sympathetic postscript. See Meeting of 17.xii.1724, fo. 442.

33. Benjamin Lay to DHMM, Letters of Condemnation, 3.i.1725/1726, ff. 38–39.

34. Ibid.

35. John Knight and Phillip Gwillim to CTWM, Letters of Condemnation, 9.xi.1725/1726, fo. 38; Benjamin Lay to DHMM, Letters of Condemnation, 21.ix.1725, fo. 39.

36. Peter Jarvis Jr. to DHMM, Letters of Condemnation, 11.ii.1726, ff. 40–41; paper on Benjamin Lay written by the CTWM, 16.iv.1723, fo. 28.

37. Essex Court of Quarter Sessions, Easter 1715–Michaelmas 1723, 12 August 1723, D/B 5 Sb5/1, ERO. Benjamin apparently did not stay in jail long for his name did not appear on the "Gaole Calendar" in subsequent Quarter Session records. Nor did the case itself reappear in later records.

38. Benjamin Lay to CTWM, Letters of Condemnation, 25.ii.1726, fo. 42; Benjamin Lay to CTWM, Letters of Condemnation, 9.iii.1726, ff. 42–43.

39. Ibid.

40. Meetings of 23.iii.1726 and 26.iii.1726, 44, CTWM Minutes, fo. 43.

41. Meeting of 5.ix.1729, DHMM Minutes, vol. V, 1727–1747, fo. 34.

42. Meetings of 7.xi.1729, 4.xii.1729, 4.i.1729/30, and 6.iii.1730, DHMM Minutes, ff. 36, 37, 40, 45.

43. Meeting of 3.ix.1731, DHMM Minutes, fo. 73.

44. Meetings of 9.i.1730 and 23.i.1730, ff. CTWM Minutes, 154, 155–56.

45. John Baker and Phillip Gwillim to CTWM, 30.x.1729, Letters of Condemnation, fo. 63; William Groom and James Catchpool to DHMM, 6.ii.1730, Letters of Condemnation, fo. 64.

46. "A Copy of Benjamin Lay's Will, Dated ye 9: 1 month 1731," folder 56; "Abstract of Benj, Lay's Will," folder 59; both SFC-UE.

47. Meetings of 5.ix.1731 and 13.x.1731, 216, CMM Minutes, 214, 216; Meeting of 5.ix.1731, CTWM Minutes, fo. 214.

48. Meetings of 7.xi.1731 and 3.i.1731/2, CMM Minutes, fo. 133, 134; Kite, "Account," 220.

CHAPTER THREE: PHILADELPHIA'S "MEN OF RENOWN"

1. Lay, *All Slave-Keepers*, 140; Hunt "Notices of Lay." Philadelphia's commercial newspaper, the *American Weekly Mercury*, noted on June 8, 1732, that "Capt. Reeves is just arrived in eleven Weeks from London, he touch'd at Bermuda." For a classic account of the early history of the Quakers in Pennsylvania, see Gary B. Nash, *Quakers and Politics: Pennsylvania, 1681–1726* (Princeton, NJ: Princeton University Press, 1968).

2. Lay, *All Slave-Keepers*, 77.

3. The portrait of the port of Philadelphia is drawn from James Birket, *Some Cursory Remarks Made by James Birket in His Voyage to North America, 1750–1751* (New Haven, CT: Yale University Press, 1916), 67 (quotation); William Black, "The Journal of William Black, 1744," *Pennsylvania Magazine of History and Biography* 1 (877): 405; Samuel Curwen, "Journal of a Journey from Salem to Philadelphia in 1755," *Essex Institute Historical Collections* 52 (1916): 79; and Edward Porter Alexander, ed., *The Journal of John Fontaine: An Irish Huguenot Son in Spain and Virginia, 1710–1719* (Charlottesville: University Press of Virginia, 1972), 118–19. For the indentured maid, the "Negro Man," and the drowned sailor, see the *American Weekly Mercury*, June 8, 1732.

4. Alexander Hamilton, *Gentleman's Progress: The Itinerarium of Dr. Alexander Hamilton, 1744* (Chapel Hill: University of North Carolina Press, 2012), 66–67. In November 1736, when Captain Reeves returned to Philadelphia from Bristol, England, one of the centers of the slave trade, Benjamin met with him to discuss the commerce in human beings. See *American Weekly Mercury*, November 18–25, 1736. Benjamin notes the meeting in an entry dated December 30, 1738, in *All Slave-Keepers*, 88. Samuel Harford signed the letter of probate administration after Benjamin's death in February 1759. See Will of Benjamin Lay, 1759, File A-55–1759, CPRW.

5. James T. Lemon, *The Best Poor Man's Country: Early Southeastern Pennsylvania* (Baltimore: Johns Hopkins University Press, 1972). For the Lenape view of the "Holy Experiment," see Jean R. Soderlund, *Lenape Country: Delaware Society Before William Penn* (Philadelphia: University of Pennsylvania Press, 2015), ch. 7. The best recent work on Atlantic ties among Quakers is Jordan Landes, *London Quakers in the Trans-Atlantic World: The Creation of an Early Modern Community* (New York: Palgrave Macmillan, 2015).

6. *American Weekly Mercury*, October 12–19, 1732.

7. Edwin B. Bronner, "Quaker Landmarks in Early Philadelphia," *Transactions of the American Philosophical Society* 43 (1953): 210–16.

8. Craig W. Horle et al., eds., "Anthony Morris," *Lawmaking and Legislators in Pennsylvania: A Biographical Dictionary*, Vol. II (1710–1756) (Philadelphia: University of Pennsylvania Press, 1997), 727–36.

9. "Robert Jordan," entry in Smith, "Lives of Ministers Among Friends"; "Robert Jordan, Jr.," entry in Frank S. Loescher, "Dictionary of Quaker Biography," unpublished compilation, FHL-SCL; "Lately Imported and to be sold by Robert Jordan *in* Morris's Alley," *Pennsylvania Gazette*, November 27, 1735; *A Collection of Memorials concerning divers Deceased Ministers and Others of the People called Quakers: in Pennsylvania, New-Jersey, and Parts Adjacent, from nearly the First Settlement thereof to the Year 1787; with Some of the Last Expressions and Exhortations of Many of Them* (Philadelphia, 1787); Will of Robert Jordan, 1742, file 291, CPRW. On Perrot in Virginia, see Jay Worrall Jr., *The Friendly Virginians: America's First Quakers* (Athens, GA: Iberian Publishing Company, 1994), 45–46. See also A. Glenn Crothers, *Quakers Living in the Lion's Mouth: The Society of Friends in Northern Virginia, 1730–1865* (Gainesville: University of Florida Press, 2012).

10. Horle et al., eds., "Israel Pemberton," *Lawmaking and Legislators in Pennsylvania*, vol. II, 824–36; Theodore Thayer, *Israel Pemberton: King of the Quakers* (Philadelphia: Historical Society of Pennsylvania, 1943), 14; Darold D. Wax, "Quaker Merchants and the Slave Trade in Colonial Pennsylvania," *Pennsylvania Magazine of History and Biography* 86 (1962): 147–48.

11. Horle et al., eds., "John Kinsey," *Lawmaking and Legislators in Pennsylvania*, vol. II, 591.

12. John Kinsey to Richard Partridge, 2 November 1742, Port 27.94, LSF; *American Weekly Mercury*, June 28, 1722; Will of Robert Jordan, 1742, file 291, CPRW; Thayer, *Israel Pemberton*, 26, 32, 33; William Bucke Campbell, "Old Towns and Districts of Philadelphia," *Philadelphia History* 5 (1942): 102.

13. Kinsey's father was a "wealthy slave-owner," according to Soderlund, *Quakers and Slavery*, 38. His own slave-ownership might have been proven in probate documents, but as it happens the materials from Kinsey's file, #41/1750 in the CPRW, are missing.

14. This and the following two paragraphs summarize an argument from Peter Linebaugh and Marcus Rediker, *The Many-Headed Hydra: Sailors, Slaves, Commoners, and the Hidden History of the Revolutionary Atlantic* (Boston: Beacon Press, 2000), 193–98. See also Barry Gaspar, *Bondsmen and Rebels: A Study of Master-Slave Relations in Antigua with Implications for Colonial British America* (Baltimore: Johns Hopkins University Press, 1985).

15. *American Weekly Mercury*, February 26, 1734, November 25, 1736, and February 15, 1737; Hunt, "Notices of Lay," 275. See Vincent Brown, *Slave Revolt in Jamaica, 1760–1761: A Cartographic Narrative*, http://revolt.axismaps.com.

16. Lay, *All Slave-Keepers*, 28, 31, 35, 82, 92; Gary B. Nash and Jean Soderlund, *Freedom by Degrees: Emancipation in Pennsylvania and Its Aftermath* (New York: Oxford University Press, 1991), 15. Soderlund shows that between 1731 and 1740,

53.8 percent of the participants in the Philadelphia Monthly Meeting owned slaves. See her *Quakers and Slavery*, 163.

17. Lay, *All Slave-Keepers*, 6; Ralph Sandiford, *A Brief Examination of the Practice of the Times* (Philadelphia, 1729), and *The Mystery of Iniquity; in a Brief Examination of the Practice of the Times, by the foregoing and the present Dispensation* (Philadelphia, 1730); Vaux, *Memoirs*, 64. Sandiford noted that he was "repulsed by the Overseers" when he submitted his first manuscript and that he was "threatened by our chief judge," John Kinsey. See *Mystery of Iniquity*, 90, 4. The London Yearly Meeting had advised the Philadelphia Yearly Meeting in 1727 that slave trading by Quakers is "not a Commendable nor allowed practice." LYM quoted in Carey, *From Peace to Freedom*, 2.

18. Sandiford, *Brief Examination*, 14, 30, 74, 94, 106; Sandiford, *Mystery of Iniquity*, 94–111; Vaux, *Memoirs*, 60. Like Lay's, Sandiford's view of animals changed over time. In 1727 his business was deeply involved in animal slaughter, as he advertised "good Hides Curried, and Calf Skins, Sole Leather, and Tann'd Sheep Skins" for sale: *American Weekly Mercury*, November 9, 1727. For George Fox's views on slavery, written after his visit to Barbados in 1671, see his *Gospel Family-Order, being a Short Discourse concerning the Ordering of Families, Both of Whites, Blacks, and Indians* (n.p., 1676).

19. Lay, *All Slave-Keepers*, 20–21.

20. Ibid., 18–20.

21. Ibid., 21–22.

22. *Ibid.*, 21–23.

23. J. William Frost has noted how strategically important it was that Sandiford and Lay went after slave-owning Quaker ministers. See his "Quaker Antislavery from Dissidence to Sense of the Meeting," *Quaker History* 101 (2012): 26.

24. Benjamin's critique of wealth and its destructive power was carried further by John Woolman and Anthony Benezet, who saw the "love of Gain" as the source of slave trading and owning. See Slaughter, *The Beautiful Soul of John Woolman*, 137, 213–17; Plank, *John Woolman's Path to the Peaceable Kingdom*, 76, 84; and Jackson, *Let This Voice Be Heard*, 63–66.

25. Lay, *All Slave-Keepers*, 194–95.

26. Ibid., 59. Benjamin was not the only voice against covetousness. Frederick B. Tolles notes that attacks on avarice increased in the Philadelphia Yearly Meeting during the late 1730s. See his *Meeting House and Counting House: The Quaker Merchants of Colonial Philadelphia, 1682–1763* (orig. publ. 1948; New York: W. W. Norton, 1963), 81.

27. The story of the pipes was originally told by Quaker John Forman in 1785 and published later in Hunt, "Notices of Lay," 274–78. The story was recounted in Kite, "Account," and Child, *Memoir*, 23.

28. Vaux, *Memoirs*, 34–35. This anecdote was repeated in the *Village Record* (Westchester, PA), February 25, 1818.

29. This anecdote was first told by "an OLD MAN," perhaps a friend of Benjamin and at the very least someone who knew him, fifteen years after his death: *Pennsylvania Packet*, February 14, 1774. The next iteration was conveyed by Rush, "Account." A third telling of the story appeared in Vaux, *Memoirs*, and a fourth in Child, *Memoir*, 25.

30. Child, *Memoir*, 22.

31. *Federal Gazette*, May 18, 1790; Vaux, *Memoirs*, viii.

32. *Daily Advertiser*, May 20, 1790; *Political Observatory*, December 10, 1803.

33. Meetings of 10.xi.1731, 7.xii.1731, 21.xii.1731, 20.i.1732, 3.iii.1732, 24.v.1732, CTWM Minutes, ff. 221, 223–24, 225, 228, 232, 238; Meeting of 12.iv.1732, "The Book of the Quarterly Meeting Minutes, Commencing 1711," EQM Minutes, 1711–1754, shelf 2, no. 1, ff. 148–49.

34. Meetings of 27.vi.1732 and 2.viii.1732, CTWM Minutes, ff. 241, 244.

35. "Robert Jordan," entry in Smith, "Lives of Ministers Among Friends." Upon his death, in 1742, the inventory of Jordan's worldly goods included a nameless "Negro boy," valued at £25, one of his most valuable possessions. See Will of Robert Jordan, 1742, File 291, CPRW. Lay also correctly identified "A——M——s" (Anthony Morris), "I——P——n" (Israel Pemberton), J——B——s (John Bringhurst), and S——P——l (Samuel Powell) as slave keepers. See Lay, *All Slave-Keepers*, 273. I thank Jean R. Soderlund for helping me to figure out the identity of Bringhurst and Powell.

36. Meeting of 29.i.1734, PMM Minutes, fo. 242; "The Journal of Susanna Morris," in *Wilt Thou Go On My Errand? Three 18th Century Journals of Quaker Women Ministers*, ed. Margaret Hope Bacon (Wallingford, PA: Pendle Hill Publications, 1994), 55, 72. On the labors of Quaker women ministers, see Rebecca Larson, *Daughters of Light: Quaker Women Preaching and Prophesying in the Colonies and Abroad, 1700–1775* (New York: Alfred A. Knopf, 1999).

37. Horle et al., eds., "Joshua Morris," *Lawmaking and Legislators in Pennsylvania*, 742–50.

38. Mielke, "'What's Here to Do,?'" 22–44.

39. "Sarah Lay," entry in Smith, "Lives of Ministers Among Friends"; Vaux, *Memoirs*, 32.

40. Lay, *All Slave-Keepers*, 33, 38.

41. James T. Mitchell and Henry Flanders, comps., "An Act for the Better Regulating of Negroes in this Province," in *The Statutes at Large of Pennsylvania from 1682 to 1801* (Harrisburg, PA: William Stanley Ray, 1899), vol. IV (1724–1744), chap. ccxcii. See also Gary B. Nash and Jean Soderlund on this "full fledged black code": *Freedom by Degrees*, 13. The practice of manumission had become common

among Quakers in the 1750s and early 1760s, but Morris remained a diehard: he refused to have his slaves freed when he died in 1763. See Horle et al., eds., "Anthony Morris," *Lawmaking and Legislators*, 735–36. For Michael the runaway, see the *Pennsylvania Gazette*, November 10–17, 1748. I am grateful to Jean R. Soderlund for information about John Bringhurst, who was a cooper and later a merchant.

42. Meeting of 27.ii.1734, PMM Minutes, 1715–1744, fo. 243, MRPh383, FHL-SCL.

43. Robert Jordan to Thomas Story, Philadelphia, 7.iv.1736, Gibson TS 730, LSF.

44. Lay, *All Slave-Keepers*, 223–24.

45. Meeting of 24.iv.1737, PMM Minutes, ff. 285–86.

46. Meetings of 24.iv.1737 and 26.vi.1737, PMM Minutes, ff. 285–88.

47. Meeting of 26.vi.1727, PMM Minutes, ff. 287–88; "Nicholas Austin," in Loescher, "Dictionary of Quaker Biography." Benjamin described his encounter in a letter to John Cadwallader Jr., printed in *All Slave-Keepers*, 262. See also "Abington Monthly Meeting Book, Containing a Chronologie of the most Material Occurrences and Transactions that have been acted and done, in the said Meeting Since the first settlement thereof, transcribed from Sundry Manuscripts by George Boone, 1718," AMM Minutes, 1682–1765, RG2/Ph/A2, FHL-SCL; Will of Nicholas Austin, 1770, File 338, CPRW; "To be SOLD," *Pennsylvania Gazette*, October 16, 1755.

48. Meeting of 30.xi.1727, AMM Minutes, 1682–1765, RG2/Ph/A2, Volume I: 1682–1746, fo. 212, FHL-SCL; Mielke, "'What's Here to Do?,'" 32. For the rule by which the disowned were barred from meetings for business and discipline (but not worship meetings), see "Meetings for Discipline" in "A Collection of the Christian & Brotherly Advices given forth from time to time by the Yearly Meeting of Friends for Pennsylvania & New Jersey," Miscellaneous Files, AMM, RG2/Ph/A2, Volume 7.9, 216, FHL-SCL.

CHAPTER FOUR: HOW SLAVE KEEPERS BECAME APOSTATES

1. Lay, *All Slave-Keepers*.

2. Carey, *From Peace to Freedom*, 143, 164.

3. Lay, *All Slave-Keepers*, 247–48; Gary B. Nash, "Franklin and Slavery," *Proceedings of the American Philosophical Society* 150 (2006): 625.

4. Lay, *All Slave-Keepers*, 3–4.

5. Rush, "Account"; Lay, *All Slave-Keepers*, 271; Frost, "Quaker Antislavery from Dissidence to Sense of the Meeting," 22.

6. Lay, *All Slave-Keepers*, 18–19, 4.

7. Ibid., 4, 5, 195.

8. Ibid., 32.

9. Ibid., 45, 136; Vaux, *Memoirs*, 43–44.

10. Anonymous, *A New Commonplace Book; being an Improvement on that recommended by Mr. Locke; properly ruled throughout with a Complete Skeleton Index, and ample Directions for its Use; Equally adapted to the Man of Letters and the Man of Observation, the Traveller & the Student, and forming an useful & agreeable Companion, on the Road; and in the Closet* (London: J. Walker, 1799); Carey, *From Peace to Freedom*, 169.

11. Lay, *All Slave-Keepers*, 11, 92.

12. Ibid., 33, 142, 105.

13. Ibid., 137, 230.

14. Ibid., 45, 31. Ralph Sandiford also emphasized the Biblical Jubilee: see *The Mystery of Iniquity*, 6, 28, 54, 66, 97, 101–2. For the broad history of Jubilee in the struggle against slavery, see Peter Linebaugh, "Jubilating; Or, How the Atlantic Working Class Used the Biblical Jubilee Against Capitalism, with Some Success," *Radical History Review* 50 (1991):143–80.

15. Ibid., 131, 266.

16. Ibid., 23.

17. Ibid., 6–9, 130.

18. Ibid., 8–9.

19. Ibid., 80–94. On Quaker slave keeping in Philadelphia, see Soderlund, *Quakers and Slavery*, 163.

20. Ibid., 85, 59. Soderlund notes that "antislavery ideals were gaining substantial support in the Yearly Meeting between 1731 and 1751." She also shows that the percentage of PYM leaders who owned slaves dropped from 58.6 (1706–1730) to 34.2 (1731–1751). These changes took place before the abolitionist "breakthrough" of 1753–1754. See her *Quakers and Slavery*, 46, 43. See also Carey, *From Peace to Freedom*, 172–81.

21. Lay, *All Slave-Keepers*, 127–28, 133, 231. See George Fox, *Gospel Family-Order, being a Short Discourse concerning the Ordering of Families, Both of Whites, Blacks, and Indians* (n.p., 1676).

22. Ibid., 80.

23. Ibid., 84.

24. Moore, *The Light in Their Consciences*, 65. Brycchan Carey also notes that antislavery ideals had spread before they appeared in sanctioned publications. See *From Peace to Freedom*, 181. See entry for "Books" in "A Collection of the Christian & Brotherly Advices given forth from time to time by the Yearly Meeting of Friends for Pennsylvania & New Jersey," Miscellaneous Files, AMM, RG2/Ph/A2, vol. 7.9, FHL-SCL. Since the 1650s Quakers had used the printing press in sophisticated and carefully controlled ways. See Kate Peters, *Print Culture and the Early Quakers* (Cambridge, UK: Cambridge University Press, 2005), 252–55.

25. Lay, *All Slave-Keepers*, 94; Robert Jordan to Thomas Story, Philadelphia, 7.iv.1736, Gibson TS 730, LSF.

26. Lay, *All Slave-Keepers*, 26–37. See also Frost, "Quaker Antislavery from Dissidence to Sense of the Meeting," 19, 22.

27. Lay, *All Slave-Keepers*, 89, 83–84, 93. See also Katharine Gerbner, "Antislavery in Print: The Germantown Protest, the 'Exhortation,' and the Seventeenth-Century Quaker Debate on Slavery," *Early American Studies* 9 (2011): 552–75.

28. Nicholas P. Wood and Jean R. Soderlund, "'To Friends and All Whom it may Concerne': William Southeby's Rediscovered 1696 Antislavery Protest," *Pennsylvania Magazine of History and Biography* (forthcoming); Drake, *Quakers and Slavery in America*, 30–32. Some kind of personal connection between Farmer and Lay seems likely. Both attended the Colchester Two Weeks Meeting, although at different times. Farmer's wife was a friend of Elizabeth Kendall, a friend of Sarah and perhaps a relative of Benjamin himself, as he named her a trustee in his will of 1731. Years later, in 1754, when one of his poor relatives in Essex fell ill and needed assistance, Benjamin sent home money through Elizabeth. See John Pemberton to Elizabeth Kendall, Philadelphia, 29.iv.1754, Pemberton Family Papers, vol. 10, page 4b, HSP. See also "The Testimony of Mary Bundock concerning Elizabeth Kendall," 1765, ff. 48–52, Commonplace Book of Elizabeth Kendall, Coggeshall Monthly Meeting, Item #1376, SFC-UE. Benjamin's niece, Sarah, daughter of his half-brother John, married Moses Kendall in 1725: Marriage licence bond and allegation of Moses Kendall and Sarah Lay, 1725, D/ABL 1725/113, ERO. See also Lay, *All Slave-Keepers*, 10–11.

29. Ibid., 76.

30. Ibid., 63–64, 58, 136, 18, 75, 84, 85, 87, 27.

31. Ibid., 136; *American Weekly Mercury*, August 24, 1738.

32. Samuel Sewell, *The Selling of Joseph: A Memorial* (Boston, 1700). See also John Saffin, *A Brief and Candid Answer to a late Printed Sheet, Entitled, The Selling of Joseph* (Boston, 1701), and, for the broader context of the debate, Lawrence Towner, "The Sewell-Saffin Dialogue on Slavery," *William and Mary Quarterly*, 3rd Series, 21 (1964): 40–52.

33. Lay, *All Slave-Keepers*, 19, 63, 68.

34. Ibid., 63–64.

35. Ibid., 137, 34; Note by John Kinsey, 19 September 1738, PYM, Miscellaneous Papers, 1731–1738 1250/D1.5 #22, PYM-SCL. In the face of such anger Benjamin comforted himself, "you shall reign over all the rage of your Enemies in the favour of God, wherein as you stand in Faith, ye are the Salt of the Earth, for many seeing your good Works may glorify God in the Day of their Visitation."

36. Ibid., 101–17. Gerrard Winstanley, the Digger-turned-Quaker who was the greatest radical thinker of the English Revolution, also used the Book of Revelation to explain oppression. See Ariel Hessayon, "Gerrard Winstanley, Radical Reformer," in Hessayon and Finnegan, *Varieties of Seventeenth- and Early Eighteenth-Century Radicalism in Context* (London: Ashgate, 2011), 110–11. The Book of Revelation was widely invoked in late seventeenth-century England, but Benjamin stood out for using it to interpret the origins of slavery. See Warren Johnston, *Revelation Restored: The Apocalypse in Later Seventeenth-Century England* (Woodbridge, Suffolk, UK: Boydell Press, 2011). Revelation was not an especially popular text in early America, though it did get significant use by ministers in the run-up to the American Revolution. See Mark A. Noll, *In the Beginning Was the Word: The Bible in American Public Life, 1492–1783* (Oxford, UK: Oxford University Press, 2016), 287.

37. Herbert Marks, ed., *The English Bible, King James Version: The Old Testament*, vol. I, Norton Critical Editions (New York: W. W. Norton, 2012), 569–72.

38. Ibid., 101–2. The Book of Revelation—an antinomian text—played a surprisingly significant role in the thinking of Quaker antislavery activists George Keith, John Hepburn, John Woolman, and Warner Mifflin.

39. Ibid., 102, 104, 107, 110.

40. Ibid., 111, 112, 60, 114.

41. Ibid., 114, 116, 117.

42. Ibid., 51.

43. Ibid., 52.

44. Ibid., 51.

45. Ibid., 111; Alan Tully, *William Penn's Legacy: Politics and Social Structure in Provincial Pennsylvania, 1726–1755* (Baltimore: Johns Hopkins University Press, 1977), 97.

46. PYM Minutes, 16–20.vii.1738; *Pennsylvania Gazette*, October 26, 1738; November 2, 1738; November 16, 1738.

CHAPTER FIVE: BOOKS AND A NEW LIFE

1. Rush, "Account"; Frost, "Quaker Antislavery from Dissidence to Sense of the Meeting," 23. For the portrait commissioned by Franklin, see chapter 6. On the subscription to Franklin's newspaper, see David Waldstreicher, *Runaway America: Benjamin Franklin, Slavery, and the American Revolution* (New York: Hill and Wang, 2005), 82.

2. *American Weekly Mercury*, October 12–19, 1732.

3. The first owner of the book was Samuel Ernow, below whose name is written "now, Benj Lays Book." Subsequent owners were George Duncan, John

Conroy, and, finally, a Mr. Foulke, who in 1916 donated the book to the Site and Relic Society of Germantown, which later became the Germantown Historical Society. Another book that seems to have belonged to Benjamin, though it has no marginalia, is *The Archbishop of Cambray's Dissertation on Pure Love*, by the French Catholic archbishop François Fénelon, published by Christopher Sauer in Germantown in 1750.

4. Dell quoted in Hill, *The World Turned Upside Down*, 42.

5. Roger Pooley, "Dell, William (d. 1669)," *Oxford Dictionary of National Biography*, http://www.oxforddnb.com.pitt.idm.oclc.org/view/article/7461, accessed July 1, 2016; Christopher Hill, "The Radical Critics of Oxford and Cambridge in the 1650s," in his *Change and Continuity in Seventeenth-Century England* (Cambridge, MA: Harvard University Press, 1975), 127–48; Eric C. Walker, *William Dell: Master Puritan* (Cambridge, UK: Heffer, 1970), ch. 4.

6. William Dell, "The Right Reformation of Learning, Schools, and Universities, according to the State of the Gospel, and the True Light that Shines Therein," in his *Several Sermons and Discourses of William Dell, Minister of the Gospel* (London: J. Sowle, 1709), 642–48.

7. Benjamin sold not only religious books in Philadelphia but also "Books of Aritmatick, Mathamaticks, Astronomy, Trogonomytry, Whistons Uclids, and others." See "To be SOLD," *American Weekly Mercury*, October 12–19, 1732.

8. Benjamin noted that he began to oppose false ministers "almost 20 [years] before I ever saw *Pennsylvania*," which would have been around 1714, a little before the first complaints were made against him for opposing "approved ministers" in the Devonshire House Monthly Meeting in London. He may have read Dell around this time. See Lay, *All Slave-Keepers*, 123–24.

9. Tai Liu, "Simpson, Sidrach (c.1600–1655)," *Oxford Dictionary of National Biography*, http://www.oxforddnb.com.pitt.idm.oclc.org/view/article/25592, accessed February 28, 2016.

10. The "bruised reed" appears in Isaiah 42:3 and Matthew 12:20.

11. William Dell, *The Tryal of Spirits* (London, 1653; rpt. 1699), iv, 24.

12. Ibid., viii, 38, 192; Lay, *All Slave-Keepers*, 53.

13. *Pennsylvania Gazette*, March 25, 1742; John Smith, *Hannah Logan's Courtship, A True Narrative; The Wooing Of The Daughter Of James Logan, Colonial Governor Of Pennsylvania, And Divers Other Matters, As Related In The Diary Of Her Lover, The Honorable John Smith, Assemblyman Of Pennsylvania And King's Councillor of New Jersey, 1736–1752* (Philadelphia: Ferris and Leach, 1904), entry for 8.xi.1746, 81.

14. We know that Lay read Stanley because he quoted from the book, precisely but without attribution, in *All Slave-Keepers* in his discussion of Pythagoras. It is likely that Lay also read [Diogenes Laërtius], *The Lives of the Ancient Philosophers,*

containing an Account of their Several Sects, Doctrines, Actions, and Remarkable Sayings (London: John Nicholson, 1702). Benjamin also had an interest in the ancient Egyptian philosopher Hermes Trismegistus, who was translated into English by the English Seeker/antinomian John Everard (1584? –1641), in *The Divine Pymander of Hermes Mercurius Trismegistus* (London: Robert White, 1650). See Lay, *All Slave-Keepers*, 166–69.

15. William Desmond, *Cynics* (Berkeley: University of California Press, 2008), 28, 82, 201–2.

16. Thomas Stanley, *History of Philosophy: Containing the Lives, Opinions, Actions and Discourses of the Philosophers of Every Sect* (London, 1701), 285.

17. See Desmond, *Cynics*, for how the Cynics waged war against *nomos* (authority): 3, 7, 84, 85, 186, 187, 189, 206, 208. In his final lectures, and in his last book before his death in 1984, Michel Foucault held up Diogenes and *parrhesia* as models for contemporary radical thinkers. See his *Fearless Speech*, ed. Joseph Pearson (New York: Semiotext(e), 2001).

18. Lay, *All Slave-Keepers*, 147, 151; Vaux, *Memoirs*, 47–49. Fasting was common among the radical Quakers of the founding generation. See Moore, *The Light in Their Consciences*, 127.

19. Vaux, *Memoirs*, 46; Desmond, *Cynics*, 98, 213; "Benjamin Lay," *Biographical Catalogue, Being an Account of the Lives of Friends* (London: Friends' Institute, 1888), 418–22. What Robert Dobbin says of Diogenes is also true of Lay: "the biographical tradition presents us with a mass of anecdotes (*chreiai*) that are often very entertaining and attest to a consistent set of habits and beliefs that, taken as a whole, inspire confidence that they are at least true to the spirit of the man and his philosophy." See his *The Cynic Philosophers: From Diogenes to Julian* (New York: Penguin, 2013), xxiv.

20. Vaux, *Memoirs*, 35; Desmond, *Cynics*, 24–5, 78–79, 85, 97, 187. Lay too made "more of an impression in person than in print," Dobbin, *The Cynic Philosophers*, xxvii.

21. Rush, "Account"; Vaux, *Memoirs*, 35–36.

22. *Pennsylvania Gazette*, March 25, 1742; Kite, "Account," 220. Benjamin's protest against tea drinking made the rounds in the London press as the article from the *Pennsylvania Gazette* was republished in the *London Evening Post*, July 6–8, 1742; the *Champion and Evening Advertiser*, July 8, 1742; and the *Universal Spectator and Weekly Journal*, July 10, 1742.

23. See John Milton, *Considerations touching the likeliest Means to Remove Hirelings out of the Church, Wherein is also Discours'd of Tythes, Church-fees, Church-revenues; and whether any Maintenance of Ministers can be settl'd by Law* (London: S. Baker, 1717). On the tradition of aristocratic and royals dwarfs in Europe, see Betty M. Adelson, *The Lives of Dwarfs: Their Journey from Public*

Curiosity Toward Social Liberation (New Brunswick, NJ: Rutgers University Press, 2005), and Deborah Needleman Armintor, *The Little Everyman: Stature and Masculinity in Eighteenth-Century British Literature* (Seattle: University of Washington Press, 2011). David Brion Davis called Benjamin the "Quaker Diogenes" in *The Problem of Slavery in Western Culture*, 323.

24. Vaux, *Memoirs*, 26.

25. The original article appeared in the *Pennsylvania Gazette*, March 30, 1738. The response appeared in the same newspaper a week later. Lay's unsigned rejoinder was published April 13, 1738.

26. Rush, "Account"; Philotheos Physiologus [Thomas Tryon], *The Way to Health, Long Life and Happiness, or, A Discourse of Temperance and the Particular Nature of all Things Requisit for the Life of Man* (London: Andrew Sowle, 1683).

27. For an excellent summary of Tryon's views on slavery, see Rosenberg, "Thomas Tryon," 609–42. The impact of Tryon on Lay, other Quaker abolitionists, and Benjamin Franklin is noted by David Waldstreicher, "The Origins of Antislavery in Pennsylvania: Early Abolitionists and Benjamin Franklin's Road Not Taken," in *Antislavery and Abolition in Philadelphia: Emancipation and the Long Struggle for Racial Justice on the City of Brotherly Love*, ed. Richard Newman and James Mueller (Baton Rouge: Louisiana State University Press, 2011), 45–65. Lay alluded to Proverbs 12:10: "A righteous man regardeth the life of his beast."

28. Jacob Bauthumley, *The light and dark sides of God or a plain and brief discourse, of the light side God, heaven and earth, the dark side Devill, sin, and hell* (London, 1650), 4. Tryon quoted in Tristram Stuart, *The Bloodless Revolution: A Cultural History of Vegetarianism from 1600 to Modern Times* (New York: W. W. Norton, 2006), 61, 73, 72; Tryon, *Way to Health*, 509–10. See also Thomas Tryon, *The Country Man's Companion, or, a New Method of Ordering Horses & Sheep* (London, 1684), ch. 5.

29. Tryon, *Way to Health*, 514.

30. Lay refers to Pythagoras in *All Slave-Keepers*, 252.

31. Stuart, *Bloodless Revolution*, xx, chs. 2–5.

32. Ibid., chs. 2, 3, 4; Roger Crab, *The English Hermite, or, Wonder of this Age: Being a Relation of the Life of Roger Crab, living neer Uxbridg, taken from his own Mouth* (London, 1655).

33. Tryon, *Way to Health*, v, 53, 136, 143, 343; Lay, *All Slave-Keepers*, 144–45. Benjamin's interest in water extended to raising money in 1744 to republish a new edition of a book by John Smith, *The Curiosities of Common Water: or the Advantages thereof in Preventing and Curing many Distempers* (London, 1723). This book was a compendium of observations by physicians about the healthful qualities of water, which was considered a "Universal Remedy." Benjamin's ad for subscriptions appeared in the *Pennsylvania Journal*, April 26, 1744.

34. Helen L. Shaffer, *A Tour of Old Abington* (n.p., 1960; rpt. 1976), available on the Abington Township website at http://www.abington.org/about-us/abington-s-history, and Edward W. Hocker, *A History of the Township of Abington* (Abington, 1956); Andrew Newman, "Treaty of Shackamaxon," *Encyclopedia of Great Philadelphia*, http://philadelphiaencyclopedia.org/archive/treaty-of-shackamaxon-2/, accessed July 9, 2016.

35. "Ann Phipps," entry in Smith, "Lives of Ministers Among Friends." Like other commoners, Benjamin organized his subsistence outside the capitalist market, but unlike others he did not cultivate land collectively but rather with Sarah and, after her death in 1735, by himself.

36. Vaux, *Memoirs*, 23, 43–44; Hunt, "Notices of Lay," 274–78; unsigned article, "Lay, Benjamin, 1677–1759," File PG7, FHL-SCL. See also "Trips Awheel: Where to go and How to get there," *Philadelphia Inquirer*, May 23, 1897; "When Philadelphians Were Cave Dwellers Along the Delaware," *Philadelphia Inquirer*, November 20, 1898; "Curious Cave Dweller Once Made Home Here," *Philadelphia Inquirer*, April 1, 1901; "Lay Denounced Slavery from Cave near Abington," *Philadelphia Inquirer*, January 12, 1903. For commoning practices in eighteenth-century England, see J. M. Neeson, *Commoners: Common Right, Enclosure and Social Change in England, 1700–1820* (Cambridge, UK: Cambridge University Press, 1996), and Peter Linebaugh, *Stop Thief! The Commons, Enclosures, and Resistance* (Oakland, CA: PM Press, 2014).

37. Julie L. Holcomb, *Moral Commerce: Quakers and the Transatlantic Boycott of the Slave Labor Economy* (Ithaca, NY: Cornell University Press, 2016), 4. There is evidence that Lay drank milk and ate honey, the only practices that would run counter to contemporary vegan practice.

38. Vaux, *Memoirs*, 32; Rush, "Account"; Hunt, "Notices of Lay," 275–76.

39. Child, *Memoir*, 14.

40. "When Philadelphians Were Cave Dwellers Along the Delaware," *Philadelphia Inquirer*, November 20, 1898. On Kelpius and others, see Douglas H. Shantz, *An Introduction to German Pietism: Protestant Renewal at the Dawn of Modern Europe* (Baltimore: Johns Hopkins University Press, 2013), 172–77.

41. Lay, *All Slave-Keepers*, 218–19, 235, 169.

CHAPTER SIX: DEATH, MEMORY, IMPACT

1. Vaux, *Memoirs*, 49.

2. Ibid., 50.

3. Ibid., 50–51; Jack D. Marietta, *The Reformation of American Quakerism, 1748–1783* (Philadelphia: University of Pennsylvania Press, 1984); Nash and Soderlund, *Freedom by Degrees*, 53–54.

4. Will of Benjamin Lay, 1759, File A-55–1759, CPRW.

5. Burials at Abington from 1758, Births and Deaths, 1670–1812, AMM, RG2/Ph/A2, vol. 3.8, FHL-SCL.

6. "A Copy of Benjamin Lay's Will, Dated ye 9: 1 month 1731," folder 5, SFC-UE. The sums specified in the will were paid after Lay's death in 1759 as executed by Samuel Cook, a weaver from North Halstead, Essex, on behalf of the late Sarah Lay. See Will of Benjamin Lay, Glover of Colchester, Essex, 2 July 1760, PROB 11/857/252, NA. See also Davies, *The Quakers in English Society*, 148.

7. A "preferential option for the poor" has been a key concept in liberation theology, a radical movement within global Catholicism that has been especially strong in Latin America. See Gustavo Gutiérrez, *A Theology of Liberation: History, Politics, and Salvation* (orig. publ. 1971; Maryknoll, NY: Orbis Books, 2015).

8. Max Weber, *The Protestant Ethic and the Spirit of Capitalism* (orig. publ. 1905; New York: Penguin, 2002).

9. *Votes and Proceedings of the House of Representatives of the Province of Pennsylvania, Beginning the Fourteenth Day of October, 1758* (Philadelphia: Henry Miller, 1775), vol. V, 35; Vaux, *Memoirs*, 43.

10. Benjamin's books were listed along with the auction sale prices of his estate sale in 1759, according to Amelia Mott Gummere in her *The Quaker: A Study in Costume* (Philadelphia: Ferris & Leech, 1901). She provides no footnote for the inventory, which has since been lost.

11. Benjamin Franklin to Deborah Franklin, June 10, 1758, London, original in the American Philosophical Society, accessed online at *The Papers of Benjamin Franklin*, sponsored by the American Philosophical Society and Yale University, digital edition by the Packard Humanities Institute, http://franklinpapers.org/franklin//, accessed May 31, 2016. See also David H. Dickason, "Benjamin West on William Williams: A Previously Unpublished Letter," *Winterthur Portfolio* 6 (1970): 133; Susan Rather, "Benjamin West's Professional Endgame and the Historical Conundrum of William Williams," *William and Mary Quarterly*, 3rd Series, 59 (October 2002): 821–64; Susan Rather, *The American School: Artists and Status in the Late Colonial and Early National Era* (New Haven, CT: Yale University Press, 2016), ch. 2.

12. Benjamin Franklin to Lord Kames, January 3, 1760, London, original in the Scottish Record Office, accessed online at *The Papers of Benjamin Franklin*, http://franklinpapers.org/franklin//, accessed May 31, 2016.

13. "A Collection of the Christian & Brotherly Advices given forth from time to time by the Yearly Meeting of Friends for Pennsylvania & New Jersey," Miscellaneous Files, fo. 292, AMM, RG2/Ph/A2, vol. 7.9, FHL-SCL. See also Dianne C. Johnson, "Living in the Light: Quakerism and Colonial Portraiture," in Emma Jones Lapsansky and Anne A. Verplanck, eds., *Quaker Aesthetics: Reflections on a Quaker Ethic in American Design and Consumption, 1720–1920*

(Philadelphia: University of Pennsylvania Press, 2002), 122–46; Anna Cox Brinton, *Quaker Profiles: Pictorial and Biographical, 1750–1850* (Lebanon, PA: Pendle Hill Publications, 1964), 1.

14. William Dillwyn to Roberts Vaux, June 12, 1816, Vaux Family Papers, Collection 684, Roberts Vaux Correspondence, 1795–1818, box 1, HSP.

15. William Dillwyn to Roberts Vaux, April 12, 1816, Vaux Papers.

16. Lita Solis-Cohen, "He Paid $4 for a Treasure of Americana," *Philadelphia Inquirer*, December 4, 1977.

17. David Howard Dickason, *William Williams: Novelist and Painter of Colonial America* (Bloomington: Indiana University Press, 1970), ch. 1.

18. Vaux, *Memoirs*, 20–21.

19. Rush, "Account"; Hunt, "Notices of Lay," 275. The prophet Isaiah (20:3) had gone "naked and barefoot three years for a sign and wonder upon Egypt and upon Ethiopia."

20. Waldstreicher, *Runaway America*, 79–82. Franklin wrote to John Wright (November 4, 1789): "about the year 1728 or 29 I myself printed a book for Ralph Sandyford, another of your friends of this city, against keeping negroes in slavery, two editions of which he distributed gratis. And about the year 1736 I printed another book on the same subject for Benjamin Lay, who also professed being one of your Friends, and he distributed the books chiefly among them. By these instances it appears that the seed was indeed sown in the good ground of your profession, though much earlier than the time you mention." The letter is available online at *The Papers of Benjamin Franklin*, http:// franklinpapers.org, accessed May 31, 2016.

21. Wilford F. Cole, "Henry Dawkins and the Quaker Comet," *Winterthur Portfolio* 4 (1968), 33–46. Cole suggests the first image was printed "probably about 1760," which seems accurate. Part of the evidence for dating the engraving is the kind of paper the engraver and printer used. Most of the surviving copies are on "laid paper," a ribbed paper created one sheet at a time before the mechanization of papermaking in late 1750s England. Thereafter engravings might appear on "wove paper," which was grained and strong, without laid lines. "Wove paper" began to be used in North America around 1795 and with increasing frequency by 1810, suggesting that the Lay engravings on laid paper date from earlier in the eighteenth century. On Benezet's likely involvement, see Gary B. Nash, "Franklin and Slavery," *Proceedings of the American Philosophical Society* 150 (2006): 628.

22. Cole, "Henry Dawkins and the Quaker Comet," 33–46.

23. See letters from Thomas Pole to Roberts Vaux dated January 8, 1818; January 19, 1819; April 25, 1819; and November 9, 1819, in the Vaux Family Papers, Collection 684, Roberts Vaux Correspondence, 1795–1818, box 1: 1795–1818, box 2: 1819–1826. How Pole acquired the painting is unclear. The most likely possibility

is that Williams either reacquired the painting from Franklin or produced his own copy. Either might serve a common purpose, that is, to prove that he had worked with the now-famous Benjamin West, whom he contacted as soon as he reached London in 1781. West gave his former teacher some assistance, allowing him, for example, to sit as a subject for a painting. Whatever West was able to do, it was not enough. In 1784 an impoverished Williams returned to Bristol and probably took the painting with him. Williams entered a home for indigent seamen, where he eventually met a Bristol gentleman named Thomas Eagles. Upon his death in 1791, he bequeathed all of his manuscripts and paintings to Eagles, likely including the portrait of Lay. A few years later, after the death of Eagles, the painting probably came into the hands of Thomas Pole. As it happens, Pole's portrait of Lay has its own fascinating history. Sometime between 1819 and 1853, the painting found a new owner who had no idea that Benjamin Lay was its subject. That owner apparently did what owners often do, he (or she) simply made up the identity of the man in the portrait. Curiously—with no apparent discernible connection—the owner glued a piece of paper to the back of the painting in 1853 stating that the subject was a "Mr. Fitch . . . one of the followers of Johanna Southcott," a controversial and well-known religious mystic of the 1790s. It was added that Mr. Fitch "has been dead about 25 or 30 years." See the Pole portrait and the file "British or American School, Portrait of Benjamin Lay, K2978," Bristol City Museum and Art Gallery, Bristol, England.

24. Lay, *All Slave-Keepers*, 58–59.

25. Horle et al., "Anthony Morris" and "Israel Pemberton," *Lawmaking and Legislators in Pennsylvania*, 727–36, 824–36; *Pennsylvania Gazette*, January 4, 1738; Gary B. Nash, "The Early Merchants of Philadelphia: The Formation and Disintegration of a Founding Elite," in Richard S. Dunn and Mary Maples Dunn, eds., *The World of William Penn* (Philadelphia: University of Pennsylvania Press, 1986), 337–62.

26. Horle et al., "John Kinsey," *Lawmaking and Legislators in Pennsylvania*, 591–607. Kinsey's daughter died in 1742, followed by his wife in 1744, a son in 1745, and another son who accidentally shot himself to death in 1748. See also Joseph S. Walton, *John Kinsey: Speaker of the Pennsylvania Assembly and Justice of the Supreme Court of the Province* (Philadelphia: Friends' Book Association, 1900); Isaac Sharpless, "John Kinsey: 1693–1750," *Bulletin of the Friends Historical Society of Philadelphia* 8 (1917): 2–10, 46–53; and, most importantly, Edwin B. Bronner, "The Disgrace of John Kinsey, Quaker Politician, 1739–1750," *Pennsylvania Magazine of History and Biography* 75 (1951): 400–415.

27. Glowing memorials of Kinsey may be found in the *Pennsylvania Journal*, May 17, 1750, and in the *New-York Gazette*, May 21, 1750.

28. Lay, *All Slave-Keepers*, 111. On Kinsey and the codification of law, see Susan A. Hoffman, "Kinsey, John (1693–1750)," *Oxford Dictionary of National Biography*, http://www.oxforddnb.com.pitt.idm.oclc.org/view/article/68175, accessed September 5, 2015; Horle et al., "John Kinsey," *Lawmaking and Legislators in Pennsylvania*, 595.

29. Lay, *All Slave-Keepers*, 59; Nash and Soderlund, *Freedom by Degrees*, 49–50.

30. Ann Emlen to John Pemberton, 15.1.1785, Pemberton Family Papers, vol. 42, 162, HSP.

31. Thomas E. Drake discusses Lay and other early abolitionists in a chapter entitled "Voices Crying in the Wilderness," in his *Quakers and Slavery in America*, 34–47. In his edited collection of documents entitled *The Quaker Origins of Antislavery* (Norwood, PA: Norwood Editions, 1980), J. William Frost includes writings by Benezet and Woolman, as well as many figures less important to the beginnings of an abolition movement, but nothing by Lay. See also Davis, *The Problem of Slavery in Western Culture*, 330, 483–93; Sydney V. James, *A People Among Peoples: Quaker Benevolence in Eighteenth-Century America* (Cambridge, MA: Harvard University Press, 1963), 125–26, 131–34; Marietta, *The Reformation of American Quakerism*, 108–9, 112–16; and David S. Lovejoy, *Religious Enthusiasm in the New World: Heresy to Revolution* (Cambridge, MA: Harvard University Press, 1985), 151–53.

32. Soderlund, *Quakers and Slavery*, 46, 163.

33. Carey, *From Peace to Freedom*, 175–76, 181, 190.

34. PYM Minutes, 1681–1746, MRPh469, fo. 412, FHL-SCL. The satisfaction of the PYM in 1738 at the lessening involvement of Quakers in the slave trade was recorded for posterity in "A Collection of the Christian & Brotherly Advices given forth from time to time by the Yearly Meeting of Friends for Pennsylvania & New Jersey," Miscellaneous Files, Abington Monthly Meeting, RG2/Ph/A2, vol. 7.9, FHL-SCL. Another possible sign of Benjamin's impact is that in 1776, when the PYM announced that slave holding was a disownable offense, the Abington Monthly Meeting was one of the first to move. Four of five enslaved Africans owned by meeting members had been freed by 1778. See Soderlund, *Quakers and Slavery*, 96, 106.

35. Vaux, *Memoirs*, 31.

36. Child, *Memoir*. Thanks to Gary B. Nash for pointing out the significance of Benjamin Rush's timing in publishing the biography amid the Congressional debates. For the crucial role of Warner Mifflin in the debate, see his *Warner Mifflin: Unflinching Quaker Abolitionist* (Philadelphia: University of Pennsylvania Press, forthcoming).

37. Rush, "Account"; Lay, *All Slave-Keepers*, 246.

38. Louise Shea argues that truth is expressed in the body of the Cynic philosopher, not as an abstract category. See her *The Cynic Enlightenment: Diogenes in the Salon* (Baltimore: Johns Hopkins University Press, 2010), 180.

39. John G. Whittier, ed., *The Journal of John Woolman* (Boston: Houghton, Osgood, 1879), 15. It should be noted that Woolman was not as deeply antinomian as Lay, but he did have the subversive approach within him, as when he explained that "laws and customs are no further a standard for our proceedings than as their foundation is on universal righteousness." When it came to slavery, upright people might have to break man-made law in service of a "higher law." See Plank, *John Woolman's Path to the Peaceable Kingdom*, 131. Thomas P. Slaughter emphasizes Woolman's "radical spirit." See his *The Beautiful Soul of John Woolman*, 389.

40. Carole Dale Spencer, "The Man Who 'Set Himself as a Sign': James Nayler's Incarnational Theology," in *Early Quakers and Their Theological Thought, 1647–1723*, ed. Stephen W. Angell and Pink Dandelion (New York: Cambridge University Press, 2015), 64–82. Lay had a much greater influence on Benezet and Woolman than did Ralph Sandiford, who had similar attitudes about slave-produced commodities, animals, clothing, and greed. Benezet arrived in Philadelphia in 1731, a mere two years before Sandiford died, while Woolman was a youth of only thirteen at the time. Both men lived, with Benjamin, in the small world of mid-Atlantic Quakerism for almost three decades.

41. Benezet quoted in Jackson, *Let This Voice Be Heard*, 19, 50. "Universal love," with its leveling embrace of toleration, went back to Ranter Abiezer Coppe, Digger Gerrard Winstanley, and James Nayler and his supporters, especially Robert Rich. See Hill, *The World Turned Upside Down*, 138, 210, 332, 338. Benjamin also appears to have influenced New Jersey Quaker minister Joshua Evans (1731–1798), an abolitionist who embraced vegetarianism, wore undyed clothes, and opposed the values and practices of the capitalist economy. See M. Ellen Ross, "'Liberation Is Coming Soon': The Radical Reformation of Joshua Evans," in Carey and Plank, *Quakers and Abolition*, 15–28.

42. Rush, "Account."

43. Benjamin's agitation may have had an impact on the "Great Awakening," the firestorm of religious enthusiasm that swept the American colonies after the arrival of the itinerant minister George Whitefield in October 1739. Beginning in 1732, Benjamin anticipated many Awakeners' messages of religious reform as he opposed conservative ministers of all denominations in the Philadelphia region. Blind, heartless, and covetous, these ministers preached people into hell; they alienated young people; they obstructed regeneration through "new birth"; they ruined the church. The New Jersey-based itinerant, Gilbert Tennent, who frequently preached in Philadelphia, used an almost identical language of critique. See Lay, *All Slave-Keepers*, 85–86, 106, 134–35, 233–35, and Milton J. Coalter, *Gilbert*

Tennent, Son of Thunder: A Case Study of Continental Pietism's Impact on the First Great Awakening in the Middle Colonies (New York: Greenwood Press, 1986).

44. Frederick Douglass, "West India Emancipation" (1857), available in Frederick Douglass, *The Heroic Slave: A Cultural and Critical Edition*, ed. Robert S. Levine, John Stauffer, and John R. Kaufman-McKivigan (New Haven, CT: Yale University Press, 2015), 133–34.

CONCLUSION

1. Rush, "Account"; *Pennsylvania Gazette*, April 13–20, 1738. A later account, published in 1805, mentioned Lay as a revolutionary alongside John Woolman, Anthony Benezet, and Warner Mifflin: "their efforts will probably, in their consequences, produce a revolution unheard of in the annals of nations—even the breaking of the yoke of oppression and willingly permitting the slave to go free." See *Independent Chronicle*, August 26, 1805.

2. Two of the great works in liberation theology are Gutiérrez, *A Theology of Liberation*, and James H. Cone, *A Black Theology of Liberation* (orig. publ. 1986; Maryknoll, NY: Orbis Books, 2015).

3. David R. Como suggests that antinomians could speak with "formidable self-confidence" because "the spirit was speaking in and through them." He suggests that "the antinomian tendency to exalt, magnify, and stress the power of the spirit" may have had "a leveling effect, which did indeed encourage and foster an unusual assertiveness among humble women and men alike." See his *Blown by the Spirit*, 52.

4. Anthony Benezet and John Woolman would carry forward the emphasis on "universal love," implying toleration and broad solidarity that defied boundaries of race, class, nation, and gender. See Jackson, *Let This Voice Be Heard*, 53.

5. Lay, *All Slave-Keepers*, 81.

6. Burrough quoted in Hill, *The World Turned Upside Down*, 386.

7. Linebaugh and Rediker, *The Many-Headed Hydra*. Brycchan Carey likewise emphasizes the American "periphery" as the driving force in Atlantic antislavery. See his *From Peace to Freedom*, 5.

8. Vaux, *Memoirs*, 25; Lay, *All Slave-Keepers*, 87.

9. Lay, *All Slave-Keepers*, 130; W. E. B. Du Bois, *John Brown* (orig. publ. 1909; New York: International Publishers, 2014).

10. Brissot de Warville, *New Travels in the United States of America*, 267. It should be noted that Brissot got numerous details of Lay's life wrong, saying, for example, that he had been a planter in Barbados.

11. I would like to thank Graham Hodges for emphasizing this important issue.

12. Rush, "Account"; Vaux, *Memoirs*, 28–29; Child, *Memoir*, 17–18; Kite, "Account," 229–30. The unpublished Quaker critics of slavery were, as Gary B. Nash and Jean R. Soderlund note, "well-situated men." See their *Freedom by Degrees*, 47.

13. Vaux, *Memoirs*, 54.

14. The Oxford-educated Anglican minister Morgan Godwyn was the odd man out in this early cohort of antislavery writers. See his *The Negroes' and Indians' Advocate, suing for their Admission into the Church, or a Persuasive to the Instructing and Baptizing the Negroes and Indians on our Plantations, with a brief Account of Religion in Virginia* (London, 1680).

15. Davis, *The Problem of Slavery in Western Culture*, 320–26. Davis also writes, wrongly, that neither Sandiford nor Lay "betrayed the slightest awareness of living in the Age of Enlightenment" (320).

16. Lay, *All Slave-Keepers*, title page.

17. Meeting of 13.iii.1717, LTWM Minutes, Book of Certificates A (1716–1767), FHL-SCL; Ian Davidson, *Voltaire: A Life* (New York: Pegasus Books, 2010), 69.

18. John Donoghue, "'Out of the Land of Bondage': The English Revolution and the Atlantic Origins of Abolition," *American Historical Review* 115 (2010): 942–74; John Donoghue, *Fire Under the Ashes: An Atlantic History of the English Revolution* (Chicago: University of Chicago Press, 2014). Around the time of Benjamin's death in 1759, philosophers in France and Germany—D'Alembert, Rousseau, Sade, Wieland, and Frederick the Great—began to revive Diogenes and Cynic philosophy within what would become the traditional enlightenment. See Shea, *The Cynic Enlightenment*.

19. Thompson suggests that Blake's antinomianism, like Lay's, was radical, subversive, and antihegemonic, helping him to break out of the "common sense" of his era. See his *Witness Against the Beast: William Blake and the Moral Law* (Cambridge, UK: Cambridge University Press, 1993), 20.

20. Lay, *All Slave-Keepers*, 51, 169; Peter Linebaugh, "All the Atlantic Mountains Shook," *Labour/Le Travail* 10 (1982): 87–121.

21. For a useful history of the boycott movement that began with Lay, see Holcomb, *Moral Commerce*.

22. Rush, "Account."

ILLUSTRATION SOURCES AND CREDITS

INSERT

Page 1–2: Portrait and details: William Williams, *Portrait of Benjamin Lay*, 1750–1758, courtesy National Portrait Gallery, Smithsonian Institution, Washington, DC.

Page 3: Thomas Clarkson, *The History of the Rise, Progress, and Accomplishment of the Abolition of the African Slave-Trade by the British Parliament* (London, 1808), courtesy Beneicke Rare Book & Manuscript Library, Yale University, New Haven, Connecticut.

Page 4: Isaac Sailmaker, *Ships in the Thames Estuary near Sheerness*, 1707–1708, courtesy Yale Center for British Art, Paul Mellon Collection, New Haven, Connecticut.

Page 4: John Cleveley the Elder, *The Royal George at Deptford Showing the Launch of The Cambridge* (1757), courtesy National Maritime Museum, Greenwich, England.

Page 5: Detail, Peter Cooper, *The Southeast Prospect of the City of Philadelphia*, c. 1720, courtesy Library Company of Philadelphia.

Page 5: G. Wood, *The Prospect of Philadelphia from Wickacove*, 1735, Philadelphia, courtesy Winterthur Museum, Winterthur, Delaware.

Page 6: Unidentified artist, *Quaker Meeting*, late 18th/early 19th century, courtesy Museum of Fine Arts, Boston.

Page 7: Artist unknown, *Friends' Meeting House, High Street, Burlington, New Jersey*, date unknown, courtesy Friends Historical Library, Swarthmore College, Swarthmore, Pennsylvania.

Page 7: William Dell, *The Tryal of Spirits, Both in Teachers and Hearers, Wherein is held forth the clear Discovery and Downfal of the Carnal and Anti-Christian Clergy of these Nations, testified from the Word of God to the University Congregations in Cambridge* (London: T. Sowle, 1699, orig. publ. 1653), courtesy Germantown Historical Society, Germantown, Pennsylvania.

Page 8: Mason Chamberlin, *Portrait of Benjamin Franklin*, 1762, courtesy Philadelphia Museum of Art.

Page 9: Charles Willson Peale, *Portrait of Dr. Benjamin Rush*, 1783–1786, Philadelphia, courtesy Winterthur Museum, Winterthur, Delaware.

Page 10: William Williams, *Self Portrait*, 1788–1790, courtesy Winterthur Museum, Winterthur, Delaware.

Page 10: Benjamin West, *Self-Portrait*, 1770–1776, courtesy Baltimore Museum of Art.

Page 11: William Blake, *The Great Red Dragon and the Beast from the Sea*, c. 1805, courtesy National Gallery of Art, Washington, DC.

Page 12: Henry Dawkins, *Benjamin Lay*, engraving, c. 1760, collection of the author.

INTRODUCTION

Page 8: Roberts Vaux portrait by Albert Newsam, lithograph, undated, courtesy Library Company of Philadelphia.

IN CHAPTER ONE

Page 18: "Above ordinances" detail from illustration in *The Quakers Dream: or, the Devil's Pilgrimage in England* (London, 1655), courtesy Haverford College Library, Haverford, Pennsylvania.

IN CHAPTER FOUR

Page 72: From Benjamin Lay, *All Slave-Keepers That Keep the Innocent in Bondage, Apostates* (Philadelphia, 1738), courtesy Library Company of Philadelphia.

IN CHAPTER FIVE

Page 102: Diogenes, from Thomas Stanley, *History of Philosophy: Containing the Lives, Opinions, Actions and Discourses of the Philosophers of Every Sect* (London, 1655–1661), 3 vols., courtesy Huntington Library, San Marino, California.

Page 112: Roger Crab, from *The English Hermite, or, Wonder of this Age: Being a Relation of the Life of Roger Crab, living neer Uxbridg, taken from his own Mouth* (London, 1655), courtesy, Huntington Library, San Marino, California.

IN CHAPTER SIX

Page 129: Engraving of Benjamin Lay by William Kneass, from Roberts Vaux, *Memoirs of the Loves of Benjamin Lay and Ralph Sandiford, Two of the Earliest Public Advocates for the Emancipation of the Enslaved Africans* (Philadelphia: Solomon W. Conrad, 1815), collection of the author.

INDEX

ABOUT THE AUTHOR

MARCUS REDIKER HOLDS a BA from Virginia Commonwealth University (1976) and an MA and PhD from the University of Pennsylvania (1979, 1982). He is currently Distinguished Professor of Atlantic History at the University of Pittsburgh and Senior Research Fellow at the Collège d'études mondiales/Fondation Maison des sciences de l'homme in Paris.

He has written, cowritten, or edited ten books: *Between the Devil and the Deep Blue Sea* (1987); *Who Built America?* (1989), volume one; *The Many-Headed Hydra* (2000, with Peter Linebaugh); *Villains of All Nations* (2004); *The Slave Ship* (2007); *Many Middle Passages* (2007); *The Amistad Rebellion* (2012); *Mutiny and Maritime Radicalism in the Age of Revolution* (2013); *Outlaws of the Atlantic* (2014); and *The Fearless Benjamin Lay* (2017). His writings have been translated into Arabic, French, German, Greek, Hebrew, Italian, Japanese, Korean, Portuguese, Russian, Spanish, Swedish, and Turkish. His books have won numerous awards, including the George Washington Book Prize, the American Studies Association's John Hope Franklin Book Prize, the American Historical Association's James A. Rawley Prize, and the Organization of American Historians' Merle Curti Award (twice). He has held fellowships from the American Council of Learned Societies, the Andrew P. Mellon Foundation, the National Endowment of the Humanities, and the John Simon Guggenheim Memorial Foundation.

Marcus worked with filmmaker Tony Buba to produce a documentary entitled *Ghosts of Amistad: In the Footsteps of the Rebels*, a chronicle of a trip to Sierra Leone in which he interviewed village elders about local memory of the shipboard slave revolt of 1839 and searched for the long-lost ruins of Lomboko, the slave-trading factory from which the *Amistad* Africans were loaded aboard slave ships bound for the New World. The American Historical Association awarded the film the 2015 John E. O'Conner Prize as the year's best historical documentary.